Word and Spi...
Woodbrooke C...

Word and Spirit at Play

Towards a Charismatic Theology

Jean-Jacques Suurmond

SCM PRESS LTD

2 69.4

Translated by John Bowden from the Dutch *Het Spel van Woord en Geest. Aanzet tot een charismatische theologie*, published 1994 by Uitgeverij Ten Have bv, Baarn, The Netherlands.

© 1994 Uitgeverij Ten Have bv, Baarn.

Translation © 1994 John Bowden.

0 334 02417 5

2029542

First British edition published 1994
by SCM Press Ltd,
26-30 Tottenham Road, London N1 4BZ

Phototypset by Intype, London and
printed in Great Britain by
Biddles Ltd, Guildford and King's Lynn

Contents

Preface

The idea for this book came from Professor Hendrikus Berkhof. He suggested that I should put my thoughts down in a 'simple but scholarly' work, 'avoiding strange words that put people off'. Whether or not I have succeeded, only the reader can judge. But at least I have done my best to avoid scholarly jargon. I have also avoided going into differing views as far as possible, in order not to tire the reader. For the same reason I have tried to limit the notes (though I have not always been successful).

The subtitle of the book is 'Towards a Charismatic Theology'. Like liberation theology, a charismatic theology seeks to illuminate scripture and the life of faith from a long-neglected aspect. This is the charism, which, as a 'gift of grace', is directly connected with God's grace, a fundamental concept in Jewish and Christian thought. Present-day Pentecostalism is again reminding Christianity of the importance of these gifts, and a charismatic theology attempts to make this fruitful for the wider church. For this it is necessary to know Pentecostalism 'inside out'. Abdalazis de Moura, the study secretary of Bishop Helder Camara, rightly remarked that as a theologian one must not begin with the doctrine of Pentecostals (which is inadequate), but with their experiences. After two decades of work in Pentecostalism, in the Netherlands and abroad, it seemed to me time to make an attempt at a Pentecostalist theology, an attempt which is also a pleasure. However, it remains no more than an approach. Often I have only been able to sketch out what consequences a charismatic approach has for the life of Christians and the church.

The fact that in addition to scripture and theology I make use of the human sciences, and especially psychology, will be attributed by some to my studies in the United States (and perhaps criticized). That is not unfair, but behind my approach there is also a deep conviction that in our time we cannot do theology without knowing about the behaviour of those fascinating beings who are called human.

It remains for me to thank Geurt van den Brink for his readiness as a non-theologian to check and correct my manuscript for readability, and my wife, Marianne Suurmond-Vonkeman, for her suggestions and critical comments – including her disturbing question whether I really live out what I teach.

Gendt, Pentecost 1993   Jean-Jacques Suurmond

Part One: The Origin and Characteristics of Present-Day Pentecostalism

The spirituality of about a quarter of all Christians goes back to the spontaneous revival which took place in 1906 in an old church building, up till then used as a warehouse, in Azusa Street, Los Angeles. The leader was the black pastor Bill Seymour, the gentle son of ex-slaves from Louisiana. His style of speaking had none of the rhetorical fireworks of the black preaching tradition, but was that of a teacher giving instruction. During the meetings he left as much room as possible for the Spirit, hiding his head in one of the wooden shoe-boxes of which his pulpit was made. In a time and country in which C.Carroll's *The Negro a Beast* was a best-seller and every week blacks were being lynched and were dangling like 'strange fruits' (the title of a spiritual) from the trees, he had to endure numerous taunts from white Christians. This was because he believed that the Spirit of Pentecost could bring about reconciliation between the races. Both white and black people met at his meetings, something quite exceptional in Los Angeles at the beginning of this century, certainly under a black leader. Above all the fact that men and women of different races touched and embraced each others was felt offensive. The front-page headlines of respectable local papers like the *Los Angeles Daily Times* speak for themselves: 'Weird Babel of Tongues'; 'Religious Fanaticism Creates Wild Scenes'; 'Women with Men Embrace'; and even 'Jumpers to Kill Children', with the sub-heading 'Holy Rollers Plan a Slaughter of Innocents'.[1]

The revival lasted three years. Three packed meetings were held in the daytime and in the evenings, seven days a week. Many people came to Los Angeles from outside to pray for the experience of Pentecost. They included not a few theologians like the Norwegian Thomas Barratt, the English canon Harford Battersby and the erudite Indian missionary Pandita Ramabai. Within two years the revival had spread to fifty countries. Seymour's paper *The Apostolic Faith* went round the world in an edition of 50,000 copies. The first issues carried the statement: 'We are not fighting against people or churches, but we are seeking to replace dead forms and dogmas with a living, practical Christianity.'[2]

I

A Fusion of Two Traditions: Africa and the Holiness Movement

Two traditions came together in the person of Seymour: African spirituality and the Wesleyan evangelical Holiness Movement. From his ancestors, who had been shipped to the New World as slaves, he inherited the African religious tradition which is handed down orally by means of stories, myths and songs. The sociologist Iain MacRobert points to the central importance of community among Africans for both the well-being of individual members and their relationship with the spirit worlds of ancestors and gods.[3] The African world-view is holistic: in other words, there is no division between the spiritual and the earthly reality. Through rhythmic drumming, danc-ing, singing and all kinds of other physical expressions people prepare themselves to be 'possessed' by a spirit (even an early white Pentecostalist like Frank Bartleman can still innocently speak of possession by God's Spirit). Under the influence of Christianity, on the American continent the spirits were in the long term identified with the apostles, saints, angels or the Holy Spirit. The world of the Bible, also of non-Western origin, in some respects tied up with the ancestral religious traditions. The interaction between the spiri-tual and the natural, the stories of miracles, healings, exorcisms and the power of the Holy Spirit, were quite recognizable to these slaves. The basic biblical story of the exodus from Egypt to the promised land did not just address them personally but also confirmed the African view of sin (in this case their slavery) as something that undermines the community and is anti-social. In Afro-American culture the liberator Moses becomes a dominant figure, sung about in popular spirituals like 'Go Down Moses' and 'When Moses Smote the Water'.

The emotional and ecstatic character of the eighteenth- and nineteenth-century evangelical revivals, in which the nearness of the divine was experienced, along with the possibility of taking part in the meeting, appealed to many blacks. This also applied to the expectation of the end of the world, which became increasingly urgent as the year 1900 approached. The imminent return of Christ would, it was thought, bring about a reversal of the *status quo*, in which God would cast down the mighty from their thrones and raise up the simple. Inspired by this vision, some slaves planned a revolt against their masters at religious meetings. The ecumenical Holiness Movement, a Wesleyan renewal movement centred on the revival campaigns of people like Charles Finney and the evangelist Phoebe Palmer, became one of the most important religious currents in nineteenth-century North America. This movement was a powerful motive for the actions for the abolition of slavery and the fight for the emancipation of women which was often associated with them.[4] Its theology was based on a somewhat simplistic exposition of the teaching of John Wesley, the founder of Methodism. Wesley had taken over from a number of Roman Catholic devotional writers the idea of a second experience of crisis after conversion which would lead to perfect sanctification. By this he understood not just the sanctification of personal life but also the sanctification of society. This emphasis on the sanctification of society implied a revolutionary criticism of the *status quo*.[5] Moreover, churches related to the Holiness Movement were also the first to open the preaching ministry to blacks and women. Antoinette Brown was confirmed in the Wesleyan Methodist church in 1853 as probably the first woman preacher in the world. The minister Luther Lee led the service and preached on Galatians 3.28: 'There is no difference between Jew or Greek, slave or free, man or woman, for you are all one in Christ Jesus.' Round about this time the Wesleyan experience of sanctification was increasingly identified with the baptism of the Spirit from the story of Pentecost in Acts 2. Moreover the significance of sanctification shifted so that it denoted being equipped with power to bear witness to Christ.

In 1905 Bill Seymour became pastor of the Evening Light Saints in Houston, an inter-racial church which, in addition to healing and prayer, expected a great outpouring of the Spirit before the end of world history. (Moreover round the end of the century the importance of the eschatological dimension of Scripture also flared up. This is evident from the work of Johnanes Weiss and Albert Schweitzer, in which there is emphasis on the future character of the kingdom of God.)

(i) A split between black and white

In Houston, Seymour went to lessons in the Bible school of the white man Charles Parham. When this school was still in Topeka, Kansas, some years earlier Agnes Ozman had been the first student to 'speak in tongues' (glossolalia). This phenomenon has occurred time and again in the history of the church. Parham taught that this gift put missionaries in a position to proclaim the gospel in languages foreign to them (xenolalia). For him, the return of this gift was confirmation of the worldwide revival which would precede the thousand-year kingdom in which Christ would reign. In the words of Jesus, the gospel has to have been proclaimed to all people before the end comes. This view of glossolalia initially gave an important stimulus to the missionary drive of the early Pentecostal believers, most of whom came from circles in which higher education and the know-ledge of foreign languages was an unattainable ideal. However, reality seemed reluctant to conform to this doctrine, so the notion of xenolalia quickly became limited to special cases. But these have never been confirmed by scientific investigation.

Still, another aspect of Parham's teaching about glossolalia has exercised great influence to the present day. This is the new idea that baptism in the Spirit would be exclusively proved by speaking in tongues. Seymour took over this idea, which from the beginning clearly distinguished the Holiness Movement from the early Pentecostal movement. This teaching has become so bound up with the identity of the majority of the Pentecostal movement that despite increasing criticism among its own members, it has still proved impossible to drop. However, Seymour gave an essentially different interpretation of it from Parham. Parham had no conception of the liberating work of the Spirit in the social sphere. Later he even sympathized with the Ku Klux Klan, and Seymour could follow his lessons only through the half-open door of the local class, sitting in the corridor. (This is reminiscent of the experience of Aletta Jacobs, the first woman in the Netherlands to be allowed to go to lectures – who had to sit behind a curtain.)

Seymour saw glossolalia above all as the sign that the Spirit was breaking through the barriers between races, sexes and nationalities and was reconciling all people with one another. When a year later (in 1906) he was in the thick of the Los Angeles revival, he saw this confirmed when blacks and whites, Americans and foreigners, professors and washerwomen prayed and sang together with sounds of glossolalia. In this way people who had no common language experienced a unity which transcended the barriers of language. For them this unity was 'the joy of union' with Christ, to quote the title of the last chapter of Hannah Whitall Smith's *The Christian's Secret of a Happy Life* (1875), a book which is still much read within the Pentecostal movement. When Parham visited the revival in Los Angeles in the autumn of 1906, at Seymour's invitation, he was utterly horrified to see 'blacks and whites mixing together' and 'lying on top of each other like pigs'. This last remark refers to a practice which is still known in Western Pentecostalism in a more stylized form as 'resting in the Spirit'. Those concerned say that they experience such a sense of the presence of God that like some biblical figures and mystics they can no longer remain standing and fall into a kind of mystical slumber.

(a) The white Pentecostal movement

During his visit to Los Angeles Parham tried to reshape the revival with its 'dumb, primitive negroes' in line with his white, middle-class views. This rapidly led to a break between Seymour and him, a foretaste of the definitive splitting of the Pentecostal movement into a black branch and a white branch.

In 1914 the Assemblies of God was established, dominated by whites. This was a Pentecostal church community which was to develop into the largest in the United States. The racist Parham became the hero of the Assemblies of God, and the teaching of glossolalia as proof of baptism in the Spirit was his banner. The black Seymour with his vision of reconciliation between races, sexes and nationalities was in practice written out of the history of the Pentecostal movement. His death in 1922 was not mentioned in a single Pentecostalist paper. Only in recent decades have researchers like the missiologist Walter Hollenweger again brought out Seymour's crucial role, so that most historians today trace Pentecostalism back to Seymour, not to Parham.[6] Cut off from its black, 'Third World' roots, the Assemblies of God, like the greater part of the Western Pentecostal movement, has become a typically white, evangelical, middle-class church, politically conservative. In its effort to become respectable it has adapted the 'Third World' liturgical elements in the meeting to the taste of the white middle class, or even dropped them completely. In the leading Assemblies of God church in Los Angeles where I myself worked as a preacher around 1980, the Sunday service hardly differed from that in an average white Protestant community. The typical 'Pentecostalist' contribution like prophecy, exclamations and spontaneous dance had been banished to a separate celebration on Monday evening! This tendency towards middle-class respectability is being considerably encouraged by the flight of the Pentecostalist movement into the dogmas of Evangelical fundamentalism, a reaction in the years around the First World War against the rise of biblical criticism, the doctrine of evolution and Communism. This fundamentalism is a system of abstract, conservative-Calvinist teachings which do not do justice to the Pentecostal experience. Sometimes they even run counter to it, as does the doctrine that the gifts of the Spirit died out with the formation of the canon of scripture. The fundamentalist view is obsessed with order and therefore tends to deny the possibility of experiences of God in the present. Many Pentecostalist believers find themselves ultimately cramped in their intellectual and spiritual development by this teaching, so that they feel forced to leave the movement.[7]

An important part of the world-wide Pentecostal movement is influenced by the Assemblies of God. However, most Pentecostal churches in Great Britain and in some other countries have never acepted Parham's dogma of glossolalic sounds as the only proof of baptism with the Spirit. Certainly they have often taken over the typical North American 'Bible Belt' morality, so that they look on the cigar-smoking and whisky-drinking members of the church charismatic renewal with bewilderment. The higher the white Pentecostalist believers climb the social ladder, and the more they begin to feel at home in the world, the more the eschatological expectation loses intensity.

(b) The black Pentecostal movement

The black Pentecostal movement has retained the 'Third World' spirituality where it has deferred less to the expectations of its white sister churches. Certainly it has often (but by no means always) taken over fundamentalist teaching, including Parham's doctrine, but this has a less prominent function than in the white Pentecostal movement. The black churches whose spirituality and liturgy corresponds most closely with those of the revival in Los Angeles are the 'Jesus Only'

communities in the United States and the Caribbean.[8] They belong
to a movement which broke away from the newly formed Assemblies
of God as early as 1916. Following the example of the Acts of the
Apostles they do not baptize in the name of the Father, the Son and
the Holy Spirit, but only in the name of Jesus. The motive behind this
is a fear of lapsing into tritheism. Their naive theological position
approaches that of Karl Barth (though few of them will have read
him). Barth does not speak of three divine persons, but of one God
who reveals himself in three 'modes of being'. Their concentration
on Jesus more than on the Father or the Holy Spirit is characteristic
of the greater part of Pentecostalism.

In these churches we still find all the 'Third World' aspects which
Seymour introduced, like an oral theology not set down in writing
which is narrative in nature and thus not abstract and dogmatic.
They express themselves in dance and other physical forms like
hand-clapping, kneeling, laughing, weeping and outcries. These are
accompanied by rhythmic music and song. Dreams and visions have
an important function. People experience the presence of spiritual
power to improve social and material reality, as for example in prayer
for bodily healing, and also in social and political involvement. The
importance of the community for both everyday life and religious
life is great. Finally, the 'Jesus Only' churches have an intense
expectation of the return of Christ, who, they believe, will turn the
present unjust order upside down. Furthermore, today one finds
these aspects most clearly in Pentecostalism in the Third World. This
is not surprising; there they meet up with the primary, religious
feeling not only of the Africans, but above all of the Indians in Latin
America and the people of Asia. Moreover Pentecostalism has a great
capacity for acculturation. The emphasis on the experience of the
Spirit means the people can become Christians without having to
abandon their own cultural identity and traditions. However, these
are critically renewed. The independent Zionists in South Africa
were once asked how they could tell the difference between someone
who was possessed by the spirit of an ancestor and someone who
was full of the Holy Spirit. They answered that the latter danced
differently (in other words, without losing his or her own
personality).[9]

However, where missionaries from the white Pentecostal movement preach their Western dogmas and morality, people become
'Americanized' and are often alienated from their own culture.

Politics has abused this. It is well known that during the years of the Cold War the American Pentagon supported training for missionaries (including Pentecostalist missionaries). So it could come about that the great Chilean Iglesia Metodista Pentecostal backed General Pinochet, who was supported by the United States, while the leadership of the somewhat smaller Iglesia Pentecostal de Chile opposed the dictator.

(ii) Social and political involvement

The inter-racial character of the revival in Los Angeles removed the props from the established theological view which uses God more or less as the legitimation for a segregated society. This also applied to the position of women, who had not yet been given the vote.

Seymour encouraged women to play a full part in the revival, even in preaching, for 'it is the same holy Spirit, both in the woman and in the man'. Even in the 1970s the Pentecostal churches in North America still had relatively the most women preachers. Seymour saw his work as 'inter-church and not sectarian'. This ecumenical attitude and the desire to bring the fire of the Spirit into the existing churches was characteristic of almost all the early Pentecostal movement. While the well-known Dutch Reformed theologian J.H.Gunning Jr was fascinated by the 'charismatic' Catholic Apostolic church, his son J.H.Gunning III felt attracted to the Pentecostalist movement. In 1922 he regarded this as a 'serious call from God to the doubting, divided, spiritually barren and lowly Christianity of our day'.[10] Gerrit Polman, with his wife Wilhelmine a pioneer of the Pentecostal movement in the Netherlands, lamented that he had hoped 'that as a Pentecostal movement we would lose ourselves in the great body of Christianity'. He wrote this in 1925, a time when the Pentecostal movement almost everywhere felt led to found its own, independent churches.[11] This development confirmed the well-known law that a renewal movement becomes independent to the degree that it is not welcomed by and integrated into the existing churches. The rejection of the early Pentecostal movement by the established churches was almost total. Reasons cited for this included the fact that the movement was thought to be inferior because of its black origins and because women and the uneducated made a contribution to worship. But above all at the beginning of the century the established churches were academic and static in their preaching and liturgy, and this was very far removed from the 'Third World' spirituality mediated through Protestantism.

(a) Meeting personal needs

The revolutionary implications of the Pentecostal revival are not (and have not been) often translated into opposition to unjust social structures. Although at a very early stage well established citizens were also involved in the revival, an important reason for this lies in the fact that the greatest support for the Pentecostal movement came (as it still does) from people who scarcely had an identity of their own.

It was above all the 'little folk' of this kind, in Scripture called the *anawim*, who seem to have been receptive to this movement of the Spirit. They belonged to the oppressed and those without possessions. They included many descendants of slaves, illiterate women and workers without a voice in society. In the revival they heard that at the heart of the universe there was a God who was concerned for them, concerned for the 'little folk'. Often the playthings of impenetrable power structures, not noticed by anyone, here they encountered a God who 'saw' them. Excluded and often ridiculed by those who guarded the entrance to the positions of power in society, in giving help they turned to those who, like themselves, had been marginalized. Thus the Reformed preacher and historian Dr G.A.Wumkes noted in a brief study of the Dutch Pentecostal movement published in 1917 that the ecstasy of the Pentecostal movement can be 'an extremely important social and ethical ferment'.[12] The first Pentecostal community in Amsterdam organized evenings for factory girls of all denominations, had a sewing school, and sent food and clothing to the poor in Germany and Bulgaria. In 1924 Wilhelmine Polman received a medal from the Austrian government for her help to malnourished children. Looking back on the Pentecostal meetings in Amsterdam, Joko Andrea wrote in 1937 to her friend, the children's author Martha Visser:

> There I had a sense of belonging to this great universal Christian church, much more than now (in the Reformed Church). When I think back to the way in which Brother Polman spoke the blessing, I felt taken up into the whole universe, and saw no horizon. When I now sit in church on Sundays it is as though the same

blessing rebounds from all the walls... The prayer is for our sick, for our elderly... for our sins of the past week. Then I say to myself, 'Mart, pray for the street girls, for those who have the itch. For all those for whom there are no prayers.' Then I have the greatest difficulty in reaching this silence where your God belongs.

Martha Visser wrote back:

I myself have so often noted precisely that strange thing that you mention, namely that you feel a kind of sectarian in the mainstream church, which is not a particularly small church, whereas in the small circle rejected by official Christianity you experienced something of the great universal Christian church. Was that perhaps a matter of feeling, or was it our youth? I don't believe that: it was true, and I would feel precisely the same thing again.[13]

It must be remembered that the struggle against unjust policies and social structures can also serve as a way of avoiding the pain and challenge of the concrete situation. Perhaps I can illustrate that with an example from my own experience, in a Pentecostal community in the Netherlands at the beginning of the 1970s. The community social services had asked the local churches to do something about the problem of the homeless who were sleeping in that port in bus shelters and sheds. The established churches, with ministries which were busy challenging poverty and oppression at a world level, could not provide any practical help. It was members of the Pentecostal community who got the vagrants off the streets and welcomed them - sometimes into their own homes. This work very rapidly grew into a developed reception centre for the homeless which was later taken over by the state.

To the present day the practical welcoming and care of the poor, the enslaved, the homeless and prostitutes is characteristic of a large part of the Pentecostal movement. However, the concentration on personal needs often coincides, as a result of fundamentalist influences, with a gloomy spirituality. Here the great world outside is reduced to a threatening sea from which 'souls' must be saved and brought into the safe haven of their own community. This preoccupation with personal salvation finds extreme expression in the 'snake-handling' churches in the poor Eastern mountain regions of the United States. The promise in Mark 16 that believers will pick up snakes and drink poison without being harmed is taken quite literally by these people. After the experience of 'anointing' with the Spirit they pass round poisonous snakes in their meetings, seize fire or drink deadly poison. Remarkably enough, people are almost never seriously harmed.

(b) Structural criticism

However, within the Pentecostal movement from the beginning there has also been a realization of the need for a more structural criticism and opposition to war, the economic system and discrimination. Before patriotism was embraced, virtually the whole of early Pentecostalism in both the United States and in Europe was pacifist. Frank Bartleman, who was involved in the Los Angeles revival from the beginning, wrote that here 'the difference between the colours has been washed away by the blood [of Christ]'. In dozens of articles he criticized capitalism and American economic policy, according to him the true motive behind the involvement of the United States in the First World War. This war was essentially 'a commercial battle... in order definitively to get the [economic] upper hand'. So the Americans might as well 'take the stars from their flags and replace them with dollar signs'. He thought the capitalist system unscriptural and condemned the policy of keeping prices artificially high, the withholding of food and the unjust distribution of agricultural land. In fact the land belonged first of all to the original inhabitants, the Indians. From his situation and time the Communism in the young Soviet Union, which strove for equal rights for all, seemed to him to be ideal.[14] Recently the Slovenian Pentecostal theologian Peter Kuzmić, following in the footsteps of the Czech Hromadka, has argued in a similar way for taking the Marxist criticism of religion seriously. Such social critics in the Pentecostal movement are motivated by their 'Third World' spirituality, in which there is no difference between the spiritual and the material sphere. Thus in principle the 'earthly' aspect of liberation in Christ can come into its own.

Moreover it is not surprising that after the split between the black and the white Pentecostalists this social and political concern faded into the background, above all in the white Pentecostal churches. Parham's doctrine of glossolalia as the only authentic proof of baptism in the Spirit made a strong contribution here. Here glossolalia is the assurance that one is baptized in the Spirit as an individual, and has no significance for the wider social context. This tendency towards the interiorization of the Pentecostal experience is further reinforced by the influence of fundamentalism, which (apart from some isolated political points of dispute at the level of personal ethics, like the rejection of the right to abortion and euthanasia) calls for a passive acceptance of the *status quo*.

Above all the non-white Pentecostalists, who have maintained the 'Third World' spirituality of the Los Angeles revival to the greatest degree, therefore strive to banish evil from social structures and institutes as well. So black Pentecostalists often played an active part in the civil rights struggle in the United States. Bishop Ithiel Clemmons of the Church of God in Christ played an important role in the 1960s in organizing Dr Martin Luther King's campaigns in New York. The evangelist Arthur Brazier began demonstrations urging civil disobedience in Chicago. Black Pentecostal communities often regard political demonstrations as one of the gifts of the Spirit. To the bewilderment of Western Pentecostalists the Brazilian Manoel de Melo brought his great Pentecostal church Igreja Evangélica Pentecostal 'Brasil para Christo' into the World Council of Churches in 1969. In amazement he noted what seemed to him to be the static way in which the celebrations in the World Council of Churches were conducted and compared them with 'pedalling a bicycle in the age of jet planes'. He hoped that it would be possible to combat poverty and oppression better in collaboration with other churches. 'While we are converting a million people, the devil is de-converting ten million through hunger, misery, militarism, dictatorships.' Why not use church buildings during the week for trade-union meetings and courses for the uneducated? De Melo regarded the former Roman Catholic Archbishop of Recife, Dom Helder Camara, who stood up for the poor, as the model of the true evangelist. Abdaliz de Moura, Camara's study secretary, in turn defined Pentecostalism as a 'conscious or unconscious protest against existing political, social, economic or religious forms'.[15] Although they do not speak very explicitly about their life in the Spirit (they have simply never learned this from the established churches), many present-day base communities in Latin America also have a charismatically structured liturgy and form of meeting. Here each can make a contribution, while the poor find courage to oppose the oppressive church and political order.[16]

In France during the 1930s and 1940s the Union de Prière, a charismatic current within the Reformed Church, was keen to have a dialogue with Eastern Orthodoxy and the Jews long before this got on to the agenda of the churches. Their 'charter' called money an idol that must be defeated in order for Christ to reign. In the 1970s Archbishop Milingo of Lusaka, Zambia, developed a liberation theology in which he sought to heal the soul of Africa, damaged by colonialism and impoverishment. He was a very popular pastor, more than a diplomatic prelate. His colleagues, mostly white missionaries, took offence at the way in which his archepiscopal palace was sometimes full of the poor and the sick. These could always count on his prayer and help, and as a result he did not always get down to his office work. We find almost all the aspects of the Los Angeles Pentecostal revival in Milingo's approach, which made him the target of Western, white criticism of his 'Africanization' of the gospel. So at the beginning of the 1980s he was summoned to Rome, where since then among other things he has been active in the charismatic renewal.[17] Another well-known contemporary model is Frank Chikane, preacher in the Pentecostal movement and secretary of the South African Council of Churches. Because of his fight against apartheid he was tortured by a police agent – a deacon, it should be noted, in the Pentecostal movement. In bewilderment Chikane had to conclude that people 'can speak in tongues and torture people at the same time'. This is above all the result of Parham's doctrine, which has had a great influence on the South African Pentecostal movement and has silenced it politically. For, as I have remarked, if glossolalia becomes the sign of baptism with the Spirit, life in the Spirit of Christ is detached from life in this world. By contrast, a Pentecostalist theologian like Chikane was inspired by Seymour's African, holistic view of spiritual and material reality. The recognition of their own, long-suppressed black origin is now slowly opening the eyes of the Pentecostal movement in South Africa. Thus Pentecostals (among them Frank Chikane) played an important role in the drafting of the Kairos Document, a critical theological evaluation of the state of emergency proclaimed by the government. In 1989 *The Relevant Pentecostal Witness* appeared, a criticism of the policy of apartheid inspired by the Pentecostal movement's own black roots.[18]

(iii) The charismatic renewal in the indigenous, non-white churches

Pentecostalism today embraces three main currents: the Pentecostal movement, the charismatic renewal and the indigenous non-white churches.[19] The charismatic renewal represents the continuation of the original ecumenical élan of the Pentecostal movement. Above all since the 1960s it has broken through into the established churches. For various reasons, of which I can mention only some here, the time had become ripe for this. During the 1960s the fruits of the Enlightenment finally became the common property of 'ordinary' (Western) people. On the one hand this accelerated secularization and repudiation of this stimulated a new quest for spirituality. On the other hand societies were going through a process of democratization, as a result of which the autonomy of the individual citizen increased. This autonomy is honoured in charismatic celebrations, in which each person has a contribution to make on the basis of his or her gifts. Increasingly during this period, above all in psychology, physics, the philosophy of science and control of the environment, the limits of the one-sided rational Western approach to reality were becoming obvious. This led to a new evaluation of the experience of faith in Pentecostalism, which is in principle holistic. Both were further advanced by the rise of the mass media like film, radio and television. Up to the 1960s, the printed word was the principal means of communication, a means which above all appeals to rational and conceptual thought. By contrast, the modern mass media are rich in imagery and appeal to more senses. They also speak not only to the understanding but above all to the feelings.

However, in the charismatic renewal, even more than in the white Pentecostal movement, holistic spirituality has remained predominantly limited to the personal integration of understanding, feeling and body. In place of a radical reconciliation between people with skins of different colours and different social backgrounds, here we find above all an unprecedented encounter between members of many different churches and groups. Not so much racial and socio-economic barriers but church frontiers fall away (although this has been less the case with Roman Catholicism in recent years). Moreover the rise of the charismatic renewal has given new stimuli to the development of a doctrine of the Holy Spirit. This emerges in Europe for example from the work of Roman Catholic theologians like

Heribert Mühlen, Piet Schoonenberg and Yves Congar, and of Protestants like Hendrikus Berkhof, Jan Veenhof and Jürgen Moltmann.

The question is why the charismatic renewal generally has little social and political involvement. There are different reasons for this, among them the fact that it mostly consists of white, well-established citizens who attach little importance to changing the social order. However, in my view the most important cause lies in the fact that the breakthrough of charismatic renewal was above all mediated through the white South African David du Plessis, a preacher of the Assemblies of God. His courageous commitment and vision of the ecumenical breadth of the work of the Spirit was almost evened out by his blind spot over the policy of apartheid in his own country. Through du Plessis the established churches received an interpretation of the Spirit of Pentecost (complete with a mild version of Parham's doctrine) which detached it from the black, holistic experience of reality. So it can happen today that in Latin America charismatic believers hold their prayer meetings in expensive hotels while at the same time actively supporting political terrorism among the poor – who include Pentecostal believers. The phenomenon of the 'charismatic' television preachers in the United States has meanwhile almost become synonymous with superficial emotional preaching, chauvinism, greed and hypocrisy. In the Netherlands, the Dutch Charismatic Association has a social and political involvement group. However, it remains difficult for charismatics to integrate this involvement into their faith. One reason for this, in addition to the white theology of the baptism of the Spirit mediated by du Plessis, is that charismatic spirituality in the Netherlands is still not welcomed consistently by local communities. So this experience of faith must necessarily for the most part remain limited to incidental conferences and retreats one step removed from refractory, everyday reality. Thus it is difficult to combine spirituality and involvement.

Finally, we find the non-white indigenous churches in the Third World, like the Zionists in South Africa, the Aladura churches in West Africa, the Kimbanguists in Zaire and the indigenous Pentecostal churches in India, Asia and Latin America. In reaction to Western paternalism, they are looking for a Christian identity of their own. Consequently indigenous religious and cultural elements are integrated into their faith. This is the reason why they have been condemned by Western theologians, who do not realize how syncretistic their own thought is (as a result of Greek, Roman and German influences). The indigenous churches often attach great importance to healing, including the healing of the social order. Like the Western Pentecostalist movement, most of them have a rigorist ethic. Today these churches form by far the greater part of Pentecostalism, which is not surprising, since this is a Christian, 'baptized' version of their own 'Third World' spirituality. Their cultures have hitherto remained free of the one-sided 'Greek' split between the understanding on the one hand and the feelings and the body on the other. Today the West is discovering how much damage this division has caused to the welfare of human beings and the environment after having great successes in the scientific and technological spheres. The independent churches founded in the Netherlands by immigrants from, for example, Ghana, Zaire, Eritrea, Surinam and the Antilles are almost all related to Pentecostalism in form, content and structure.[20] Bill Seymour acculturated Christianity into the African religious tradition in such a way that a spirituality arose with an appeal and intercultural breadth unprecedented in church history.

(iv) Growth and diversity

The statistician David Barrett became widely known in 1982 as a result of the publication of his *World Christian Encyclopedia*, which provides a documented survey of Christianity worldwide. One of the great surprises produced by this work was the enormous growth of Pentecostalism. Fascinated by this phenomenon, since then Barrett has regularly published a scholarly account of the latest state of affairs.[21]

It emerges from this that in the year 1991, around 392 million people were involved in Pentecostalism, and that the annual increase amounted to nineteen million. There are still no signs that this growth will diminish in the immediate future. It is expected that before long the number of Pentecostals will exceed that of the total membership of the Protestant churches. Of these sixty-six per cent are in the Third World, often in unexpected places. Thus there are around a million Pentecostalists among the old civilization of the Tamils in South India, more than the number of Anglican charismatics in Great Britain. In Korea there are thirteen million Pentecostals. Thousands of these are active as qualified workers in the Middle East, which is closed to Christians, where they spread the gospel at their places of work. Today Pentecostalists are found in all the traditions, churches and groups of Christianity, in about eight thousand different ethno-linguistic cultures and seven thousand languages (about five per cent of all the languages spoken on earth). Pentecostals live more in the city than in the country, and there are more women than men among them. Barrett points out that in our century perhaps more of them have been persecuted, tortured and killed for their beliefs than Christians from any other tradition. One shocking fact, which prosperous Western members of the Pentecostal movement and the charismatic renewal have seldom stopped to consider, is that fifty per cent of all Pentecostals have to live in shanty-towns in the depths of poverty. These amount to more than two hundred million people, nineteen million of them among the poorest of the poor, who have to scrape through the rubbish heaps each day in search of food.

This enormous ethnic, linguistic and social difference seems to be the world-wide, twentieth-century counterpart of the Pentecost event in Acts 2, in which the Spirit is poured out on people from different lands, peoples and languages. Hollenweger's account of a consultation which was organized by the World Council of Churches at Bossey in 1980 illustrates this clearly:

There were well-known [white] theologians from Roman Catholic and Protestant Charismatic Renewal groups ... In addition, a nuclear physicist, who happened to be the chairman of the cabinet of the chef spiritual of the Kimbanguist church, and the General Secretary of the Israel Nineveh Church (two independent African churches, both members of the WCC) were present. A black choir from the Church of God in Christ in England came with their pastor, a driving instructor by profession. One of the worship services was led by the Senior Apostle [in daily life a book-keeper] of the Cherubim and Seraphim Society from England (an African Independent Church widely known throughout West Africa) according to the liturgy of his church, which is word for word identical with the old Anglo-Catholic liturgy – except that he celebrated it without reference to a printed liturgy and with all the dramatic panache and deeply felt reverence of an African who actually knew and experienced that he was praying in the presence of angels and archangels, the cherubim and seraphim and all the company of heaven. Prophecies and speaking in tongues fitted easily into this age-old liturgy. At the final eucharist the Anglican

Archbishop of Cape Town [Burnett] confessed that the Scripture reading of that day had spoken personally to him.[22]

Hollenweger remarks that from the communal experience of the Spirit, Pentecostalism can build a bridge between the different cultures, in the same way as happened in the Los Angeles revival (and in the New Testament communities). Such an inter-cultural dialogue should not only relativize particular theological presuppositions determined by culture but also contribute to an increasingly mutual understanding and actual solidarity – not least between the rich West and the poor masses in the southern hemisphere. In Pentecostalism, religion, so often used as an occasion and justification for war, has the potential to make an essential contribution to world peace.[23]

Now precisely what is the essential contribution of Pentecostalism? As I have said, this lies above all in the 'Third World' spirituality mediated through the black Seymour. The well-known rabbi Abraham Joshua Heschel compares the blacks with Joseph, who becomes the saviour of those who had sold him into slavery. 'The great spiritual resource of the negroes, their ability to be happy, their closeness to the Bible, their aptitude for worship and enthusiasm could prove to be a blessing for all humankind.'[24] Pentecostalism is essentially a gift from the Third World to the West with its poverty of feelings and its fear of the body. Its spirituality is expressed most clearly in celebration.

2

Charismatic Celebration

The participants themselves experience the essential contribution of Pentecostalism, but do not (or hardly ever) put it into words. If asked what they see as the most important characteristic, members of a non-white indigenous church might for example answer 'Healing through prayer'. Someone involved in the charismatic renewal would mention the baptism and gifts of the Spirit and the renewal of the churches as the most important contributions, whereas a Pentecostal would think of the proclamation that Jesus is Lord and baptism in the Spirit together with speaking in tongues. However, in my view this does not yet get to the heart of the matter. And since one of the tasks of a theologian is to express human experiences in words, I shall make an attempt to describe the essence of Pentecostalism. For an experience only comes into its own when it finds emotional, physical and intellectual expression to match. In Pentecostalism, however, expression through feelings and the body is better developed than conceptual expression. (We find the opposite in the established churches: there intellectual expression comes first and emotional and bodily expression comes much lower down the scale.)

So the real contribution of Pentecostalism does not lie in a doctrine. The ethnic and cultural diversity of this trend finds its counterpart in a great theological difference. So most Pentecostalists practise water baptism with a confession of faith and their community structure is made up of a mixture of congregationalist (the community has the say) and presbyteral (the elders have the say) influences. But there are also major Pentecostal church communities which recognize infant baptism and are governed by bishops (mostly an influence of Methodism). From a theological perspective there is a great difference between the 'Jesus Only' churches and, for example, the Kimbanguist churches in Zaire, which seem to place their founder and prophet Simon Kimbangu close to the triune God. For North American

Pentecostalists, but also, for example, for Roman Catholic charismatics, the faith of the non-white indigenous churches is often so far removed from their own Western theological presuppositions that they sometimes find difficulty in recognizing the members of these churches as fellow Christians. And the charismatic renewal knows almost as many different theological views as the churches involved. Certainly all forms of Pentecostalism regard the church as normative for belief, and in connection with the knowledge and service of God they attribute a crucial role to Christ and the Spirit. But there is no generally accepted interpretation of this from the Bible. Moreover, as I have said, the secret of Pentecostalism lies in its 'Third World' spirituality, which is experienced above all in charismatic celebration. By 'charismatic' here I do not just mean the charismatic renewal, but the kind of celebration which is characteristic of almost all Pentecostalism. Here are meetings in which the gifts (Greek *charismata*) function explicitly.

(i) Characteristics

At this point I want to go more deeply into the most important aspects of charismatic celebration.[25] Although a written description is no substitute for personal acquaintance with such a celebration, it is good to begin with an eye-witness account of a Pentecostal meeting in Chile. Here Hollenweger is again our reporter:

> An ocean of faces floated before my eyes, 2000 to 3000 faithful, some with car-tyres on their feet instead of shoes. But as soon as the trumpet blew the first melody, those faces, creased with the signs of age-long oppression, came to life. In a circle the people danced slowly the dances of their Indian ancestors. Those who did not dance stood reverently and clapped their hands slowly. A woman prophesied in a deep, soul-searching voice. All of a sudden there was silence! The whole congregation fell down on their knees in order to thank God for the dance he had given them ... The most important element of the Pentecostal worship is the active participation of every member of the congregation, even if this amounts to several thousand people ... In the structure of the Pentecostal liturgy one might find most of the elements of historical liturgies: Invocation, Kyrie, Confession, Gloria, Eucharistic Canon and Benediction. Yet these parts are hardly ever so named ...

[They are linked together with the help of] so-called choruses, i.e. short spontaneous songs, known by heart by the whole congregation . . . If someone sings a song of praise in the Kyrie part, or gives a prophecy in the Invocation part, he will be corrected either by the pastor, or by an elder, or, if he persists, by the immediate and spontaneous singing of the whole congregation. Most Pentecostals are not aware of the liturgical function of these choruses, yet they are clearly observable. The Pentecostals thus demonstrate that the alternative to a written liturgy is not chaos, but a flexible oral tradition, which allows for variations within the framework of the whole liturgical structure, similar to the possibilities in a jam session of jazz musicians.[26]

Five characteristics of charismatic celebration spring particularly to view.

1. The celebrations have an oral liturgy which is not set down on paper and therefore is accessible to people who have little or no literary training. This liturgy is led by the president but it is also as it were in the people themselves and allows much room for spontaneous contributions and improvisations. This encourages personal involvement and interaction between the participants. In the established churches which are involved in the charismatic movement the traditional liturgy is often experienced in a new, more personal, manner and internalized in a way which corresponds to an oral liturgy. In addition, in these churches room is deliberately made for the spontaneous contribution of believers, for example before or directly after the celebration of the eucharist.

2. The main characteristics of charismatic celebration are a narrative theology and testimonies. The central place is not occupied by Western concepts and dogmatic teachings but by the existential conviction of 'what God can do for you' and the corresponding story of 'what God has done for me'. In the Pentecostal movement this narrative structure usually takes the sharp edges off imported fundamentalism. Scripture then is not treated as a legal code but expounded with the aid of a charismatic exegesis which resembles that of the prophets, the New Testament writers and rabbinic midrash.[27] This includes a playful interaction between the text of the Bible and the present situation, in which the story of scripture is interwoven with that of the community. Conversely, the believers recognize themselves in the text. The story is best suited for expressing

communal experiences in a way which not only encourages the building up of the community but are also makes these experiences accessible to newcomers. The story communicates better than an abstract theological argument because it resonates with the human depth-structure. In the words of the literary critic Paul Ricoeur, human beings are a 'living text', complete with a beginning, middle, end, and a plot that supports the life story. Hence also the abiding fascination of proverbs, novels, films and even jokes, which can be regarded as 'mini-stories'. Moreover the testimonies (like, for example, the Heidelberg Catechism) are also constructed according to the universal scheme of being lost, redeemed and giving thanks (the happy ending). Here the account is not as objective as possible but is a form of proclamation in which – in the rhetorical desire for the message to come over but also in sheer pleasure at the story itself – the darkness of the wood in which people are lost is made extra thick; the unexpected redemption through Christ takes on a fairy-like gleam and the newly found life with God becomes a palace of enchantment.

3. On the basis of the gifts of the Spirit there is the maximum possible participation at the level of prayer, evaluation and also the making of resolutions. This can lead to a community which is attentive to differences and is therefore reconciling. However, as free groups Pentecostal communities are vulnerable to authoritarian leaders, people who take on a paternal or maternal role which limits the autonomy of the members of the community. This sometimes causes divisions. But even in such Pentecostal communities the possibility of a personal contribution to the celebration is always greater than in moderate traditional church worship. In the latter the role of believers usually remains limited to singing hymns given out by the priest or preacher and saying fixed responses and prayers. If here in word and sacrament there is a deliberate emphasis on the objectivity of the salvation that comes upon believers which can make the worship rather static, in the charismatic celebration the flexible liturgy also leaves room for the dynamic, spontanous response of the participants. Already in preaching, as in the early church, there is the possibility of reacting with approval, in applause, laughter, exclamations or laments. At other moments the response can be a prayer, praise in glossolalic sounds, a dance, prophecy, testimony, a song or a text from scripture. Those present can experience these expressions as gifts of the Spirit through which such a subjective

response can in turn become the vehicle of objective salvation and take on the character of proclamation, encouragement or admonition. These gifts function above all in the celebration, but they can also emerge in, for example, a pastoral conversation or a meeting of the community. It is obvious that where there is more room for a subjective contribution, greater reference is made to the different capacities of the community. In reaction to all kinds of mistakes which have been made here, within Pentecostalism today the functioning of the verbal gifts is sometimes restrained or their truth-content is relativized in advance. Instead of this it seems better to reflect again on the nature of the charisms, as I hope to begin to do later in this book.

4. A good deal of space is made for intuitive communication, for example in the form of dreams and visions. The function of these can be compared with that of icons. The typical light that is characteristic of an icon is God's light, which for the believing eye shines throughout creation and can be perceived particularly in Christ and the saints. So, too, the intuitive images which are 'seen' in dreams and visions of angels and the like can have a divine radiance, as a result of which they have been experienced as a special encouragement and sometimes instruction. The opposite also happens. Then there are threatening or demonic manifestations without any radiance, which are experienced as a warning or judgment. So the images are often vehicles and typifications of existential experiences of God's presence or, negatively, God's absence.[28] This non-rational, intuitive dimension in human beings, in which the damaging Western abstract gulf between subject and object is overcome, is clearly stimulated by charismatic celebration. From the experience of a bond with God and the world new insights into reality well up from the unconscious which can help people further on their way. This liberation of the power of the imagination can lead to liberation in the political and social sphere, as often happens with black and Latin American Pentecostals. This begins the moment people can imagine a different order from that of today.

5. Finally, body and spirit are experienced as one whole in the charismatic celebration. The sense of this unity is now also beginning to penetrate into the West, but it has not yet become common property. Our body ties us to the world, so that this holistic view, as we have seen, can lead within Pentecostalism to all kinds of activities at the social level. This unity is most clearly expressed in the

celebration in the prayer for healing, which includes bodily ailments. In the charismatic renewal, to a greater extent than in the Pentecostal movement, this prayer is taken up into the whole of the liturgy, with reference back to traditions from the early church. This helps to avoid an unhealthy fixation on the healing of a specific ailment (the organically directed approach) and opens the eyes to the importance of healing the wider sphere of life with its elements which produce illness, like the excessive pressure of work, discrimination and pollution of the environment. I once watched Archbishop Milingo as, faithful to his African tradition, he laid hands on someone whose business had gone bankrupt. The prayer for healing is in principle at the same time a prayer for the healing of creation. For, with a variation on a saying of Paul's, where the body of the world suffers, our bodies also suffer. So when hands are laid on someone in a charismatic celebration with a prayer for healing, in an extension of the kyrie prayer, at the same time hands are laid on the world of which the person concerned forms a part. So both fulfil a priestly function. The one who prays represents the God who is concerned for healing, while the one for whom the prayer is said represents in his or her sick body the suffering world. It is an old Jewish notion that our pain can only truly be healed when this is experienced as the pain of the world and is thus connected with the whole creation in need.

Now it is striking that all these characteristics, most of which Miskotte counts as part of the 'surplus' of the First Testament,[29] have an element of play in them. The oral liturgy corresponds to rules which make a personal contribution possible (and does not everyone learn as a child to play in a verbal milieu?). Narrative theology can have the tension and intensity of a good story. The greatest contribution on the basis of charisms has many elements of a team game and strengthens the team spirit. The intuitive level as this is expressed in images and visions but also, for example in glossolalia, is essential for a good game, where it can produce surprising upsets. And the unity of body and spirit is also experienced when one is wholly caught up in a game. So it is not surprising that some observers, like the English bishop John Taylor,[30] have recognized just how like a game charismatic celebration is. What is perhaps surprising, though, is that hitherto no one has worked this out as the most important contribution of Pentecostalism. The main reason is that the Pentecostals do not do this themselves, whether because of their fundamentalist presuppositions, because (in the charismatic renewal) they are too much influenced by their church traditions, or simply because they do not feel the need to reflect on their experience. But the essential importance of play for human beings and their society has been demonstrated by all kinds of researchers (above all in the Netherlands), and has more than ever taken on prophetic weight in our modern, technocratic age. Already in scripture play occupies a more important place than is often imagined. So we shall now turn our attention to that.

Part Two: Sabbath Play: Biblical Notes

The time of great systems is also past in theology, and their place is being taken by a broad spectrum of interpretations, each of which puts existence in a different light. Now the model of play is certainly not new in itself, but it has taken on a new relevance because of both present-day Pentecostalism and modern, reified society. In this part I shall above all investigate the biblical evidence, and in the next part look at church history, as well as go more deeply ito play and the playful character of charismatic celebration.

I

The Uselessness of God

A prominent characteristic of play is its uselessness. It serves no purpose, but is an end in itself. This attitude of play seems to be the only right attitude to God, to our fellow human beings and to creation generally.

Anyone who tries to prove God's existence by demonstrating the need for God makes the same mistake as those who claim that in our modern secularized society God no longer has any function and has thus become superfluous. Both begin from the usefulness of God. But God is not useful.[1] God does not serve any purpose, since God is an end in himself. However laudable our striving may be, as soon as God is used to achieve one purpose or another, we reduce the divine to an instrument. Then God is no longer God. Moreover it is not surprising that in a technological culture like ours, which is obsessed by purpose and achievement, God has often either been reduced to a useful, predictable idol, or is experienced as absent. Using a term from the Jewish thinker Martin Buber, this last sensation is called a darkening of God. One could see this as the cultural counterpart to what the sixteenth-century Spanish mystic John of the Cross called the 'dark night', a night (or wilderness) through which every believer has to go on his or her way with God. This is a period of dissociation from the God who above all satisfies our needs, and of learning to cope with God as God is in himself. In the first instance this is experienced as a loss, just as the liberated Hebrews longed for the fleshpots of Egypt because they could not yet appreciate the taste of the manna in the wilderness.[2] Although unfamiliar with the great mystics, the Pentecostal movement has generally retained this truth better than the charismatic renewal. It knows of wilderness experiences and has prayer meetings in which sometimes a whole night is spent 'waiting on God'. Certainly Pentecostal believers, like all Pentecostals, bombard God with questioning prayers, but a fixation on the desired answer is usually avoided by the play of the celebration. They are like a lover whose beloved refuses to fulfil certain wishes, but who gladly accepts this and forgets it in the joy of the love-play. By contrast, in circles of the North American charismatic renewal, which is often more permeated with the dogmas of the consumer society than the Pentecostal movement, it has proved possible for a 'Positive Confession' movement to form. This is a form of positive thinking carried to absurd extremes which starts from the presupposition that everything that is 'claimed' in the name of Jesus will be received. Here God is reduced to a magical answer to prayer. The meetings have become a means to an end, namely the satisfaction of often crudely materialistic desires. The Assemblies of God (albeit after some hesitation) have condemned this approach as unscriptural.

The tendency to identify God with usefulness emerges above all from the primitive, animal drive towards the satisfaction of needs. Everything that an animal does, like graze, hunt, sleep and couple, is directed towards need, in other words towards the survival of the species. The play of young animals is also subordinate to this goal. Now the desire to see our needs satisfied is in itself legitimate, just as it is not wrong that most relationships begin at the point where two people discover that they fulfil each other's needs. However, if things stop here the relationship remains purely functional: the one is reduced to an extension of the other's ego, and vice versa. The other is then important because of the need that the partner has, not because of who he or she is in themselves. There is no question of a real encounter. So partners can essentially remain strangers to each other. This same, primitive dynamic also works towards God, who is needed to satisfy needs which cannot be met by human beings, like the desire to know why one exists and to overcome the pressure towards death. In addition to its many positive contributions to humanity the modern scientific approach has encouraged this instrumental attitude through its thought in terms of cause and effect. The word 'God' becomes the explanation of everything that cannot be explained, a means of filling the gaps in our knowledge. This view is no different from that of primitive people who spontaneously attribute what to them is the incomprehensible working of lightning to a deity. The question 'how?' asked by scientific investigation not only banishes God to the limits of our knowledge but also reduces the divine existence to an instrument for satisfying our needs. In that way it is difficult for us really to know God.

In the same direction, the philosopher Kant (who recognized that he had not kept up with the development of Christian theology in his time) made religion a moral doctrine, useful in order to restore the original human tendency towards the good. In the third book of his *Religion within the Limits of Reason Alone*, 'God' in fact becomes a designation of this moral disposition in human beings. Kant's reduction of God to an instrument to serve morality was only partially compensated for by his view that the moral commandment is an end in itself and must be obeyed uncon-ditionally, or it does not produce a result (see his *Critique of Practical Reason*). The nineteenth-century theologian Friedrich Schleiermacher, in his *Speeches on Religion to its Cultured Despisers*, was the first to criticize this distortion of religion by the rationalistic approach of the Enlightenment, with its orientation on utility, and to emphasize the importance of the existential experience of God.

Only when the question 'How does the world work?', aimed at controlling it, is transcended in the more fundamental question 'Why does the world exist?' can God be known. The answer to the last question is: for no reason at all. The uselessness of God implies the uselessness of creation. Creation exists only because God takes pleasure in it: God finds the world 'good', according to the refrain in Genesis 1. And Psalm 104, which is about the creation, celebrates God in v.26 as a God who has made Leviathan (some kind of giant sea creature) 'to play in it'. From moment to moment the world is called into being 'for nothing' in a pure game of love through God's Word and Spirit (compare verses 29-30). To use a traditional theological term: we exist by grace. For God there was and is no need at all to create. God is a playful God. As the Reformed theologian Van Ruler wrote: the world has no reason and no basis, and precisely for that reason, on the one hand it is open to complete meaninglessness, but at the same time, on the other, it is open to the free play of the totally other God.[3] This emerges most clearly in human beings who, being in the image of God, are God's 'kindred spirits'.

(i) The play of the sabbath

We can conclude from the creation stories that God meant the world as a game. Thus in the first chapter of Genesis we find a more or less rising line in which God creates ever higher forms of life. For a long time it was thought that human beings were to be the crown of creation. This notion was also stimulated by the influence from humanism which gives human beings a central place, but we are now aware of the serious consequences of this for the environment.

The Tübingen theologian Jürgen Moltmann rightly points out that the crown of creation is not human beings, who were created on the sixth day, but the sabbath, made on the seventh and last day of creation.[4] On this day God 'rests' from his work and 'takes breath', enjoys his creation. The sabbath was so identified with God that not to celebrate this day was even regarded as a lack of faith in God himself and was to be punished accordingly (Exodus 31.12-17). In the later Jewish tradition, 'sabbath' is even one of the names of God. The weekly sabbath points to the eternal sabbath rest and keeps alive the notion that human beings, and thus the whole of creation, are on the way to perfection. The world is governed by the messianic time: orientated on being with God in complete freedom and delight. In a working week characterized by necessity and achieving, the celebration of the sabbath creates as it were a free space in which God's purpose with the world becomes transparent. For a whole day people abandon their work in the belief that it is not their work but only grace that can save them. This intuition is also expressed in the so-called second creation story (Gen.2), which breathes an atmosphere of play. We read about a garden in which the trees are not what they seem, a paradise with gold and chrysophrase. The man gives names to the animals, the man and the woman enjoy each other and run naked through the garden like children – together with God. It was the kind of frivolous way of living that the ancient Greeks revered in their immortal gods, with a degree of distaste. In the biblical story of paradise the sabbath play is spoiled in the next chapter when men and women no longer listen to God. The free innocent game is exchanged for the need for clothing and sustenance. Peace gives way to dispute and greed. Human beings are pursued by the definitive necessity of death: they will 'surely die' (2.17), 'dust you are and to dust you will return' (3.19).

At a very early stage the rabbis made a connection between the sabbath and the exodus from Egypt and thus the end of all disruption, injustice and violence. The sabbath is about no less than the humanity of existence and creation coming into its own. Moreover, the sabbath also has a derivative, the sabbath year, in which once every seven years no work is done on the land. What grows of its own accord was for the poor and after that for the animals. The sabbath year culminated (at least in theory) every fiftieth year in the year of jubilee, in which, moreover, all debts were written off and Hebrew slaves freed (Ex.23.10-11; Lev.25.8-55). The sabbath points to the perfect bond between God and creation, and thus between all parts of creation. The evangelist Luke (4.18-19) makes Jesus pronounce his messianic programme in the synagogue of Nazareth where he stands up on a sabbath and reads from Isaiah 61:

> The spirit of the Lord is upon me, because he has anointed me to preach good news to the poor. He has sent me to proclaim release to the captives and recovering of sight to the blind, to set at liberty those who are oppressed, to proclaim the acceptable year of the Lord.

The evangelists describe how Jesus healed people on the sabbath and allowed his disciples to pluck ears of corn. This brought him into conflict with some legalistic Pharisees (it is not improbable that Jesus himself was a member of another group of Pharisees). In their zeal to hallow the sabbath they had protected it from the working week with so many regulations that contrary to the original intention this day had become just one more observance and had a less human character. In his answer to them (Mark 2.23-28) Jesus first recalls David, who upset the priestly order by taking the dedicated show-bread and eating it with his hungry men. Jesus thus relativizes the zeal for the divine which can so easily turn into a rigid order at the expense of humanity. Then he refers to the creation of the sabbath: 'the sabbath was made for man, not man for the sabbath'. Here Jesus has no intention of abolishing the sabbath, nor is he claiming that human beings should be the criterion of all things. He is recalling the real significance of this day. The sabbath points people to the kingdom of God, to true humanity: to the enjoyment of creation, if only by eating ears of corn, and to freedom from sickness, alienating order and compulsion (see also the following story, Mark 3.1-6). So Jesus interprets the sabbath in the light of the creation story and of his own service to God and human beings.[5] In his own person and work he embodies the meaning of the sabbath. More than David, 'the Son of Man (a term Jesus used to refer to himself) is lord also of the sabbath'.

Although its origin is different, the Christian Sunday cannot therefore be understood properly without the Jewish sabbath. Sunday is a radicalization of the sabbath and can best be understood as the beginning of the fulfilment of the sabbath hope, in the belief that in his resurrection Jesus became the 'firstfruit' of the perfected creation (compare I Cor.15.20-28). The necessity of death has in principle disappeared, and above all on Sunday Christians take breath, and already experience in Christ a foretaste of the kingdom of God. However, Christianity, too, has its oppressive forms of hallowing Sunday. Here a legalistic stress on order has robbed the celebration of its essentially playful character – and thus its real meaning – and banished that to the sports field. Compared with the average church service, in charismatic celebration this element of play is fully present. It is no coincidence that Pentecostalism is one of the few Christian currents which is named after a festival (Pentecost). This playful character is the first thing that strikes people who visit a charismatic celebration and was an important reason why the established churches initially rejected Pentecostalism.

(a) Human play

So human beings are not the crown of creation; the sabbath is, and on it the whole creation is focussed. In other words, human beings are crowned with the 'glory and splendour' of the sabbath and are thus priests of creation, as Psalm 8 has it. The word sabbath does not occur in this psalm, but its meaning is all the clearer. In verses 1c and 2a the poet writes: 'Your glory above the heavens is chanted by the mouths of babes and infants.' But another translation of verse 3 can be: 'By the mouths of babes and infants you (God) have established strength.'[6] Both meanings are possible and in fact supplement each other. In useless worship of God human beings place themselves on the same footing as the unpretentious little child. In worship human beings recognize the gratuitous character of their existence. Nothing in the universe makes human existence (and that of the world) necessary. Life is a disinterested gift from God. To recognize this is God's power. In contrast to the 'strength' of God's enemies, who in their purposeful, aggressive striving live at the expense of other human beings and nature, God's 'strength' is grounded in babes and infants, symbols of vulnerability and play. Human beings are not called to dominate and to manipulate but to allow the creation to have its due by playing a game with it. The awareness that existence is not necessary leads on the one hand to the sigh, 'What is man that you are mindful of him?' But on the other hand that same sense leads to the conclusion that human beings have been made 'almost godlike' (v.6), for they are an end in themselves and are crowned with the radiance of the sabbath through which they are priests of creation. Many early translations, like the Greek Septuagint on which the New Testament writers drew, toned down this radical statement: here human beings are made 'almost like angels'. In the New Testament this is said of Jesus himself, the true human who was 'weak' and precisely in this way king of God's kingdom and lord of the sabbath. The expression is always used in passages about his death and resurrection, in which the vicious circle of necessity is broken through and the fulfilment of the sabbath hope is begun (I Cor.15.27; Eph.1.19-22; Heb.2.6-9).

As priests of creation, human beings are called to live in a way that the rest of the world as yet cannot, so that the purpose of creation becomes clear. The lives of plants and animals are dominated by necessity and utility and directed towards the preservation of the species. However, the activities which most distinguish human beings from animals transcend this and have the free character of a game: worshipping, celebrating festivals, creating art, loving without an object or a reason. Animals have no festivals and create no art: they couple but do not love. The more human beings learn to live playfully, the more human they become and the more they begin to resemble God, who has directed creation towards the sabbath game. This is the new Jerusalem where the music never stops and mature wine flows; where the lion lies down with the lamb and humankind plays the game of bride and bridegroom with God. As the poet and theologian Charles Williams wrote (in *The Founding of the Company*), the human being, consisting utterly of love, is then the 'prime and exalted image of perfect superfluity'.

Johan Huizinga, the historian of culture, has shown that the essentially human element does not just lie in thought (*homo sapiens*) or in the capacity to make things (*homo faber*), but above all also in the fact that human beings can play (*homo ludens*).[7] Play is fundamental to our humanity and our society. Unlike animals, moreover, human beings create culture. Culture, Huizinga demonstrates, is in fact a game. It differs from art and music to the degree that legislation differs from table manners. Present-day psychologists generally see the capacity for play as characteristic of sane people. No one is more obssessed with order and concerned with the consequences of his or her behaviour than the neurotic. The healthy person is someone who can live day by day and receive existence as a gift with open hands. Anyone who arrogantly says 'But it's only a game' is perhaps betraying the degree to which he or she is infected by our neurotic civilization, deluded by purposefulness and utility. This is often characterized more by animal instincts than by human freedom. The Jewish philosopher Martin Buber, a contemporary of Huizinga's, made a distinction between culture, as an expression of superfluity and play, and externalized civilization focussed on utility. Society with its fixed forms and 'dead conventions' which must protect individuals from one another's self-interest corresponds to civilization. By contrast, culture is bound up with the community which has nothing but itself, and thus life, in view. According to Buber, within civilization and society religion is determined by 'dogma' and the static 'God enthroned from eternity' (this becomes an impersonal 'it'). On the other hand, within culture and society religion is characterized by the 'personal revelation of each individual' and 'God coming to be in whose development we can share' (God as personal 'You'). Only from a renewal of the interpersonal relationship in which the other is no longer regarded as an object and instrument but is respected as an end in himself or herself can orderly society become a worthwhile human society.[8]

Huizinga wrote that play is of a higher order than seriousness. 'Seriousness seeks to exclude play, whereas play can very well include seriousness.'[9] And indeed, employers want their people to feed information into the computer at the office during the day with the same dedication and concentration that they devote to putting a ball in the net in the evening in their free time. Only a playful way of living does justice to the seriousness of life. In making this observation Huizinga was standing on the shoulders of the Greek philosopher Plato. In his last dialogue, written shortly before his death, Plato concludes that all human beings must make the best possible game out of their lives, because God is the real goal of any serious activity directed towards the good. Here Plato remarks directly that this is a complete change from the present state of things which is dominated by a concern for superficialities, and also for war.[10] Preoccupation with gossip and endless television series is symptomatic of a lack of that intensity of life which can alone help a playful approach to existence. War is originally a playful testing of power (think of the ancient virtues of chivalry and fair play) which has degenerated into a dispute. This happens whenever a game is no longer an end in itself but becomes completely subject to the purposes of the players. Then they are no longer concerned with the game but with their own personal advantage.

The tendency for what Plato called the 'game of peace' to degenerate into a dispute is always present. Thus sporting fixtures can sometimes end in a blood bath. The so-called play of the free market economy is essentially little more than a bitter struggle for survival at the expense of ecological balance. Instead of being a fellow player in society our neighbour has often become a contender, a threatening rival and competitor. Even the intimate game of loving is often corrupted by the desire to dominate and perform. Where play degenerates into an ordinary dispute, people lower themselves to the level of animals. We are not as far removed from the higher animals as we sometimes like to think. Very realistically, the creation story in Genesis sees us as having been created on the same day (the sixth) as them. When human play degenerates into war, culture, like nature, becomes stained with blood. Human beings themselves have been the greatest corrupters of the creation principle, and the question arises how they can exercise their function as priests of creation. Heavy hangs the head that bears the crown of creation. I think a beginning of an answer lies in becoming conscious of and experiencing the dynamics of the Word and the Spirit.

(b) God's Wisdom: the Word and the Spirit

Although the First Testament is dominated by the Hebrew prophets and the prophetic interpretation of history, we also find the tradition of the wise men. This wisdom tradition produced among other things the books of Job, Ecclesiastes and Proverbs. Here a good deal of material was used from the ancient Near East, like instructions from Egypt and sayings from Babylon and Assyria. This was subsequently interpreted in the light of the revelation of God to Israel. The wisdom literature is primarily interested in the question 'What is wise?' 'How must human beings live in this world?' Wisdom also represents the creation principle. For the wise person lives in accord with God's wisdom, in other words God's purpose with the world. So it can be said that God creates the world in, through and with wisdom (which is often personified).

In Proverbs 8.22-31, Lady Wisdom says:[11]

> Yahweh created me at the beginning of his work
> ...when he laid the foundations of the earth
> then I was with him as the apple of his eye
> and I was daily his joy;
> constantly playing before his face,
> playing in his inhabited world
> and rejoicing in the children of men.

God's creation principle is playful Wisdom. The person who plays is wise, knows how to live, since he or she lives in harmony with God's world order. Moreover, often the teaching of the wise is a bit like a literary game, as emerges from the use of fables, playing with words and numbers, and also practical examples which often have a farcical element. The foolish man tumbles like a jester through the books of Proverbs and Ecclesiastes. In Proverbs exciting scenes of seduction do not fall short of those produced by the modern film industry: the lazybones sees 'a lion on the street' and turns over again in bed like a door on its hinges (26.13-14); and the workaholic is told, 'The blessing of the Lord makes rich, and he adds no sorrow with it' (10.22).

The book of Proverbs opens with an introduction from which it emerges that in Lady Wisdom there is both a 'spirit' which she wants to pour out, and 'words' with which she calls loudly in the streets (1.23). God's Word and Spirit come together in the concept of wisdom, which emerges above all in the later (inter-testamental) wisdom literature.[12] Wisdom is not a fruit of human study or experience, but comes as a guest to live with men and women (compare Sir.39.6; Wisdom 1.4-6). Indeed, 'from generation to generation she enters holy souls and makes them friends of God and prophets' (Wisdom 7.27). 'In her is a spirit' (Wisdom 7.22; see also 9.17), but Wisdom is also seen in parallel to the creative Word of God (Wisdom 9.1-2). God's Wisdom is given to human beings so that, like Solomon, they can rule over creatures (Wisdom 9.3-18).

Later a split will develop, and most church fathers will identify Wisdom with the Word (but some, like Irenaeus, identify her with the Holy Spirit). However, in scripture Wisdom is above all a combination of the Word and the Spirit. Moreover throughout the Bible these are as it were in tandem. Neither can do anything without the other, just as a word without breath (spirit) remains unexpressed, and breath without a word is inaudible and empty. Spirit and word belong together like breath and voice. Where God's Spirit is named, God's Word is not absent, and vice versa (II Sam.23.2; Ps.33.6; Matt.10.20). The Spirit gives life (Ps.104.30; John 6.63), but this is also said of the Word (Deut.32.46-47). Jesus frees people from demonic powers by the Spirit of God (Matt.12.28), but the Word also heals (Ps.107.20). Like Wisdom (Wisdom 9.10), the Word of God comes to earth with a dynamic mission. As the rain and snow which fall and make the earth fruitful, 'so shall my word be that goes forth from my mouth; it shall not return to me empty, but it shall accomplish that which I purpose, and prosper in the thing for which I sent it' (Isa.55.11). The book of Isaiah prophesies that the land shall be taken away from Edom and will teem with jackals, snakes and kites, 'for (God's) mouth has commanded it and his Spirit has gathered them' (34.16). The 'Spirit of the Lord' brings about the prophetic 'Word of the Lord' that Ezekiel speaks against the leaders of Israel (Ezek.11.5-13). Certainly early writing prophets like Amos, Zephaniah, Nahum and Jeremiah avoid the term spirit (*ruach*). This word was probably tainted by its misuse by pseudo-prophets who claimed the spirit for their verbal fancies and were known among the people as maniacs and windbags (*ish haruach*, see Hos.9.7b). Moreover certain prophets also used synonyms for 'spirit': first among these was the other member of the tandem, the 'word' (*dabar*, a dynamic word). If the Spirit of God came to the prophet (I Sam.19.23-24), now the same thing is said of the Word (Hos.1.1). Other terms are also used to denote the Spirit like 'visions' (Hab.2.2) and 'hand of God' (Jer.1.9). From the exile on, the authentic prophets again felt free to use the term 'spirit'.

This pairing of Word and Spirit in Wisdom corresponds to the combination of order and dynamics which is the fundamental characteristic of play. With the word things are named and thus separated from the rest: defined, limited and objectified. Moreover for the philosopher Heraclitus of Ephesus, in the midst of all movement and change in the world the Word (*Logos*) was the eternal ordering formula which makes the world a cosmos. For the later Stoics the Word stood for the rational, ordering and divine principle that pantheistically penetrates and dominates all things. I cannot go here into the many nuances of meaning which the term *logos* has in Greek thought, but in general it can be said that it represents the world order and thus law and structure. In short, the Word stands for the order in play. The Hebrew term for spirit by contrast denotes air in movement. Spirit is dynamic, surprising, unifying and conveys enthusiasm. Incomprehensible as the wind and breath of life (Gen. 2.6: here the word *ruach* is not used but *neshamah*, which is almost a synonym), 'spirit' also denotes the level of feeling, and thus the tension of play. As I have said, in scripture the Word and the Spirit are always thought of together, a combination which finds expression in playful Wisdom. If for the Greek freedom stood for insight into the necessary ordering of the cosmos, for scripture freedom is the unnecessary play opened up by creative possibilities. The tension between rules and spontaneity characteristic of play, the tension between the necessary and the possible, between structure and dynamics, is the tension between the Word and the Spirit. This creative tension vibrates in creative wisdom, the world order as God means this to be.

The world-view of modern science seems to be surprisingly in accord with this. The earth is not simply the stage on which the drama of life is performed. No, the world seems to be built up in accordance with the structure and dynamics of play. In contrast to Newton's one-sided orderly mechanical picture of the world, modern physics and biology stress the idea of indeterminacy. This is not a matter of blind chance, since there are fundamental limitations like the limits of species and of space and time. These represent as it were the 'rule' of the cosmic game in which the element of indeterminacy represents the creative possibility of something new, of a surprising shift (as in a mutation). We find a similar tension between order and indeterminacy in modern system theory. This sees all healthy organisms, societies and eco-systems as characterized by the tension between manipulation of their own order (self-confirmation) and interaction with a greater whole in which they change (integration). Thus for example the Netherlands is trying both to maintain its own national identity in the growing European Community and to take an active part in the greater whole of the EC, which is changing our country. Order and indeterminacy or self-confirmation and dynamic interaction – in short, the Word and the Spirit – are, in a telling remark of Irenaeus's, the two creative hands of God. They are as it were the Yin and Yang of evolution which together develop and work out life like a cosmic Bach fugue. Here the creation shows a gratuitous surplus which seems far to surpass what is required by the purposeful existence and continuation of the species. The Dutch philosopher Buytendikjk made a famous remark, that the birds sing far more than Darwin allows them to. Word and Spirit are present at every level of creation, and work towards the eternal sabbath which has already become visible in a unique way in a man from Nazareth. Jesus is as it were a mutation of human life, a protest against the utilitarian principle of selection and a successful 'adaptation' to the central reality of God's kingdom. Therefore he is the definitive revelation of God.[13]

Jesus, the Wisdom of God

In the New Testament, Lady Wisdom becomes the Lord Jesus. In itself this relativizes for theological thought the fact that Jesus was a male. It also opens up perspectives for the dialogue with other religions, and not only because the Qur'an too (4.169-171) sees Jesus as created by God's Word and Spirit. As I have said, numerous elements from other cultures than that of Israel (including religious elements) play a part in the concept of Wisdom. The sense that Jewish-Christian belief owes much to other religions can only benefit inter-religious dialogue.

Now it is said of Jesus, 'the image of the invisible God', that God has created all things in, through and with him, as in the hymn in Colossians 2.15-20.[14] This passage is coloured by the wisdom tradition, with the help of which Jesus' whole existence and mission is interpreted (see also I Cor.8.6). So reference is made back to the inter-testamental book of the Wisdom of Solomon, in which the divine Wisdom is called the 'image' of God's goodness (7.25). But there are also echoes of the creation story in Genesis 1 here. Jesus is the true image of God 'in whom the whole fullness was pleased to dwell' (v.19). The word fullness (*pleroma*) points to the presence of God in the world (see Jer.23.24; Ps.72.19). The redundant expression 'whole fullness' probably seeks to emphasize that the Christians in Colossae need not be afraid of all kinds of heavenly powers which might mediate and control access to God. No, God's Word and Spirit are now fully present 'bodily' in Christ (see 2.9). Through the crucifixion God has reconciled all things in creation with himself and made it capable of the interplay of peace. As 'the beginning, the firstborn from the dead' (v.18), Christ is the origin of a new humanity, the community, in which God's purpose with the creation already becomes visible. This emerges clearly from the letter to the Ephesians, which in many respects is related to that to the Colossians. In the lyrical meditation of 1.3-14 the author writes – at a time when Christians formed a negligible minority in the great cities of the ancient world and humanly speaking did not have a hope of being of any significance to wider society – that the church of God is a preparation for the fullness of the times (v.10). The church is the divine means for renewing the whole cosmos through the guarantee of the Holy Spirit. In it God sums up everything in heaven and on earth – the whole cosmic difference – under the charismatic kingly rule of Christ (see 4.7-16).

Not only Colossians and Ephesians, letters which breathe the tradition of the apostle Paul, identify Christ with God's Wisdom. Other New Testament authors, above all John and the author of the letter to the Hebrews, do this.[15] Just as Lady Wisdom was already with God from the beginning (Prov.8.22-23), so too Jesus is the Word with God from the beginning (John 1.1-2; Heb.1.10 – a quotation from Ps.102 applied to Christ). Through Wisdom God has given a foundation to all things (Prov.3.19), and so too all things have come into being through the Word (John 1.4; Heb.1.2). In Wisdom is life and light (Prov.8.35; Wisdom 7.26), and so too Jesus is the life and light of men (John 1.4; Heb.1.3). Wisdom descended from heaven to dwell among human beings (Prov.8.31; Sir.24.8; Wisdom 9.10) and this is also said of Jesus (John 1.14; 3.31; Heb.1.1-3). Wisdom teaches people about truth, how they can do God's will and thus lead a life which even overcomes death (Prov.4.13; 8.7; Wisdom 6.18-19; 8.4). All these things are also said of Jesus in the Gospel of John (see also Heb.2.14-15). There are many other parallels. Thus bread and wine (or water) symbolize the teaching of both Wisdom (Prov.9.5) and Jesus (John 4.13-14; 6.51-59). Like Wisdom, Jesus wanders through the streets in search of people whom he can win (Prov.1.20-21; see John 1.36-38), so that they become friends of God (Wisdom 7.14, 27; see John 15.15). It is clear how much the writers of the New Testament draw on the existing wisdom tradition to describe Jesus the Messiah, a tradition which in turn also coloured their vision of him.

We saw that God's Word and Spirit work together in playful Wisdom. The same thing is also said of Jesus in the New Testament.

(i) A one-sided Word christology

In theological discussion the Word and the Spirit were very soon separated, above all after the Council of Nicaea (325), at which under the influence of the Greek concept of the Word (*Logos*), the divinity of Jesus was attributed to the Word. The result was a one-sided Word christology which found its full formulation at the Council of Chalcedon in 451. The text strongly suggests the work of a committee in which account is taken of the wishes and concerns of all parties. It had the good intention of guarding against wrong ideas of the person of Jesus, but as a result it has a defensive character. The Spirit, and thus Jesus' life and work, are not discussed in this definition. Even the resurrection is not mentioned. The person of Jesus is reduced to a static and bloodless formula remote from the lively person who according to the Gospels roamed through the streets, sorrowing with the sorrowful and rejoicing with the happy. Not only the challenge of communicating the gospel in a culture which thought in Greek terms but also the interests of the emperor furthered this emphasis on the Word at the expense of the Spirit. The councils were called by the emperors of Rome, who detested the theological disputes over the person of Jesus. Such divisions threatened Christianity as a state religion and a political instrument and made it impossible to maintain order in the empire. The emperors themselves exercised a good deal of influence on the course of the councils. In the fulsome description by the historian Eusebius, who was present, the emperor Constantine appeared at the council in Nicaea as a 'heavenly messenger from God'. At the end the emperor declared that the resolutions of the council were inspired by God, and imposed them on all the churches. In a similar way the Eastern Roman emperor Marcian threatened anyone who deviated from the resolutions of the Council of Chalcedon with heavy penalties, after which the participants exclaimed to him: 'You are both priest and king, conqueror in war and teacher in the faith!'

This one-sided Word christology orientated on order has since then dominated the church's view of the person of Jesus.

In reaction to this (and in our time under the influence of Pentecostalism), theologians have attempted to develop a Spirit christology in which the divinity of Jesus is not attributed to the Word but to the Spirit. However, this approach threatens to become as one-sided as the Word christology. The Dutch theologian

Piet Schoonenberg has criticized me for not regarding a Spirit christology (like an exclusive Word christology) as being a sufficient christology in itself.[16] In my view only a Wisdom christology, one in which both Word and Spirit are honoured, does complete justice to the person of Jesus.

(ii) Word and Spirit christology

The traditional Word christology is strongly influenced by the Gospel of John, which begins in a majestic way with strophes suggestive of the creation story: 'In the beginning was the Word and the Word was with God and the Word was God.' We saw that the church fathers interpreted this Word above all in the light of the Greek concept of Logos (which in general was static), but in John the significance is above all Hebrew.[17]

In Hebrew thought Wisdom is not identified with God, as happens with the Word in John, but is regarded as divine (Wisdom 7.25-26; cf. John 1.14). It is also said of Wisdom that she is 'unique' (only-begotten, John 1.14). Both Wisdom and the Word play an active part in the creative activity of God, and descend to earth (Prov.8.31; John 1.14). Both have 'tabernacled' among human beings (Sir.14.8-10; John 1.14) and both were rejected by them (Sir.15.7; John 1.11). Almost every important aspect in the prologue of the Gospel of John (1.1-18) thus has a counterpart in the Wisdom tradition. Why did John give preference to the Word over Wisdom? There may have been various reasons for this, including the simple fact that 'word' in Greek is masculine and therefore better suited to denote Jesus than the feminine term wisdom (*sophia*). Moreover, the leap was not so great for John because the Hebrew 'word' (*dabar*) is close to wisdom. I have already pointed out that where God's Word is mentioned in scripture the Spirit is not far away, and vice versa, so that they could later come together in Wisdom. Moreover *dabar* does not denote a static word but an active word. It means both word and deed. So the psalmist (33.9), in the style of the creation story, can sing that God 'spoke and it came to pass'. The Hebrew 'word' is as it were permeated with the dynamic power of the Spirit. In contrast to most church fathers, for John, who thought in Hebrew terms, the Word also had connotations of the Spirit and thus of Wisdom. His contemporary Philo, a Jewish scholar who lived in Alexandria, also saw the Logos as both the creative Word of God and personified Wisdom (and also the all-pervading ordering principle of the Stoics), while on the other hand he could identify the divine Word and Wisdom with the Spirit. Under the influence of Greek thought he contrasted the spirit with the body. For John, however, Wisdom (Word and Spirit) became 'flesh' in Jesus.

That both the Word and the Spirit were present in Jesus in a special way is also confirmed in other places, particularly in the same Gospel of John which is so often used to support the claims of an exclusive Word christology. So we read in 3.34: 'he whom God has sent utters the words of God, for he gives the Spirit beyond measure'. Most reliable manuscripts do not indicate the subject of the second part of the sentence. It could be either God or Jesus. If Jesus is the subject, then he speaks the words of God because he gives expression to the Spirit in an unparalleled way. The power of the Spirit then endorses the divine authority of his words, which are 'Spirit and life' (6.63, compare I Cor.2.4). However, if God is the subject, then it is not in the first place Jesus' audience but Jesus himself who receives the Spirit beyond measure. He can speak the Word of God because he himself is boundlessly filled with the Spirit of God which 'remains' on him (1.33). This corresponds with the following verse, in which God has given him all things [i.e. beyond measure] into his hand so that 'whoever believes in the Son has eternal life'. This eternal life is the life of God's kingdom which is brought to earth through Jesus. Death has no power over this life (11.25). So this life, as we saw in another connection, is the eternal sabbath play which is now already being manifested in Jesus' person and preaching because not only God's Word but also God's Spirit dwells 'beyond measure' in him. Were that not the case, then he would not be able to speak the 'words of God' and give the Spirit. Thus, as so often with John, two interpretations are possible and in fact presuppose each other. The Word that Jesus proclaimed was a creative Spirit-Word which changed people.

This emerges, for example, from the conversation with the Samaritan woman by the well. The water that Jesus is to give is 'living water' which in the one who drinks it becomes a fountain that 'springs to eternal life' (John 1.14). Already from the second century this 'living water' is interpreted as either the Spirit which Jesus gives or his revelation by means of his preaching. In the First Testament and the intertestamental literature, however, Wisdom is a symbol of both the Word of God (Amos 8.11-14; for the Torah see Sir. 24.23-24) and the Spirit of God which is 'poured out' like rain (Isa.32.15; Joel 2.28). So these are two aspects of one and the same event. Jesus' gift of Spirit and Word becomes a fountain which 'springs' to eternal life, a word which recalls the Greek translation of e.g. Judges 14.16 and I Sam.10.10, where God's Spirit 'springs' upon people and makes them 'charismatic' leaders. Spirit and Word issue from Jesus of Nazareth as a prelude to the eternal sabbath play and liberate the Samaritan woman from her dead end (John 4.16-30, 39-42). She knows that she has been 'seen' by him (4.17-19). Living from the Word and the Spirit (the true self, see the next chapter), she can now worship only 'in Spirit and in truth'. According to 17.17-19 the truth 'hallows' and thus puts people in a position to encounter God (worship): Jesus himself is called the truth (14.6), in the sense that he makes God's truth known (8.45). On the other hand the Spirit is both the Spirit of Jesus and the Spirit of truth (14.15-17). The terms Spirit of God, Word ('truth') of God and Jesus the Messiah thus blend into one another in the Gospel of John.

We find this tandem relationship between the Word and the Spirit more or less explicitly in the other Gospels as well. Like the Gospel of John, all announce Jesus as the one who wil baptize with the Holy Spirit (Matt.3.11; Mark 1.8; Luke 3.16; John 1.33). However, he gives not only the Spirit of God but also the Word of God. So the earliest Gospel, that of Mark, states directly after the announcement that Jesus baptizes with the Spirit that he preaches 'the gospel of God' (1.14), that people are 'amazed' at his 'teaching with authority' (1.27) and that his word healed a leper (1.41-42). More could be said about this, but I shall end with a passage from a sermon of Peter which breathes the spirit of the earliest apostolic proclamation and leads to the outpouring of the Spirit on the Roman centurion Cornelius and his household:

You know the word which [God] sent to Israel, preaching the good news of peace by Jesus Christ – he is Lord of all – the word which was proclaimed throughout all Judaea, beginning from Galilee after the baptism which John preached: how God anointed Jesus of Nazareth with the Holy Spirit and with power; how he went

around doing good and healing all that were oppressed by the
devil, for God was with him (Acts 10.36-38).

The Word that God has sent to Israel in Jesus is not simply a verbal
word but an active word, because Jesus is 'anointed' (*echrisen*, from
which the word Christ comes) by God, 'with the Holy Spirit' and
with power. So as Lord of all he could liberate all those who were
oppressed with evil.

(a) God's troubadour

Moreover Jesus emerges in the Gospels as God's troubadour *par
excellence*. He is the perfect 'charismatic' who in miraculous healings
and preaching with authority manifests both the non-rational and
the rational aspects of the Word and the Spirit.[18] His life displays the
creativity, the passionate dedication and the surprising twists of a
game.

In an early text (Luke 7.31-35), Jesus compares the people of his
generation with children calling to one another in the market place:
'We played the flute for you and you did not dance; we sang laments
to you and you did not weep.' This simile can be interpreted in
different ways, but it is probable that the children who invite others
to play (first at a wedding and then at a funeral) primarily represent
Jesus and John.[19] 'The people of this generation' (v.31) are then those
who rejected both the strict and sober John and the free, wine-
drinking Jesus. They have turned down the invitation from both to
play. In a saying of Jesus which was added at an early stage we then
hear: 'Wisdom is justified by (all) her children' (v.35). So originally
these children are John the Baptist and Jesus. As so often, Luke has
added the word 'all', so that their followers, too, including all the
'tax collectors and sinners' (see vv.29,34), are regarded as children
of Lady Wisdom. Here Jesus identifies himself explicitly with playful
Wisdom. He came playing the flute and eating and drinking, but no
one wanted to dance. The foolishness of his words and actions, to
which people react as mocking spoilsports, seems to be the sign of
Wisdom, who with her game makes tax-collectors and sinners the
friends of the Messiah. So she is proved right (Wisdom 'is justified').
Later on, Luke writes that the kingdom of God is for people who are
willing to dance and play; in short, those who are ready to receive
this kingdom 'as a child' (18.16-17). Jesus presents the children here

as a model for any adult who wants to enter his kingdom. Here he will have been thinking of specific properties, for of course not all aspects of a child are positive (think only of sibling rivalry and the tendency to see oneself as the centre of the world). Now what is indubitably characteristic of a child? That it plays. For a child, the whole of life is a game. People who are not open to play cannot enter into the kingdom of God. For the kingdom of God is the sphere of the eternal sabbath, the interplay of creation in which each and everyone gets his or her due: a situation of complete union which the Jews call *shalom* and the Africans *umbuntu*.

Jesus' teaching, like that of the old sages, had a playful style. The Sermon on the Mount undermines the dictatorship of necessity and order by challenging people to play the sabbath game now: 'Why are you anxious... See how the lilies of the field grow. They do not toil or spin, but even Solomon in all his glory was not clothed like one of these' (Matt.6.28-29). He spoke about the kingdom of God above all in parables.[20] In a parable the kingdom of God is compared with this world in the sense that a parable reflects our world with a shocking 'kingdom difference'. Like a game, a parable is set in this world (as might be, for example, a bowls competition in a village), but is not of this world (bowls is not part of ordinary social life) and precisely because of that, it is in a position to change it. Like an icebreaker, a parable makes a gap in our closed order and thus creates room for God's rule.[21] So we know what a vineyard worker is, but here Jesus tells of one who is paid a full day's wages for working only one hour (Matt.20.1-6). We understand the joy of a father over the homecoming of a runaway child (Luke 15.11-32), but not why the child does not seem to feel the need to say somewhere between the party dinner and the dance floor, 'Why have you done this for me?'. And a story in which the sinful tax-collector is justified and the pious Pharisee is not (Luke 18.9-14) plays games with the existing order and opens up unsuspected possibilities for those who are oppressed by the order, or stand outside it. Like a game, a parable reflects our world in the light of its consummation in the eternal sabbath. Therefore a parable also has therapeutic power, since it puts us in a position to stand back from the present situation, perceive possibilities we had not dreamed of, and thus understand ourselves and the world in a new way. The stories about Jesus's miracles also have a similar power to change the world and are as it were parables of action. Against a passive acceptance of the *status quo* they proclaim that the possessed can be freed, the hungry fed and the sick healed. As the German theologian Gerd Theissen writes: 'The miracle stories will rather deny the validity of all previous experience than the right to eliminate human suffering'.[22] The passion of Jesus breaks through the closed walls of necessity, surprisingly bringing in the healing light of God's kingdom.

Through the Word and the Spirit Jesus not only preached in parables; in his own person he was a living parable. He was a human being as we are, but with that crucial 'kingdom difference' that within the limitations of our world made him already the eschatological, perfect human being. As the mystics say: Jesus *is* the image and the parable of God while we are made *towards* the image and likeness of God and thus still have a way to go to reach perfection. He was *in* this world but not of this world, and therefore in a position to change it. Nowhere is there ever a person so free as Jesus. He was not attached to some moral code or or other, or to human traditions and conventions. So he has been called the great model breaker. Jesus was not a slave of the established order, and was seen by its guardians as a troublemaker. But unlike the fool from the wisdom tradition who denies God's wisdom, Jesus himself represents the wisdom which is regarded by an unfree society as folly. In contrast to the sheer utilitarian thought of some of those present (like Judas Iscariot according to the Gospel of John), he welcomes the prodigal, precious anointing by a woman in Bethany. He even says that her deed will be spoken of wherever the gospel is proclaimed (Mark 14.3-9). Her anointing is a living illustration not only of the freedom and super-fluity of his own life and message but also of the response which these aim to produce among his followers. Jesus reacted spontaneously to any new, concrete situation, was unconcerned about possessions or reputations and felt completely free to identify with the outcasts of his time. He was also free to learn from others in an ongoing reciprocal activity, even from a non-Jewish woman who pointed out to him that God's involvement with people did not stop at the frontiers of Israel (Matt.15.21-28). Although he could share his own pain and sorrow, he never claimed the role of victim. Although he also knew anxiety (see Gethsemane), he did not feel any need to persuade Pilate to save him from death. In short, his life had the playful quality of God's kingdom. He was 'Lord of the sabbath', and therefore his presence was experienced as liberating, healing and re-creating. The British feminist theologian Mary Grey points out that

Jesus' relations are characterized by a redemptive mutuality in which people came into their own.[23] Moreover his life had an irresistible attraction for those who were pushed aside by the established order. In his presence they felt free to make themselves known in their brokenness, sickness and demonic possession. As in a real game the outcome was open for them: tax collectors become Robin Hoods who returned their own money to the poor; common sluts become princesses of the resurrection preaching. For those who were ready to be involved in the gracious game of Jesus' life, proverbs became reality. In his first book on Jesus, Schillebeeckx describes the freedom that he brought under the telling heading, 'The existential impossibility of being sad in Jesus' presence'. So this man from Nazareth already embodied the eschatological sabbath play, that generous kingdom which is God's wisdom, but folly to a world imprisoned in a rigid order and unable to play.

Those who play will, moreover, constantly find their play thwarted by the dominant order, sometimes with fatal results. Jesus did not live in order to die, as some theories of reconciliation fixated on the cross seem to say. He died as he lived. Whereas while going round Israel he welcomed need and death in the form of the poor and outcast and liberating them from it, now he welcomed death in his own life in order to transcend it. For here Jesus' existence, as a living parable, took a definitive, shocking turn: he rose from the dead. Although the patristic theory of redemption that God disguised himself in Jesus as human bait and thus caught the devil on the hook seems to us to be crude and simplistic, at all events it still communicates an awareness of the element of play in the cross and resurrection. Something of the feeling comes through that he who laughs last laughs longest. This sense, moreover, remained alive in the Greek Orthodox tradition, where believers meet to tell jokes on the second day of Easter.

3

The Church as a Liberated Community

After his death, Jesus' life and mission, the liberating game of the coming kingdom, were continued by the community. Moreover this initially consisted of people who had been excluded by the prevailing order.

(i) The last come first

In his first letter to the community in Corinth Paul calls Christ 'the power of God and the wisdom of God' (I Cor.1.24).[24] Here this is meant not so much as a definition of the person of Christ but as an indication of the nature of the liberation that he brings.

The cross of Christ is the wisdom and the power of God (v.18). This was folly for the Jews, who expected signs which would announce the coming of the unconquerable Messiah. It was also nonsense to the Greeks, who could not understand how God can suffer and be bound up with human beings (1.22). The preaching of the cross of Christ was foolishness to the religious and philosophical systems of both the Jews and the Greeks. If these did not legitimate the prevailing order (through the static Greek image of God), at least they kept it in being (through the often passive wait for the signs which would precede the coming of the Messiah). These 'rulers of the age' had crucified Christ (2.8), for they did not know the 'hidden wisdom of God' (2.7). This wisdom means that God does not justify, sanctify and liberate those who maintain the *status quo* but rather the weak and the oppressed who, like Jesus, have been denied or oppressed by the established order (1.30). Hence Paul reminds the Christians in Corinth, against the triumphalism of some of them (cf. 1.12; 3.1-9), that they certainly do not belong among the wise, influential and respectable of this world. Indeed they were useless, 'of no account', but precisely for that reason were called by God to become the nucleus of the greatest liberating revolution the world has ever known. Moreover Paul relates this to himself: he did not come with 'brilliant words' but 'in weakness, with much fear and trembling'; however, it was precisely in this that the Spirit and power of God could manifest themselves (2.1-5). The life of the apostle as bringer of the gospel is, as with Jesus, in accord with this gospel, and in its simplicity is closer to the poor than to established citizens. Moreover today this is also part of the secret of the attraction of Pentecostalism for the poor masses. These feel little attraction to what to them are rich Western missionaries, but are attracted to the popular Pentecostalist preachers who are recognized by them as 'one of us'.

For Paul, the Spirit discloses the divine wisdom. This is not the spirit of this world order but the 'Spirit of God' which makes known to us God's free gift (2.12). Here the apostle uses the verb *charizomai*, which is related not only to the word 'grace' (*charis*) but also to 'gifts of grace'. It is probable that here he was thinking of these gifts. Somewhat earlier he already thanks God because the community in Corinth 'falls short in no single gift of grace (*charisma*)' (1.7). In chapters 7 and 12-13 he will go into these gifts at still greater length. Here the Spirit puts us in a position to think God's deepest thoughts (2.10-12), in other words God's 'hidden wisdom' which chooses those who are 'of no account' in this world to manifest all the more clearly the unconditional character of grace, so that 'there is no room for boasting before God' (1.29). In the useless weak who cannot find any foothold in the dominant social order, God's grace emerges most strongly as the power which creates something out of nothing, life out of death. This becomes manifest in the resurrection of the failed Jesus, so that Paul calls him 'the wisdom of God'. For the activity of this wisdom has the character of a game. The last unexpectedly become the first on the basis of the unconditional gifts of God, through which they can play a full part in the society which is called church. The necessity imposed by the ruling order is relativized by God's choice of the victims of this order (and those, according to Paul, who feel associated with them) and his gift of charisms to them. The powerless thus shed the yoke of anxiety which constricts their freedom and grow in pride and self-esteem). Moreover, the playful character of present-day Pentecostalism is the most powerful reason for its attraction to the poor.

So the great prophecies are fulfilled in a community which is already living 'in the last days' because it has a share in the sabbath play of God's kingdom. Moreover Paul later writes in his first letter to the Corinthians that they function as members of Christ's body on the basis of the gifts of the Spirit (12.1-26, 28-31). I shall be returning to these gifts, but here it is important to note how much this interplay of gifts brings people to liberation. They are redeemed from the need to entrench themselves in a rigid order which makes human differences a cause of division and oppression. On the contrary, when these differences become gifts of grace, they keep in being the one body with its differences among members. 'All are baptized in one Spirit into one body, whether Jews, Greeks, slaves or free'(I Cor.12.13). It is just as in a game of football, where the differences between defence, forward, goalkeeper and so on do not prevent the one game but make it possible. However, for this unity in difference a 'team spirit' is necessary. So too people are liberated in the spirit of Christ to become a gift for others in their own specific identity, and thus to make a contribution to the celebration of community life. The early Christians did not strive for a society in which the model of masters and slaves would be replaced by the liberal model in which each is his or her own master, detached from their neighbours. No, God is concerned for the whole creation, and therefore for an interplay with one another and with the earth. Like Jesus himself, the early church was therefore a crazy, living parable in which the masters served the slaves and women with no rights prophesied. The awareness that one is a gift of God and thus has the same right as others to play in the community has an emancipatory power. So Paul writes to Philemon that he must welcome his runaway slave back, 'now no longer as a slave but as more than a slave, as a beloved brother [in the Lord]' (Philemon 16).

(a) No one is left out of the game

Luke shows how liberating this was in the Acts of the Apostles, in which he brings together the two great traditions of early Christianity: the recollections of Jesus and the life of the Pauline communities. The more the community spread, the more one order after another which had brought slavery and division was overcome by Christians inspired by the Word and the Spirit.

In chapter 2, first the followers of Jesus and then the Jews from the Diaspora, present in Jerusalem to celebrate the feast of Pentecost, are baptized in the Spirit (cf. 1.5, 8). These Jews were regarded as somewhat inferior in Israel because they lived in non-Jewish 'unclean' lands. In general this Pentecost event is seen as the counterpart to the story about the tower of Babel (Gen.11.1-9). This story tells in a mythical way how chaos in the human race is the consequence of the attempt to be 'one people' with 'one language' (Gen.11.6). The attempt at unity all too often degenerates into a totalitarian order which takes on a divine authority and always provokes opposition and splintering; their language is confused and they are 'dispersed over all the earth' (Gen.11.9). In history almost every overthrow of the dominant order leads to a new order which oppresses its own children. Not uniformity, but unity in difference is the way of living together in which people also come into their own as unique individuals. This dynamic unity exists only through the Spirit, which makes the many human differences gifts for the one society. In Luke's view the languages, confused by the totalitarian order of Babylon, become one as the disciples of Jesus are 'filled with the Holy Spirit' and speak 'in other tongues' (Acts 2.4). This last is probably a reference to glossolalic sounds which are understood by those present from all kinds of language area (through the charism of translation?, compare I Cor.12.10). The working of Spirit and Word leads to a playful language which is attributed by some to drunkenness (2.13) but is experienced by others as a sign of union between Jews, proselytes, Cretans, Arabians (cf. 2.11), and so on.

In accordance with the programme which Luke has set out at the beginning of his book (1.8), subsequently in 8.4-25 the Samaritans are approached. They certainly possessed the Torah (i.e. the first five books of the First Testament), but had founded a rival temple on Mount Gerizim and were therefore regarded by the Jews as schismatics. They were open to the word of the gospel proclaimed by Philip. Accustomed as they were to being treated by the Jewish community as outcasts, they needed Peter and John to come from Jerusalem in person to confirm them in their status as members of the new community of Christ. Thereupon they received the Spirit, which seems to have been accompanied with external manifestations, since Simon the magician 'saw' that the Spirit was given to them (8.18). This may have been glossolalia, but also prophecy or both (cf. 19.6). In the same chapter (8.26-40) the Spirit (according to the variant in the so-called Western text) falls on a chamberlain from Ethiopia. He was black and a eunuch, someone who was sexually different and therefore according to the First Testament excluded from God's community (Deut.23.1). He too received the word preached by Philip, accepted baptism and 'went his way rejoicing'. The next order which brought about the greatest division is overcome in chapter 10. Here Cornelius and members of his family, uncircumcised non-Jews to whom the temple was therefore closed (see Ezek.44.9), received the Spirit when Peter preached the word. Thereupon they spoke in tongues and praised God (10.46), an event which made Peter think of the first outpouring of the Spirit on the day of Pentecost and convinced him that the non-Jews too had access to the community of Christ (11.15-18). Finally I might mention the story of the (sectarian?) disciples of John the Baptist in Ephesus, who were baptized by Paul in the name of Jesus. They received the Holy Spirit, spoke in tongues, and also prophesied (19.1-7).

Luke clearly wants to indicate that through the new experience of the Word and Spirit of Christ people in all their difference are encountered as equals and that no one need any longer be left out of the game. In the book of Acts, one order after another that had brought oppression and division between people falls away. It is striking that in this liberating breakthrough Luke on various occasions mentions the gift of glossolalia. This corresponds closely with the experience of Bill Seymour in the Los Angeles revival, for whom glossolalia was the sign that the Spirit was breaking down the barriers between races and peoples. Even if we take account of the fact that the book of Acts is also preaching and that Luke is therefore not giving us an 'objective' account, it is clear that among the early Christians, as with their master, there was a radical transcending of self, inspiration, and great joy. Even during persecutions they are 'filled with joy and with the Holy Spirit' (13.52), a joy which is experienced above all in celebration (2.46; 5.42-42; 11.23). According to Acts and various letters in the New Testament the church is a consistently charismatic community and as such equipped for play in God's coming kingdom. In the community God's Spirit and Word which bring the whole creation to consummation are intensely present. Like Jesus, the community is a living parable. This emerges clearly from the miracles which according to Luke accompanied the gospel word of the early Christians. The first healing, that of the man at the temple gate whose lameness is cured, illustrates the resurrection of Jesus from the dead (3.15-16) and thus that of all people who are bowed down and hemmed in by an oppressive order. Although the couple Ananias and Sapphira pretend to take part in the new life of Christ, they cling to the old order of anxiety and death, withholding part of their possessions; so in accord with the order that they obey, they meet their end (5.1-11). On various occasions the apostles are freed from dark prisons as a surprising resurrection from the dead (5.17-25; 12.6-12; 16.23-26), to the despair of the authorities, whether these are the Sanhedrin (the Jewish senate and chief court of justice), king Herod or Roman officials.

However, very quickly the word of the gospel became an oppressive law and the established political and social order embraced the church. The Spirit was forced to the periphery of the church, where it was welcomed by those who were excluded. Time and again charismatic counter-movements came into being here in which the revolutionary sabbath game again became visible to a greater or lesser degree.

Part Three: Sabbath Play: A Closer Look at Church History

Down to the present day the greater part of the church is hampered by the misunderstanding that there is no alternative to order than disorder. Hence the church conservatism and institutionalism that is present everywhere. We find the same misconception among critics of the churches fixated on law and order, like the Pole Leszek Kolakowski.[1] He defines God's grace as the absence of order, and concludes from this that the institutional church as a proclaimer of this grace finds itself in an impossible dilemma. But this grace is not without order; it knows the order of the play of Word and Spirit. In Plato *charis* ('grace') already denotes the pleasure of the useless game.[2] However, a real game is not dominated by order or by chaos. It consists in the creative integration of order (word, rules) on the one hand and the spontaneous contribution and dynamic (enthusiasm) of all participants on the other. Only in the play of Word and Spirit can human beings blossom in church and society.[3]

Church History

(i) Emphasis on the Word at the expense of the Spirit

Because the church rapidly put all the emphasis on order, the Word and the Spirit were set against each other, or at least openness to the work of the Spirit was limited. However, without the Spirit the Word becomes a law. It becomes static and legitimates the established order. The Word becomes the word of the elite who have to learn to write, to preach and to discuss. The word of dogma begins to justify the exclusion of those who think differently, a development which reached a climax in the church of Rome in the last century in the Pope's claim to infallibility. This makes opposition *a priori* impossible. The fixation on order makes the church often slow and inert. This is evident among other things from the fact that it took until 1992 for the Roman Catholic church officially to revoke its condemnation in 1633 of the astronomer Galileo to lifelong imprisonment – because he wrote that the earth goes round the sun and not vice versa, as the hierarchy believed. We also find a similar one-sided attachment to the order of the word in the Eastern Orthodox churches, which often take the statements of the Greek Fathers absolutely, and in the Netherlands among the strict Reformation Christians whose faith seems to be clad in the literal doctrinal rules of Dordrecht from 1619.

However, the Spirit is poured out uncontrollably on 'every living creature'. So all down history uneducated men and women began to prophesy. Those without a voice lifted up their voice without having undergone higher instruction sanctioned by the elite. Thus Hollenweger writes about the Pentecostal movement:

> Whether it exists among the agricultural workers of Chile, the Indians of Argentina, the proletariat of North America, the masses of African cities, the gypsies of France, the members of Swedish

trade unions, or the poor of Britain, the function of the Pentecostal movement is to restore the power of expression to people without identity and powers of speech, and to heal them from the terror of the loss of speech.[4]

The Belgian priest José Comblin, who has been working in Latin America since 1958, tells how today the poor are getting a voice in such a way in their base communities, which often have a charismatic structure.[5] For centuries they have been regarded by politicians and landowners as dumb instruments, and that is also how they saw themselves. Their voice was unimportant, and in the presence of the authorities they were intimidated and kept their mouths shut. However, in the celebration they learned to pray in their own words (not with the words of the priests), to give a prophecy and to read the Bible. They have a contribution of their own to make which helps other people, and so they discover that their voice really does count. Then for the first time they also begin to speak in public against the political and social distress in their country. Here they follow Peter who, 'filled with the Holy Spirit', surprised the Sanhedrin with his address, since he was 'one of the illiterate and simple men of the people' (Acts 4.8-14). No wonder that the Spirit makes those who maintain order nervous. Therefore down through history attempts have been made to keep this dangerous spirit from people by caging it in the Word, in doctrine and structures. Of course we do not do justice to church history by imagining it as a dark spiritless period after the (imaginary) charismatic 'golden age' of the New Testament, as Pentecostals sometimes do. For example, Martin Parmentier, Professor of Charismatic Renewal at the Free University of Amsterdam, finds the first centuries of church history a source of inspiration for his theological work.[6] But to a large extent it can be said that above all from the third century on, in an over-reaction to charismatic Montanism, the church has put a disproportionately heavy emphasis on the Word, order – at the expense of the Spirit which brings life. Thus the church denied its identity as bringer of the sabbath game and sold its soul to the *status quo*. In history the expressions and activities of the church are often indistinguishable from those of the political authorities. More often than not the church was like the world instead of being a crazy parable of the kingdom of God.

(a) The hierarchical church

At a very early stage, in an attempt to emphasize its identity as the 'new Israel' in its polemic with the synagogue, the church introduced the static priestly system from the First Testament, complete with male priests, a sacrificial cult and (later) a high priest. This tendency is already evident from the first letter of Clement of Rome to the community in Corinth, written around thirty years after the death of Paul. The dispute with the Gnostics encouraged the formation of a fixed, closed canon of scripture and the notion of a literal apostolic succession as a hallmark of the church. Cyprian, bishop of Carthage, wrote around 250 that the bishop, hitherto above all a symbol of unity, also legitimates the true church.

The challenges with which the young church found itself confronted were met by institutionalization and an excessive emphasis on order at the expense of the essence of the gospel and the church. All this took on its definitive stamp when from the time of the emperor Constantine the church acquired the status of a state church and conformed its organization to that of the Roman empire. Rigorous public disciplinary measures made their appearance, with an extended system of penance which the guilty had to undergo before they were accepted as full members of the church. From the sixth century, individual penitential practice entered the church from the monasteries. Although there was an honest pastoral concern behind this, in practice penance degenerated into a legalistic weighing of every sin and the quest for an appropriate penance for it. Unconditional forgiveness by God and the freedom of the Spirit seem a long way off here. In the meantime the framework of Stoic philosophical thought had been adopted in theology. In this philosophy, order, the Word (the Logos), was central. God was increasingly seen as a rational creator, in place of the God who is concerned for community. That emerges, for example, from the Apostles' Creed and the declaration of Nicaea both of which open with this statement. This idea of God as a self-sufficient creator and monarch has since then legitimated the absolute authority of the one pope, king and emperor. As far as christology is concerned, we already saw how at the councils of Nicaea and Chalcedon the person of Christ was defined in static, abstract terms. In christology the Spirit played less and less of a role until around 1100 Anselm of Canterbury worked out a theory of redemption in which the Spirit does not even occur. Hence the charge of Eastern Orthodoxy that the West thinks one-sidedly in terms of Christ. Anselm imagines God as a feudal lord insulted by his subjects. Here God is on the side of the mediaeval rulers. The Spirit also vanished from the teaching of the church. Around 1600 Bellarmine, a cardinal and the Pope's personal theologian, defended the hierarchy God-Christ-church, in which the Spirit is not mentioned. God is revealed through Christ and Christ is proclaimed by the church. The Spirit is degraded to being an assistant of the hierarchy. Theologically this development was encouraged by the addition made by the Western church to the creed of Nicaea and Constantinople to the effect that the Holy Spirit 'proceeds from the Father *and the Son*' (*filioque*). This extension also became a cause of the great schism in 1054 between the Eastern Orthodox churches and the Western Roman church. Although the Gospels make it clear that the Son also proceeds from the Spirit (for example in the birth narratives and Jesus' experience by the Jordan), here the Spirit is one-sidedly made dependent on the Son and on the Pope (with his bishops and priests) as his 'representative'. The papal power and the distinction betwen priests and laity are emphasized above all after the Gregorian reform, which took place around 1100. The aim of this was to improve the deplorable condition of the church, above all by an increase in the administrative and legal authority of Rome.

This emphasis on order, the Word, the Neoplatonic Logos separate from our reality, at the expense of the Spirit which is poured out on 'every living creature', leads to a dangerous dualism. In christology Christ is separated from the historical Jesus as the divine Word. In the doctrine of redemption attention was no longer directed forwards, towards the coming renewal of this earth, but fixed on heaven in the expectation of the escape of the soul from the corruptible body. So personal justification was detached from doing justice in history. In the doctrine of the church the church as the mystery of Christ was separated from the institution as a sociological fact, which according to Bellarmine was no different from the kingdom of France. The result was that the Christ of faith, justification by grace and the church as the body of Christ were taken out of history and became irrelevant to this world. On the other hand the concrete life of the historical Jesus, the struggle for the liberation of the world and the church as an institution were secularized.[7] The relationship between the 'vertical' and the 'horizontal' dimension, or the bond between God and the world, was largely lost. Moreover scholastic theology hardly referred to contemporary history. Theology remained hovering about a metre above the earth, on the high altar. That is the price which must be paid if the Spirit is quenched. Without Spirit no dynamic inter-relationship, no interplay is possible between Word and reality, between God and the world, between believers and their history. For as Paul Tillich, whose theology is by his own confession 'essentially (but indirectly) influenced by the spiritualist movements', writes, the Spirit in particular is the integrating principle which binds together faith and life, the ideal of God's kingdom and everyday reality.[8] Without the Spirit which inspires a way of life, the Word itself remains meaningless, for significance always grows in, and out of, the context of a particular practice.

Since the Council of Trent in the sixteenth century this absence of the experience of the Spirit has been legitimated by the Jesuit school – at the time the guardians *par excellence* of the papal order. In the polemic with the Reformation, with its emphasis on the inward testimony of the Spirit that endorsed only Scripture as the highest authority for believers, this school made a radical distinction between sanctifying grace and religious experience. The word 'spirit' was now replaced with 'grace', and grace, it was taught, is not experienced. The difference between Christians and non-Christians is thus unconscious. In this way order was objectified to an extreme degree. Faith becomes a rational observance of the rules of the game, i.e. obedience to the hierarchy. This was the culmination of the development already indicated, in which, above all in the struggle with the Holy Roman Empire, the Spirit was increasingly identified with the hierarchical order. In 1215, at the Fourth Lateran Council, the hierarchy had itself forbidden the formation of new religious orders (and therefore new movements of the Spirit). Mystical experiences, which reached a climax in the sixteenth century, were thus made quite exceptional. The hierarchy kept them away from ordinary people, whose religious experiences were condemned as superstition.[9] Of course the mystics themselves could not go along with this theology. They saw themselves compelled to work out their experiences in a (proto-) psychological way rather than in terms of a doctrine of the Spirit. However, Scripture was the most important source of the thought of a mystic and monastic reformer, the poet John of the Cross. He experienced the Spirit as a 'living flame of love', a scorching awakening by God in his innermost being. But the renewal movement of which he was a member, along with Teresa of Avila, was swiftly directed into legalistic channels. He was put on one side as superfluous and his writings attracted the attention of the Inquisition (the church judges). Because the mystics did not speak very explicitly about the Spirit, present-day Pentecostalism finds it difficult to come to grips with them and can hardly profit from the treasury of wisdom and knowledge to be found in them.

The result of all this was that up to and including the Second Vatican Council in the 1960s there was no real Catholic pneumatology. The council itself took over the Augustinian and Thomistic notion of the Spirit as the soul of the church. While this emphasizes the intimate bond betwen Spirit and church, in practice it meant that the Spirit becomes a kind of automatic divine stamp of approval on everything that the Roman Catholic church says and does. For, the notion is, its actions emerge from its soul. Thus the Spirit is no longer a critical counterpart and can hardly inspire the practice of the crazy sabbath game in which each person has his or her rights.

(b) The churches of the Reformation

The Reformation came into being above all as a reaction to this Roman Catholic emphasis on order which preached, sometimes to an absurd degree, the ascetic method and the need for 'good works' in order to come to God. Over against this the tormented Luther set his mystical rediscovery that God accepts human beings out of grace, 'for nothing'. Calvin developed Luther's notions of the unbreakable bond between the Word and the Spirit in his doctrine of the indwelling testimony of the Spirit. In the interplay between the Spirit at work in human beings and the Word of Scripture, men and women become convinced of the biblical truth and are accepted as children of God.

But although the Reformation had the slogan 'Word and Spirit' on its banner, it changed little in the Roman Catholic emphasis on order and structure. In Hendrikus Berkhof's words, the Catholics imprisoned the Spirit in the church and the Protestants imprisoned it in the Word.[10] Certainly, now people were left out of the game rather less; but their role remained limited. They could sing psalms again in worship, but Calvin thought that because of its sins the church was finished with charisms, so that the interplay of gifts faded away. Luther was more open to the possibility of the functioning of the gifts of grace. Thus in the last couplet of his hymn 'A Mighty Fortress is out God' he could write (in the original version), 'The Spirit and the gifts are ours/ through him who with us sideth'. However, like Calvin, he too did not really see that the structure of the community of Christ is in principle charismatic.[11] The community does not really become a subject. The rediscovery of the priesthood of all believers is in practice limited to prayer and Bible reading at home. When in 1524 the German Peasant Revolt broke out under the leadership of the militant Thomas Münzer because the serfs, inspired by the Word and Spirit, grew up and wanted relief from their inhuman situation, Luther mercilessly settled the matter with an appeal to the established order. Since then the Lutheran church has remained politically conservative and in the shadow of the authorities. This goes a long way towards explaining its bewildering obedience to the Nazi authorities in Germany during the 1930s and 1940s. This static atitude was further intensified by theological developments in the seventeenth century. In both Lutheran and Calvinist theology the élan of the Reformers gives place to rationalism and a neo-scholastic emphasis on order of a kind which Luther himself had opposed. The living truth of God's Word and Spirit is reduced to the printed truth of the Bible, which is made a legal code. Justification by faith was largely objectivized and represented by the Word and sacraments of the church. This increased the desire on the subjective side for liberation through Christ, as is evident from the rise of pietism. In scholastic thought the Holy Spirit was seldom considered separately, and was treated as an extension of the doctrines of scripture and of Christ. With its idea of predestination, Calvinistic theology here legitimated the *status quo*. To put it in popular terms: anyone who is born a nickel can never become a dime. In a sense this was a Calvinistic version of the ancient idea of the 'ladder of being' (*scala entium*) in which the dominant social order is seen as being willed by God. Any attempt to change this order must therefore be of the devil. Shakespeare several times in his plays echoes (ironically) fear of the breakdown of this order. In *Troilus and Cressida* (I, iii) Ulysses remarks in a famous speech to the Greek leaders during the siege of Troy:

O when degree is shaked
which is the ladder to all high designs,
the enterprise is sick! How could communities...
the primogenitive and due of birth,
prerogative of age, crowns, sceptres, laurels,

but by degree, stand in authentic place?
Take but degree away, untune that string,
And, hark, what discord follows!
...the bounded waters
Should lift their bosoms higher than the shores,
and make a sop of all this solid globe.

Moreover, in North America in the last century Calvinistic theologians of the old school like Hodge and Warfield were the greatest opponents of the (proto-)charismatic Holiness Movement which was intent on a just society. The reason for this was their emphasis on God's sovereignty and predestination and reservations about experience, miracles and attempts to change the *status quo*. The maintaining of a one-sided emphasis on Christ as the Word in Protestant theology generally results in the Spirit being given a merely instrumental role. Here the charisms are limited to the early community. Although for example Karl Barth says splendid things about the dynamic self-revelation of God, for him the Spirit remains predominantly an extension of Christ, the Word.[12]

(c) Eastern Orthodoxy

The Eastern Orthodox tradition is literally and figuratively a separate story. For geographical and political reasons, for a long time this rich tradition was isolated from the West, so that very little interchange took place. Such interaction could have preserved both the East and the West from one-sidedness. The recent opening of the frontiers of Eastern Europe has a certain promise in this respect.

The West begins from the Augustinian starting point of the sinful individual who, condemned by the Word of God, must be justified by Christ and sanctified. This led to a strong emphasis on human guilt and unworthiness, and faith often degenerated into a joyless moral code. By contrast the East always drew far more on the festal stream and because of that has preserved better the early Christian emphasis on the Spirit. There the coming of the Spirit of Pentecost is the festival of the world, the festival of the resurrection of Jesus and with him of the whole creation, which is celebrated in the liturgy. Moreover the Eastern Orthodox celebration has kept more the character of play. Whereas in the West the gifts of the Spirit rapidly came to be regarded as a kind of accessory which was no longer needed since the church could stand on its own feet, the East always continued to see the charisms as constitutive of the church. But the Eastern Orthodox celebration had little liberating influence on history. That is above all because like the church in the West from the time of Constantine, it entered into a marriage with the ruling order, i.e. with the Byzantine and Russian empires. Here we must also remember that until very recently the Eastern Orthodox Church was the most and longest persecuted church in Christianity. All attention and energy was often concentrated simply on survival, which encouraged an inward-looking attitude and compromises with the *status quo*.[13]

After this summary survey, which inevitably is full of generalizations, generally speaking we can conclude that the Catholics imprisoned the Spirit in the church, the Protestants in the Word and the Eastern Orthodox in celebration. That hindered the church from recognizing the liberating play of Word and Spirit in the world, as in the democratic intentions of the French and American revolutions. The church even opposed this (which it saw as disorder). Only after the devastations of the Nazi dictatorship did for example Pope Pius XII somewhat unenthusiastically recognize the justification for a democratic form of state. To the present day, almost five hundred years after the playful humanist and martyr for his Roman Catholic faith, Thomas More, argued in his *Utopia* for democratically elected priests (and high priests), it is still almost impossible to discuss the distribution of power within the church of Rome.

The prophetic voice of the church is often stifled as a result of its entanglement with political and economic interests. The newly elected, consciously charismatic, Archbishop of Canterbury, George Carey, discovered this. When in 1991 he attributed the riots by young people in English cities to high unemployment and poverty, the government told him that such remarks played into the hands of the opposition. There is no doubt that in its role as the bulwark of the established order the church has been the most important cause of the rise of atheism, and also of the ideologies of the Enlightenment. These can be regarded as the stepchildren of a Christianity which denied its own dream of the freedom, equality and community of all men and women.[14]

(ii) Charismatic counter-movements

The relative independence of the Spirit is evident from the rise of numerous counter-movements in history. Almost all the renewal movements in the church in the Netherlands, from the itinerant Irish monks in the seventh century, the monasteries, the Reformation, the Second Vatican Council, up to and including the base communities, have also been inspired by the radical charismatic community of the New Testament. The explicitly charismatic movements were mostly lay movements which were characterized by the same ideals as those striven for by the ideologies of the Enlightenment: freedom, equality and brotherhood and sisterhood. People on the margin could certainly play a part in the evangelical sabbath game, which constantly seems to have had an emancipatory force. Thus the Montanists, a trend which among other things strove for a church without a hierarchical structure, still had women bishops up to around the year 500. I myself worked in the 1980s in a North American Pentecostal church with a woman who was celebrating her sixtieth (!) anniversary as a preacher. In the summary which follows, I cannot be complete, and must limit myself to mentioning some of the most important figures and movements.

(a) Before the Reformation

The well-known martyr Perpetua and her slave Felicitas, who met their deaths in the amphitheatre around 200, were members of the Montanists whom I have already mentioned. In the early church, martyrdom was seen as a charism. According to the acts, *The Suffering of Perpetua*, when they had come to God after their deaths they were told, 'Go and play.' Whereupon Perpetua replied: 'Thank God! As I once delighted in earthly play, so I will be even more joyful.' This playfulness is characteristic of many charismatic figures and trends in history.

In the twelfth century the Italian abbot Joachim of Fiore announced that the time of the Spirit was near. He distinguished three phases in salvation history. Each phase prepared for the next and was transcended in it. His dynamic view of history contributed to the later, modern belief in the progress of humankind. In his thought the kingdom of the Father was the period of subjection to the Torah; the kingdom of the Son was that of obedience to the priests of the church. Finally, the kingdom of the Spirit would be a time in which believers were no longer regulated by the ruling order of the church hierarchy, anxiety, law and punishment. No, in a kind of equal play all believers would be led by the Spirit and have direct knowledge of God. The fact that a learned and pious monk like Joachim thought that the Spirit really still had to be poured out shows how little the church lived by the Pentecostal experience. His notions influenced some later Methodists like John Fletcher, John Wesley's official successor, who were opposed to the established English state church. This idea that the time of the Spirit was still to dawn also exercised a great influence on Francis of Assisi, one of God's troubadours, and the spiritual figures inspired by him who went around proclaiming the gospel. Their way of life, free of the pressure of possessions, shows apt similarities to that of some early preachers in the Pentecostal movement. The sociologist Robert Anderson writes: 'While the Pentecostal movement had perhaps more than its share of venal and sordid preachers, it had, too, men and women of solid character. These lived often in extreme poverty, going out with little or no money, seldom knowing where they would spend the night or how they would get the next meal.'[15] How much the playful, laid-back way of life of the then spirituals confused the established church order has been attractively described by Umberto Eco in his well-known novel *The Name of the Rose*. In it the old monk Jorge murders anyone who wants to read a book by Aristotle (which does not in fact exist) about laughter. According to him, laughter liberates from fear of – and thus subjection to – God's law, which would reduce the world order to a state of chaos. The great theologian Thomas Aquinas condemned Joachim of Fiore with the same argument, and Luther later used it against Thomas Münzer; later still the established churches were to use it against the rising Pentecostal movement. This argument was that all that can be expected of the Spirit has already been given and is present in the church. It was unimaginable for them that the Spirit, which in their view legitimated church authority, could criticize this same authority through people who were often even on the very edge of the established church. The pretensions of this view are revealing. For it is not the church which possesses the Spirit, but the Spirit the church – and this last time and again proves to be rather broader than the official church order indicates.

(b) After the Reformation

In the radical Reformation (the left wing of the Reformation) the Anabaptists practised glossolalic prayer. In their meetings each person had the right to expound scripture, guided by the Spirit. In the sixteenth century the Polish Brethren, forerunners of the Socinians, had a community in which masters lived with serfs and peasants and listened with respect to the contributions of even the most illiterate participants. In seventeenth-century England we meet George Fox, pioneer of the Quakers. On the basis of the activity of God's Spirit in all people (the 'inner light') he thought that everyone was completely equal. In the third part of his *Apologia* (1676), their best-known theologian, Robert Barclay, wrote that Christ's Spirit is a more important guide than Scripture. For the Spirit, 'no one is so young, no one so untrained, no one so far off that he cannot be reached by this and properly instructed'. Moreover in a Quaker meeting everyone can contribute a word of God from the silence. They are in favour of consistent pacifism and feminism and against slavery. In addition I will just mention the Camisards, a radical branch of the Huguenots who after the revocation of the Edict of Nantes rebelled against the brutal repression of their worship. Count von Zinzendorf tried to change the whole life of his Moravian Brethren in one great liturgical game as a result of which this church became more liberated and equipped for service to the world than perhaps any other church since the Reformation. Initially the Moravian Brethren had a great influence on the Anglican priest John Wesley. After his experience of the Spirit in which he felt his heart 'strangely warmed', Wesley wrote that he regarded the Montanists as 'truly scriptural Christians'.[16] Early Methodism was a movement which was familiar with charismatic expressions like glossolalia, prophecy, resting in the Spirit, dreams and visions. It anticipated the achievements of the French Revolution and brought about such a renewal of English social life that some historians see Methodism as the reason why England was spared the bloody revolution that happened in France. Wesley was against slavery. With his preaching of a 'religion of the heart' (and thus not of static doctrine) he emancipated a working class which at a time of rising industrialization was living in deep poverty, though his preaching was rejected by the state church. At the same time (above all at a later stage) he encouraged women to preach and lead classes – something which at that time was thought immoral. Regardless of their origins or social status people were liberated in order to become involved and make a contribution, to become a gift. Nor is it surprising that the first leaders of the British trade unions and the Labour Party were predominantly Methodists.

At the beginning of the nineteenth century Edward Irving became minister of the Caledonian Chapel in London. With great eloquence he condemned the chilly indifference with which the rich treated the poor. Among his large congregation were British Members of Parliament, and his circle of friends included writers like Thomas Carlyle and Coleridge. When some of his friends in the West of Scotland began to speak in tongues and healed after prayer, after a thorough investigation Irving concluded that this had to be an authentic work of God's Spirit. Thereupon in his church services he began to make room for the functioning of gifts like glossolalia and prophecy. This, together with the dynamic christology which he developed, became a reason for dismissing him as a preacher. The witnesses declared that they believed in the authenticity of the charismatic expressions concerned, but found it unacceptable that they 'interrupted' the order of service. Moreover the fact that he encouraged 'laity' and women to speak in services on the basis of their gifts contributed to his condemnation. When he was dismisssed, Irving was followed by the majority of the congregation. From them arose the Catholic Apostolic Church, in which Irving himself accepted the modest position of deacon. Remarkably enough there is no demonstrable connection between Irving and later Pentecostalism, though their spirituality is related in many ways.[17] Also in the last century the Holiness Movement, which has already been mentioned, arose in the United States; this was an ecumenically orientated renewal movement which grew to be the most inportant religious factor in nineteenth-century North America. We have already seen how a fusion between this Holiness Movement and Seymour's black spirituality led to the rise of Pentecostalism at the beginning of our century.

As a result of the defensive attitude of the established churches, the charismatic movements were time and again forced into a sectarian isolation. Here the play of Word and Spirit became chaotic or turned into its opposite, legalism. They were hardly helped by the church theologians to integrate their experience of the Spirit with the Word.

In the Netherlands, too, the request made by the Pentecostal pioneer Polman to the established churches for help in interpreting the baptism in the Spirit biblically and theologically was rejected.[18] So Pentecostalism became vulnerable to fundamentalist influences and, as for example happened with the Reformation, a legalistic teaching and method ('ten steps to baptism in the Spirit') could encapsulate or stifle the liberating experience of God. However, today we live in a unique time. For the first time the established churches are no longer simply rejecting charismatic spirituality, but are ready to investigate it.[19] In addition to the causes of this openness mentioned earlier (like the effect of the Enlightenment ideas of autonomy and democracy and a revaluation of the holistic approach to reality) there is the fact that as a result of secularization the church is dropping its interest in the established order. It is emerging time and again that only a church which knows that it is poor really stands open to the crazy play of Word and Spirit. All this gives hope that the dynamic of the Spirit will finally once again be fully integrated into the church, so that the church becomes fully liberated to play the creative sabbath game. Twenty-five years ago no one would have expected that towards the end of this century the Holy Spirit would again be playing a prominent role in Christianity. If the present tendency continues, this means no less than a revolutionary change in the direction which the church has taken, above all since the third century. That would be a deeper event than the Reformation, because the Reformers left intact the fundamental structure of the church, one-sidedly focussed on order (the Word).

Play and Humour: A Closer Definition

Before we return to celebration, we need to spend a little longer on the nature of play. We saw that this does not consist in order or in disorder, but in the play of the creative activity of the Word and the Spirit, so that God's purpose with human beings is fulfilled.

The historian of religion Gerardus van der Leeuw has pointed out that being human involves *becoming* human.[20] The animal does not *become*, but *is*; it remains one with its world. Animals can play to a certain degree, as is evident, for example, from the sometimes very complicated rituals which some animals perform at mating time. However, their play always remains the same. Animals remain in the world as a part of it and do not distinguish themselves the world, as human beings do. Unlike human beings, they do not know the word that names and makes a difference, as a result of which the world becomes something 'over against' and fellow human beings become a 'you' so that one increasingly becomes 'I'. Human beings are constantly in movement, going to and fro between the world and themselves. This play is in fact an abiding effort to transcend themselves. People become more human in their play. That already emerges from the playing of the small child which makes itself room by moving, by reaching for things around it and finally by going through this room. In the end the child also 'takes' time to play by not only moving spontaneously but arranging its actions in accordance with a process which is aimed at achieving one end or another. In this way it conquers space and time and gets a hold on the world. However, human beings do not just have a hold on the world; the world also has a hold on them. In this constant interaction, both the world and human beings are shaped. This is what is called *yihud* (union) by the Hasidim, a Jewish mystical movement which came into being in Eastern Europe in the eighteenth century and whose celebrations, with their dance, raising of hands, clapping and prayer for healing, show many parallels with Pentecostalism. The way in which God deals with human beings is the way in which human beings deal with the world and the potter deals with her clay. The slightest gap between her hand and the clay brings the process of creation to a halt. Therefore the hands remain joined to the clay, but at the same time the clay which is being formed leads the hands of the potter. For the hands do not go to work according to a predetermined intellectual scheme: the form is as it were caught surprisingly in the dynamic interaction with the clay. In the creation of their world human beings constantly create themselves. So unlike animals, human beings not only receive their life but create it. In the shaping of the world they 'make something of their life' by creating clothes, tools and other forms of culture which in their turn influence people. Thus human beings, unlike animals, also make history. History does not consist in a total of merely being born and dying but of what human beings add to these natural events: art, war, religion, science. Human beings grow in this play of giving to the world and receiving from it.

Tillich pointed out that we can speak of being human only if there is also a prescribed, distinctive identity by which the change can be measured.[21] There is an ongoing tension between one's own identity and interaction with the world. This characterizes the human self and makes real growth possible. There are many different descriptions of the human self around, but in this book I shall begin from the fact that this tension between an ordered recognizable identity and change in relationship to the world represents the dynamic between Word (identity) and Spirit (interaction with the world). I have already observed that in creation any sound organism and social system or ecosystem is characterized by the tension between maintaining its own identity (order) and the dynamic relationship with the environment in which it changes (integration). This is the play of Word and Spirit which, as God's creative principle, finds its highest expression in the human self. And because the Word and the Spirit (Wisdom) are an expression of God's being, the human self in this way participates in God's self. Moreover, the Irish theologian Johannes Scotus, who worked at the court of the Emperor Charles II, rightly concluded that we are most the image of God in our inability to get a grip on the core of our humanity as this, precisely because it is the image of God, always escapes our grasp. However, here we must add that human beings as male and female are the image of God (Gen.1.27), which means that the human self is essentially relational (Word and Spirit). In forming the other/the world and therefore in forming themselves, human beings are thus co-creators with God.

(i) The heavy, false self and the light Spirit

The free interaction with the world and the self-transcendence which is characteristic of human play are clearly expressed in the capacity to laugh. In addition to the spoken word this distinguishes people most clearly from the animal kingdom. As far as we know, animals do not really laugh. In laughter human beings transcend their bond with the world and relativize this without escaping it. However, those who take themselves too seriously, who cannot play or laugh, continue to coincide with the world and cannot transcend it. Therefore those who can laugh at themselves are the freest and most human.

Doris Donnelly points out that humour is a condition for healing, understood as serious and often painful change in accordance with the image of Christ.[22] The target of the healing process is our false, 'animal' self which absolutizes the instinctive pressure towards selfhood. It is false because it parades as our true human self where it is actually suppressing this. The difference between the false self and the true self is that between individual and person; the individual places himself or herself in the centre, whereas the person is concerned for others. The false self constantly aims to preserve itself and therefore opts for routine and predictability, nestling in the apparently safe haven of possessions, reputation, status and achievements. It cannot accept that its existence is not necessary, and therefore makes itself indispensable. A false self tilts heavily towards itself, is incessantly occupied with itself and tends towards an oppressive, formal piety. This is far removed, for example, from the spirituality of the Hasidim, whose prayer to God often twinkles with humour, precisely because they know their limits. They know that they are creatures and so they can relativize themselves and let God be God: 'Be still and know that *I* am God' (Ps.46.11). Nothing less than a shock therapy is needed to unmask the false self and bring God, in Word and Spirit, into the centre of our life. This shock breaks the anxious need for rational control and helps us to let go of our life. In this the false self dies, along with the rigid order which it imposed on reality, and God can give new life from the dead. The newborn self is free from the need to justify itself and to entrench itself in a massive order: free recklessly to wager all on God's promises and to regard everything as 'refuse' for Christ's sake; and free to live in a playful interaction with the world, with courage, surrender and great joy. The lightness of the Spirit redeems us from the heaviness that condemns us to live by a false, 'important' self.

(a) The foolishness of Christ

The surprising twist in a parable or a joke (think also of the Zen *koan*) can provide the necessary 'shock therapy'. Both relativize the order of this world which we regard as unchangeable and natural and can give us a surprising new perspective on reality.

It is not the good, obedient oldest son who is given a feast, but his brother, who had run away and had thrown all religious and moral codes overboard. It is not the important, pious Pharisee who goes home justified after his prayer, but the bad, wordless tax-collector. A remark by the well-known Trappist monk Thomas Merton gave a similar shock: he said that in American society the monk is the true prophet because he is the only one who is free to do nothing and not feel guilty about it. Humour is characteristic of the playful, true person and Jesus, as a living parable, was ready with his answers, witty and unpredictable. Anyone who has ears to hear can see his sense of humour in his conversations with some Pharisees fixated on order. Thus in Matthew 22.15-22 he is asked whether it is permissible for a Jew to pay tribute to the Roman emperor. In his reply Jesus laconically asks to be shown a coin, which his opponents produce. So they seem to have with them a coin which no pious Jew would carry around because it had on it not only the image of the emperor but also the inscription that he is both king and God, and thus breaks two commandments of Moses. After this witty unmasking his partners in the discussion are hopelessly lost. In Matthew 5.22 Jesus turns upside down the legalistic, Pharisaic hierarchy of sins and the punishments which go with them: the greatest sin gets the lightest punishment (anyone who lives in anger with his brother will be convicted in court) and the lightest sin gets the heaviest punishment (anyone who says 'you fool' is condemned to hell fire). Moreover, in the Christian tradition Christ is sometimes portrayed as a clown, as someone who at the same time both belongs and does not belong in the present-day order and thus criticizes it.

The Eastern Orthodox tradition still knows the (rare) office of the *salos*, the prophetic fool for Christ's sake. So in the sixth century the monk Symeon felt called to play a 'game' with the world. He really challenged all the rules which guarantee order in society and in this way roused many people from their self-satisfaction. He made the kingdom of God as it were visible by means of a topsy-turvy world. He made his entry into a city dragging behind him a dead dog on a string. He entered the women's baths naked, relieved himself in the market-place, forced his way into a room where a woman was sleeping and made as it he were going to take off his garments, and during a church service mounted the pulpit to pelt the congregation with notes.[23] Another well known *salos* was Nicolas of Pskov who put a piece of meat, dripping with blood, into the hands of the murderous Tsar Ivan the Terrible. Pentecostalism, too, knows its fools for Christ's sake, like Homer Tomlinson, head of the Church of God (Queens, New York). From 1954 to 1966 he visited 101 large cities. In each city he first notified the press, then went to a central open place and there crowned himself 'king of the world'. After that, holding an inflatable globe, he took his place on a portable throne and spoke a message of peace to his audience. A less dramatic folly is speaking in tongues, to which Pentecostals often react with mockery. Glossolalia is the charism which is most similar to laughter. It is spontaneous, useless (because it consists of meaningless sounds) and is experienced as broadening and healing. Furthermore the stories in charismatic celebrations often have a comic twist, while participants in a prayer meeting can burst out laughing spontaneously in the middle of a prayer. Other charismatic expressions are also often regarded as foolish by outsiders, like raising hands in praise and resting in the Spirit. These 'foolish' expressions help to break through the excessive control of the analytical intellect and to make us open to an encounter with God in the deeper levels of our being. Richard Baer Jr has pointed out that the extended Catholic and Eastern Orthodox liturgy and the silence of the Quaker meeting in principle have this same function.[24]

(b) Coping with the absurdities of existence

Another important aspect of play that is also clearly expressed in humour is the capacity to see the absurdities of life. We burst out laughing when the everyday and the unexpected, the ridiculous and the sublime occur together. In this sense, too, in Jesus a laugh went through Israel. The Sermon on the Mount (Matt. 5.1-12) is an absurd blessing on poor people who possess the kingdom of God, gentle people who inherit the earth and mourners who are comforted. But can the play of humour also do justice to the basic absurdities of existence, like a newly married young man who dies in an accident, a small child which has a malignant tumour and a continent whose death by famine is watched on television by the rich West?

All his life, the American theologian Reinhold Niebuhr was impressed by the human capacity to do evil. As he never paid much attention to the doctrine of the Spirit his ethics sometimes seems not only sober but also sombre. Nevertheless, directly after the Second World War he could write that humour is the gateway to belief.[25] Both are a response to the absurdities of existence, humour being our reaction to the superficial everyday absurdities and faith to the essential absurdities of life and death which threaten the meaning of our existence. The understanding (a willing instrument of the false self which is obsessed by control) can only look at these absurdities from one side or the other, at the same time denying the absurdity which it seeks to resolve. According to Niebuhr, even humour cannot give an adequate answer to the basic absurdities of existence. Then humour is twisted and the laugh becomes bitter or shrill with despair. So humour, confronted with the essential absurdities of life, must turn into faith. But we can also put Niebuhr's view that humour is the gateway to faith the other way round: faith makes authentic humour possible. All humour presupposes a basic trust in the goodness of existence. When suffering and evil wreak their devastations, humour refuses to draw what rationally is the logical conclusion that life is meaningless and without hope. Humour bears witness not to what is before our eyes but to trust in the good things which are unknown and not yet visible. According to the developmental psychologist Erik Erikson, this basic trust in all cultures is derived from religion.[26] This basic trust is consolidated concretely and radically in Jewish faith in the belief that God is a God of the Exodus who leads his people from oppression, slavery and death to the eternal sabbath. Hence the well-known remark by the London rabbi Lionel Blue that humour is the most characteristic weapon of Jewish spirituality. This trust in the goodness of God is further intensified by the Christian faith that Jesus, unjustly condemned and executed, was raised from the dead. As the Irishman

Patrick Kavanagh sings in his song 'Lough Derg', Jesus' resurrection is 'a laugh freed for once and for ever'. Christian existence is fundamentally a laugh. But the resurrection is taken seriously only if the crucifixion is also looked at seriously, Play must constantly remain open to suffering, otherwise it becomes superfluous and laughter becomes hollow and smooth. This happens even in the circles of prosperous Western charismatics who shut themselves off from the need in the world.

Over against the inescapable fate of tragedy stands the unpredictable surprise of comedy. Humour stakes its money on what is good and is still to come and is thus an act of opposition to the absurdity of evil. It does not deny this absurdity, as superficial and also strictly rational attitudes do, nor does it let itself be overcome by it, as in a purely emotional approach. Humour does justice to the absurdity, for despite the evil which is present it continues to believe in the good. In humour, human beings continue to confront the evil which by definition can never really be integrated. They relativize it without trivializing it and can therefore forgive. They do not accept the situation and as a result do not allow themselves to be stopped or paralysed by it. In commitment they remain free so that they really can suffer with others and attack the evil in righteous anger. Both humour and anger are nurtured by faith – faith that things can be different. In this way faith holds open the possibility of creativity, of a surprising shift to the good – as a resurrection from the dead. Pastors know how even at the most tragic sick bed, in an unexpected humorous event or statement the deep suffering can be transcended for a moment which is liberating both for the patient and for the visitor. In such a gratuitous moment, there is the unconscious experience that evil does not have the last word. There is a vague, deep trust that all will still be well, that the Word and the Spirit can make something new even out of this destructive experience. Humour is what Peter Berger called a 'rumour of angels'. This trust inspires an opposition which is not fixated on evil and does not deny it. In such a way believers do not allow an action to combat the need in the world to be paralysed by the weight of the problem. They do not take all the responsibility for it on their own shoulders, but on the other hand they are not deaf to the urgent appeal which comes from this need. Both reactions are typical of the false self which takes itself too seriously and therefore knows only an 'all or nothing' attitude. But people who really make some contribution (however modest) to the relief of need in the world are usually people who are aware of their finitude. Therefore they can put even the most extensive suffering in the perspective of the God who transcends it. Only this relativization of one's own importance takes not only God but also the distress seriously. Relieving it need no longer serve to prove the importance of one's own contribution, which can easily lead to discouragement, since the pain of the world seems infinitely great. This relativization of one's own importance is characteristic of humour and makes possible a free, creative, interaction with the suffering of others. Thus human beings are like potters who do not deny the unwilling clay, but enter into an interaction with the clay and continue the creative process in which they themselves are formed. Through this play of giving and receiving, human beings can become themselves even in the most barren, disastrous situations and really be of significance. The attitude of play (which does not exclude anger but includes it) makes possible a true human response to the seriousness of suffering and evil.

To sum up, I conclude that only a playful approach does justice to reality by not reducing it to a rigid order which must give the false self the illusion that it has ground beneath it. Here it critically confronts any ideology and political or religious system which has absolute claims. Nor are playful human beings out to dominate reality and exploit it, to justify their own existence with the result. This implies a criticism of technocratic utilitarian thought and achievement which attacks both the nature and the quality of human life. Both approaches are typical of the false self, which not only wrongs reality (and thus the truth) but leads to an absolutization of one's own interpretation of existence. This, added to the need for self-justification, can in extreme instances easily result in violence. Behind an attitude which does violence to the fellow human being who is different there is always a view of existence which violates humanity, since it excludes whatever is 'different'. Attentive receptiveness of the truth of the other, and thus of God as the Other, is by contrast the heart of all spirituality, as Simone Weil remarked.[27] Thus the attitude of play is characteristic of the true, free self which is grounded in God. It uses reality, not as an instrument for grounding and justifying itself, but first of all as an end in itself. In the Word and the Spirit the true self shares in the outgoing movement of God which creates creation and makes it blossom. The true self consists in the dynamic of Word (identity) and Spirit (relationship) with the world which makes possible a reciprocal interaction with reality. This play of giving and receiving, in which both the world and we ourselves are formed, is an expression of the nature of God as it is revealed in Jesus Christ. Love is therefore another word for this playful way of life which seems to be stimulated above all in charismatic celebration.

3

Celebration as Sabbath Play: Huizinga's Definition

In the beginning was the celebration. To an important degree the liturgical festivals have governed the structure of scripture. Scripture is a liturgical book, full of songs, prayers, poems, visions, laments and drama. There is an interaction. The liturgy puts the stories of the Bible in their place, that is, with human beings in their history. On the other hand the Bible stories support the liturgy and put it on the track of the history which God writes. Important theological conceptions are born from this creative play of the liturgy.[28] Above all in the Eastern Orthodox tradition the sense that the liturgy is not only the source but also the expression of church theology is still clearly present. The word liturgy (*leitourgia*) originally denoted a service performed for the people. In ancient Greece it denoted the service of a well-to-do citizen who paid for the religious ceremonies associated with the games so that these could take place. Although we may not apply this significance directly to the Christian liturgy (for the meaning of a word is also dependent on the time and context in which it is used), it does, I think, touch on a fundamental truth. In and through the Word and the Spirit, revealed in Christ, God serves his people in the celebration so that they can already play the sabbath game. By way of summary I shall now investigate once again the main characteristics of charismatic celebration but now from another perspective, starting from Huizinga's definition of play:

> Play is a voluntary activity or occupation executed within certain fixed limits of time and place, according to rules freely accepted but absolutely binding, having its aim in itself, accompanied by a feeling of tension, joy and the consciousness that it is 'different' from 'ordinary life'.[29]

(i) A voluntary occupation

Play is a voluntary occupation and therefore neither necessary nor imposed by an order coming from outside. Although there is social control even in Pentecostal communities, most Pentecostals do not go to their assembly out of a feeling of guilt or duty but simply because they want to go. Most of the participants do not feel that the celebration is too long because for them the celebration is an active *occupation* in which they are totally involved. Characteristic of a charismatic celebration is the 'jazz factor', the creative integration of order and the spontaneous contribution of the participants. The Spirit is experienced as 'team spirit' which involves everyone in this crazy sabbath game. This is in marked contrast to the services of most of the established churches, which are one-sidedly orientated on order. There the focus is really never on one another, as in a team game, but on the one priest or preacher who presides. Many people find this emphasis on order burdensome and do not really feel free. They do not have the feeling that they can be themselves in the service. When a child says or does something spontaneously, sometimes the whole community lights up. Too much emphasis on the objective Word or the sacraments excludes the subject. No wonder that people in such a service begin to look at their watches after about an hour. An authentic Christian celebration is a feast of freedom which celebrates the fact that existence is given by grace and therefore is without necessity or purpose.

(ii) Within fixed limits of time and place

A game is played within definite, fixed limits of time and space. The celebration is held at a time and place which are *in* this world but not *of* it. It takes place above all on Sunday, which has no purpose, the day of the resurrection of Jesus and the radicalizing of the sabbath. The sphere of play is also clearly marked out from the rest of the world and is often a building which really has no other use. The church building is a holy space, in the sense of a space that is set apart, just as the time of play also falls on a separate, holy day. If the Jewish sabbath is the 'circumcision' of time, then the Christian Sunday is the 'baptism' of time. Above all in some Protestant traditions, however, Sunday has come to be burdened with an order as a result of which to a considerable degree it has lost its holy, set apart character. Like working days, Sunday has taken on a necessary, legalistic character to which men and women must conform. In this way Sunday loses its prophetic content. Such a Sunday is not only *in* this world but, contrary to all intentions, also *of* this world. The many people who do not go to church on Sunday but have recreation in sport and games do more justice to the significance of this day than Christians who have reduced it to a means to an end, even if that end is pious. Sunday is the day of the resurrection of Jesus, on which the definitive necessity of death is overcome. Sunday is a forerunner of the eternal sabbath play and therefore a protest against the grain of a social order which reduces people to useful instruments.[30]

This significance of Sunday is focussed in the celebration. Here the essentially playful structure of creation is clearly visible. The play of Word and Spirit creates what McLuhan has called a 'counter-milieu' and therefore has a recreating, healing power. For charismatic celebration, too, there remains a challenge here to maintain the tension between the 'not *of* this world' and the '*in* this world'. For the prophetic content of the celebration is not only lost if it is too much *of* this world, as in church services orientated on order and utility, but also if it is too little *in* this world. Bonhoeffer pointed out that there are not two realities, a divine and a human, which stand over against each other. In Christ there is simply one reality, this world, and the task of the church is at the same time both to confirm this and to criticize it.[31] However, quite a few charismatic celebrations contribute uncritically towards maintaining the dominant order. Like the practice of modern sport, they simply function as an outlet for the ideas, emotions and bodily expressions which have to be suppressed during the week at school, business or office. Then Sunday is not a day set apart which criticizes the working week, but stands isolated from the rest of the week. The 'not *of* this world' does not fully work through into the '*in* this world'. As we have seen, the main reason for this is the 'whitewashing' of the 'Third World' spirituality, as a result of which the experience of the Word and the Spirit is detached from earthly reality. The reflection on its black roots which has recently begun in Pentecostalism will anchor the charismatic celebration much more firmly in this world. This will increase its prophetic content, as is already happening, for example, in South Africa.

(iii) Freely accepted rules

Furthermore, according to Huizinga's definition play is played according to rules which are freely accepted but absolutely binding. This is the element of order, of the Word that together with the Spirit can create its own bewitching order of play in which all things are possible. Through the one-sided orientation of many traditional church services on the Word, faith remains on a rational, abstract level. It does not 'land'; the words do not become 'flesh'. A one-sided emphasis on the rules kills the sabbath play. This also applies to the liturgical rites, which are for movement what words are for sound. Rites also make possibly the creative interplay in celebration, but if they become formal, they cut off the experience of God, produce rigidity and take the pleasure out of the game.[32] By contrast, if they remain living and serve the liturgical game, then – like parables, humour, glossolalia and the foolishness of other charismatic expressions – for a moment they take us out of our automatic way of living in accordance with the order of this world and open us to the possibilities of the kingdom of God.

Whereas the established churches often put one-sided emphasis on the rules of the game, the liturgical rules of the Pentecostal movment are often inadequate. In both cases the game is spoilt, as any child knows. Although Pentecostals tend to deny this, their meetings follow a liturgical order which largely corresponds to that in other traditions. This also applies to the liturgical year, though an individual Pentecostal sometimes will not have Christmas carols sung at Christmas because 'for us every day is Christmas and Easter and Pentecost'. But these are exceptions. In general, Pentecostal communities, above all when they have been in existence for some time, tend like the established churches not towards chaos but towards too much order. They too do not escape the sociological law of institutionalization. But because they do not recognize that they are following an order in the liturgy (albeit an oral one), they cannot reflect critically on it. The consequence is that insufficient resistance is offered to the gravity of the order, which can degenerate into domination by the minister, rigid views about baptism, or legalistic rules calling for the wearing of hats by women in meetings (for example in the French Pentecostal movement). This tendency is further strenghtened by the influence of fundamentalism, so that not a few Pentecostal meetings have become as static as an old-fashioned Protestant preaching service. Even the charismatic renewal is not free of this bias towards order, which has recently become clear in the so-called Restoration Movement. This movement, which is above all making progress in England (in the House Church Movement) and in the United States (in the Shepherding Movement), has tried in different ways to restore the pastoral ministry, complete with an almost apostolic authority. So most parish members of the episcopal, charismatically renewed Church of the Redeemer in Houston must at a given moment ask permission from their ministers for example to buy a new car or even to marry a partner they have their eye on. After criticism from the charismatic renewal itself, this movement has abandoned its most extreme views. However, it remains remarkable that the very people who have experienced the Spirit seem to be so receptive to authoritarian and legalistic views. Moreover that applies to almost all the charismatic currents in history, beginning with the first Christian communities. I shall be investigating this later. Here I would also like to remark that in general the play of Word and Spirit seems likely to find most room in the charismatic renewal. The combination of a traditional liturgical order used critically and openness to the charismatic Spirit often inspires a creative sabbath play which leaves few people indifferent.

(iv) Having its aim in itself

Huizinga also remarks that play is an end in itself. In the period of the rise of modern Pentecostalism, the Roman Catholic theologian Romano Guardini described celebration as a game.[33] In his view, in celebration we waste time before God. We recreate without reason or purpose. The liturgy has no aim, to make it subordinate to something outside itself. No, the liturgy itself has an indispensable significance and is therefore an end in itself. As a child pours itself out in its play, in celebration we express our true selves, giving ourselves to God and to one another. Of course this rings out like a curse in the ears of our purposeful 'time is money' society, which constantly pursues a goal that it will never reach because it can only be received in the welcoming of life now. Only in the useless play of celebration is life taken seriously as a true gift of God. Here God's kingdom already breaks through to some extent, so that the celebration is itself both already eternal life (the Eastern Orthodox view) and the means to salvation and liberation (the Roman-Catholic view). Here, through the Word and the Spirit, God's people are increasingly tuned to the eternal sabbath play so that the celebration in principle has power to change the world. A celebration makes you human again, since the game is fundamentally for our humanity. (We can find a theological translation of this insight in Karl Barth's *Church Dogmatics* III/4, in which he begins his teaching on ethics with a discussion of Sunday.) In celebration nothing less than the world is at stake. Nor is it surprising that people in other religions, and even atheists, have always felt an intuitive need for liturgies of their own. People from primitive antiquity already believed that rituals (according to Plato identical with play) could guarantee the well-being of the world.[34] This often degenerated into magic (even in Christianity): in an effort to dominate reality personal advantage (power and order) began to be more important than the play. This fact further emphasizes how essential it is that there is also room for the Spirit alongside the Word. In the celebration the minister is therefore a kind of religious producer who helps people to play their own roles convincingly in church and society.

Experience in the celebration of God who is useless, because God is an end in himself, can liberate us from our purpose-orientated attitude which destroys play. Then we can give to the world in a creative way and receive from it. For our fellow human beings who are created in God's image are ends in themselves – and in the end that applies to all creation. The play of celebration is therefore the Protestant doctrine (which is essentially also that of Eastern Orthodoxy and the Roman Catholic Church) of justification by faith (grace) alone brought to life.[35] This runs counter to the notion underlying our Western culture, namely that human beings should be their own autonomous creators (Aristotle's *causa sui*) and thus are what they produce. When work no longer needs to be a way of proving ourselves, it can become more of an expression of our self-development. This not only gives more room for creativity, since the quality of the work improves, but also furthers human well-being. For those who have eyes to see, in our modern technocratic society the children, the aged, the unemployed, the handicapped and the poor have become prophetic signs. They remind us that it is not our useful work but only unmerited grace that can justify our existence. Moreover it is not by chance that people from these categories are so abundantly represented in Pentecostalism. For to a greater degree than the worship of the established churches, often orientated on order and achievement (as sermons can suggest), charismatic celebration is characterized by useless play which has no purpose. The participants simply express themselves in the celebration and thus become free gifts (*charismata*) for God and for one another. Bonhoeffer wrote that life is an end in itself, but not in an absolute sense. Purely in itself, life has no significance and becomes a destructive 'movement into nothing'. Therefore as an end in itself life is at the same time also a means to the end of participation in God's kingdom. As an end in itself, a gift of God, life has unassailable rights. As a means to the end of God's kingdom, as a gift of God, it also has duties.[36] As bearers of the sabbath crown, men and women are called to respect the interplay of creation and to further it by giving themselves to it – beginning with celebration.

Anyone who lives playfully will not easily be discouraged by the question of the utility of the struggle for truth, justice, peace and a healthy environment. For the struggle for these things does not depend on whether it achieves visible results; they are important *in themselves* (what Gandhi called *anasakti*). A playful approach to existence transcends the superficial, pragmatic attitude of Western culture in which the meaning of each activity is judged by the contribution that it makes. In a speech given in 1992 to the French Académie des Sciences Morales et Politiques, Vaclav Havel, the Czech president, emphasized this. He related how as a dissident he had learned that speaking the truth had a significance in itself without 'knowing whether this would ever triumph or whether it would be choked – as so often happened'. The technocratic approach fixated on results betrays a lack of humility and patience with respect to the distinctive dynamic of the true, the good and the beautiful, because it wants to reduce these to something over which it has control and which it can use at will.[37] The attitude of play respects this distinctive dynamic and remains a zeal for truth and justice, even in times and situations in which this seems useless and crazy. So people become living parables which can turn the world upside down and renew it. The remarkable thing is that the less we are bothered about the result, the more quality our contribution has. Those who are no longer fixated on a goal will achieve it unexpectedly.[38]

(v) Tension and joy

Huizinga's definition also goes on to note that play is coupled with feelings of tension and joy. In the celebration God gives himself in Christ's Word and Spirit, so that the participants are liberated to play the play of the kingdom of God. The intensity and joy with which this is accompanied bring about an asceticism of this world order with its utilitarian thought and thus an openness to the holy. People become free to praise God for God's sake, not for what God does: free to welcome the neighbour as an equal partner and also to involve the non-human creation in the play in the form of bread, wine, water, incense, icons and so on. A charismatic celebration is characterized by joy. This can take on a triumphalistic form in the sectors of Pentecostalism where people forget their black roots. Nevertheless the participation of very many poor people who do not have the luxury of being able to avoid or suppress their persistent suffering and wants suggest that the charismatic joy is in principle authentic. Of course here too worship can become an opium, and celebration a trick in which one forgets the misery of the everyday. More than being a criticism of their experience of faith (which at least helps them to survive), this implies a condemnation of the unjust economic conditions in the world. As a result of these the poor have no chance of a worthwhile human existence and are forced to seek the consolation of drink.

However, evil cannot authentically be confronted without joy. If it is, what is usually left is the Stoic atittude which has become so characteristic of a large part of Christianity. Here people attempt, come what may, to preserve an internal emotional order, so that, unlike Jesus (Luke 1.21; John 11.35), they avoid both excessive praise and deep sorrow. This gives the church service a stylized and emotionally flat character. Confronted with intense suffering these Christians can usually react only with dignity and reassurance. The Stoic atittude is by definition static; it can at best keep evil in check, and cannot offer any real resistance to it.[39] That is possible only through the joy which finds its origin in the God of joy, whose Word and Spirit can constantly create something new. Only those who can laugh can also really feel the pain of others and mean something for them. For sorrow presupposes joy, and despair presupposes hope. Without joy and hope there is no deep sorrow and no screaming despair, just as only the experience of justice makes righteous anger possible. So only in a process of emancipation, in increasing awareness of one's own freedom and dignity, can discrimination and oppression can be painfullly perceived. If it is good, this stimulates opposition to injustice, but many people break off through lack of courage and support from their surroundings and continue to live unchanged – plagued by the melancholy recollection of the fleeting freedom which they once breathed. Only the experience of joy in the play of God's kingdom makes it possible to experience the battlefield of evil and suffering in this world in all its despair and pain. So not only joy but also sorrow and indignation are expressed in the charism of the celebration. Lamentation and anger are the obverse of praise, as emerges abundantly from the Psalms.

One important cause of the omnipresent Stoic attitude is that for modern people there is little difference between good and evil. These are so mixed in their thoughts and feelings that they cannot experience goodness openly as good. Psychological investigation has shown that even the noblest deed is not without inferior motives (Paul also already knew this, see I Corinthians 13.1-3). And Auschwitz made it abundantly clear that good, respectable citizens can in some circumstances turn into horrible monsters. No wonder modern people have become mistrustful, and when something good happens they immediately think, 'Yes, but...' The heart of the problem is that this mixture of good and evil is projected on to God, so that people cannot surrender to God's goodness, and continue to maintain a Stoic attitude. However, with Pentecostals this mixing is very much less. For them, in general good comes from God and evil from the devil. Their belief in the devil sometimes seems mediaeval and can lead to a simplistic black-and-white ethics, but it puts them in a position to give a place to evil and fully to experience joy in God's goodness. This makes them capable of tackling the evil in their immediate surroundings, as is witnessed by the great amount of work by Pentecostals among the enslaved, the homeless and the like. At the deepest level, joy is the meaning of human existence.[40] As the Westminster Confession of 1646 put it: 'Man's chief end is to glorify God and to enjoy him for ever' (alas, in this Calvinistic confession this is limited to those who 'are elect to salvation'). It is this joyful experience of God which attracts to charismatic celebrations people who thought that God was dead, simply because they did not know any place where the divine presence was experienced and celebrated. Moreover, the accent on experience seems timely in an age in which truths of faith are no longer accepted on authority but must be experienced personally as true.

(a) Dance

This joy is expressed in charismatic celebration not only by means of enthusiastic songs (with texts and melodies which sensitive ears can sometimes find painful), extravagant praise and hand clapping, but also in dance. This can sometimes be classically trained dance but more often is a spontaneous folk dance in which everyone can join. Huizinga saw dance as one of the purest and most perfect forms of play.[41] Dance was already central in the liturgy of ancient Israel. The call 'rejoice in [or before] the Lord' which is repeated many times in the books of Deuteronomy and Psalms was an invitation to dance. Mystics and some church fathers describe the new creation as a dance, and there was much dancing in churches up to the Reformation.[42] The meetings of the eighteenth- and nineteenth-century Shakers (a movement influenced by the Quakers and Camisards) consisted exclusively in dance. According to them this was the only right form of celebration for a church which lived 'in the last days' and was thus close to God's kingdom. But similarly many church fathers, on the basis of Greek thought which puts the spirit above the body, rejected dance, and the teaching of the philosopher Descartes, in which there is an emphasis on the intellect at the expense of the body, has led in recent years to a discouraging of dance in church. The body was no longer welcome in church services and this has contributed to an intellectualization of faith at the expense of the body and, in the same direction, of nature. Moltmann writes that the exploitation of nature is the counterpart of the subjection of the body.[43] People have subordinated their bodies to the purpose of functioning in industrial society, in which they have to sit in an office day by day or stand on the factory floor hour after hour. As a reward, their restless false self can satisfy the demands of consumer ideology: the possession of the most recent product praised by advertising. Because we treat our bodies as a means to an end, we do the same with the nature of which our bodies are a part. Nature is in the first place an object to use, not creation which arouses wonder and amazement. In principle there is no difference between smoking a cigarette and poisoning nature with exhaust fumes. We have become strangers to our bodies and therefore cannot live in friendship with the earth. We spoil the interplay of all things, what Moltmann calls 'the community of creation', with serious consequences for the environment.

However, our body comes into its own again in liturgical dance. We are detached from our remote, reflective attitude which makes our bodies and nature objects. In dance people learn to live directly and spontaneously again, instead of in a derived sense with ideas *about* life. Dance is a confirmation of our existence as creatures and a celebration of the flesh in which in a priestly way we express the joy of the whole creation at the fact that it is a dwelling-place of the Word and Spirit. We move in a harmonious interplay with the creation in rhythm, space and time. Moreover in dance the holistic 'Third World' spirituality with its integration of Spirit and matter (body) has its highest liturgical expression. As joy made flesh, dance is also opposition to suffering and evil. Therefore the Pentecostals, who are the very Christians who in recent history have had to endure the most mockery, persecution and suffering, are the ones who dance. And the Jewish Hasidim, whose meetings, as I said earlier, can have a playful character which in some respects suggests a charismatic celebration, understood dance in this way. So the following story is told of Rabbi Naphtali of Robsitz who, on the evening of the feast of the Joy of the Law (*simchat torah*), heard that a pupil and friend had died:

> The Hasidim don't have the heart to go on with the festivities. So he scolds them angrily: 'Are we not at war – at war with destiny, with the entire world? What does one do at the front when an officer falls? What does one do? Does one run away? On the contrary, one closes ranks and fights even harder. So close your ranks and dance, dance with more vigour than ever; dance like you have never danced before!'[44]

(vi) 'Different' from normal life

Finally, according to Huizinga, play is felt to be 'different' from ordinary life. That is already evident, as we saw, from the fact that the celebration takes place in a separate 'holy' place on a 'holy' day. According to Scripture, God alone is holy and what is hallowed shares in God's being, like the people of Israel, the sabbath, the land of Israel, the community of Christ and Sunday. What is hallowed is 'different' from the world that does not know God. This applies above all to the 'holy meeting', which therefore has the character of a parable, a 'kingdom difference' which makes the celebration crazy in the eyes of the present world order. The celebration is *in* this world but not *of* this world, a tension which is caused by the fact that the kingdom of God has 'already now' broken through in the guarantee of the Spirit (II Cor.1.22; 5.5) but 'not yet' completely. Moreover in the perfected creation there will be no temple or church building, with a celebration apart from the world. God himself will be their temple and the whole creation a wedding (Revelation 19.7-9; 21.1-3, 13, 22). However, like Jesus, the church, too, still lives in the old world order which, as a living parable, it constantly breaks open to the order of the eternal sabbath game that becomes most clearly visible in celebration. The regular celebration maintains the awareness that God's kingdom is 'other', living. This prevents us from coinciding with the purposeful, rigid order of this world whose gravity constantly pulls on us. So whenever the celebration is not sufficiently 'other', the church lapses into activities which can be engaged in just as well or better by other groups. It is equally clear that the present world is more like a battlefield than a playing field, and it is evident that many church services do not realize their potential to change the world. Moreover a number of churches are experiencing an identity crisis and are asking whether they still have anything to say to the world.

In my view the most important cause of this crisis lies in the fact that celebration has lost much of its playfulness and therefore no longer has any power to change. In an attempt to be relevant, churches have introduced the instrumental thinking of the world and thus have become irrelevant. The priest or preacher tells too few parables and moralizes too much. Celebration is subordinated to all kids of didactic, social or political ends. However well meant this may be, it cannot really inspire people. Through the week they are treated at their work as a means to an end (to produce) and now they have to expect the same instrumental treatment on Sundays. The celebration is no longer foolish enough, so that it no longer proclaims God's wisdom. The balance has been shifted in the direction of the Word, order, utilitarian ethics and didacticism, at the cost of the Spirit who inspires, surprises and renews. Certainly in the Pentecostal movement and in the non-white indigenous churches, too, the sermon is often too moralistic and aimed at results. But this fixation on 'utility' finds a counterbalance in the extended play of the meeting.

Moreover Pentecostal ministers are really evangelists. Their preaching is addressed to the bystanders drawn into the game by means of conversion or baptism in the Spirit, and thus does not affect the uselessness of the celebration itself. Roughly speaking, it can be said that by contrast the celebration in the established churches is not sufficiently 'different'. The service, like a modern carnival and the sporting world, which is bureaucratic and orientated on money, has become culturally sterile. I am aware that this is a generalization which does not do justice to the playful initiatives which are developed here and there. But in general the traditional church services provide too little counterbalance to the present technocratic society, which is inhuman in various respects. When the order of celebration has become a copy of the order of this world, the otherness of the neighbour as a fellow-player cannot be honoured, and unity in difference gives way to uniformity or uncommitted toleration. Only in the play of Word and Spirit can human beings grow as human beings, in other words in a playful interaction with one another in which their unique identity is given as a gift and shaped by the reception of the identity of the other.

A celebration which is insufficiently 'different' cannot well proclaim the otherness of God's kingdom and thus the otherness of God himself. In that case God becomes a useful idol, or is regarded as superfluous – witness the practical atheism of so many churchgoers. So many traditional churches in Western Europe today are feeling a 'dark night of God', whereas the Pentecostal communities in the same cities or the charismatic conferences in the same areas are sometimes overwhelmed with the abundant 'outpouring' of God's Spirit. The liturgical movement in our century has done a good deal to involve God's people more in the liturgical game, but with its catholicizing tendencies it is orientated on order and therefore cannot solve our present-day problems. The increasing use of albs, stoles and the like in Protestant worship is in itself a festal sign, but does it stimulate the priesthood of all believers? Celebration must again become what Harvey Cox described as a 'feast of fools', a playful protest that disturbs the social order and sets it moving with a view to its liberation and healing. This is God's mission and the task of the church as the community of Christ, the Wisdom of God.

It can be concluded that charismatic celebration generally matches Huizinga's definition of play better than moderate traditional church worship. Alongside the Word, it also clearly makes room for the Spirit, and these together inspire a 'Third World' spirituality which puts people in a position to play, sing, dance and leap before the Lord. Already alluding to the eternal sabbath play and as disciples of Christ, the participants in this way become more human and in principle are equipped, in priestly concern, to contribute to a more humane society and to the preservation of creation. Moreover, it is not surprising that charismatic celebration has recently become an important factor in the renewal of the liturgy of, for example, the Protestant churches in the United States.[45]

Now that we have noted the crucial importance of play and its realization in charismatic celebration, it is time to go explicitly into the question of how it is that Pentecostals can play so strikingly. The answer lies in their expectation and experience of the baptism with Word and Spirit, which manifests itself in numerous charisms.

Part Four: Baptism with Word and Spirit

Where Catholics ask whether one has received the sacraments and Protestants inform one about the correct doctrines, the first question that Pentecostals ask is 'Did you receive the Holy Spirit when you came to believe?' (see Acts 19.2).[1] This experience of the Spirit already occupies a prominent place in the prophetic expectation of the First Testament. However, as a result of a one-sided stress on order (Word and sacraments), 'baptism with the Spirit' has hitherto received too little attention in theological reflection. This is now beginning to change only through the rise of Pentecostalism. In a recent study the South African Henry Lederle has surveyed the most important interpretations of baptism with the Spirit within the Pentecostal movement and charismatic renewal.[2] Here I shall distinguish three main approaches: the doctrine of the Pentecostal movement, the sacramental interpretation and the critical organic approach.

The majority of the Pentecostal movement sees baptism in the Spirit as an experience different from and following on rebirth, confirmed by speaking with glossolalic sounds. We have seen that Charles Parham formulated this doctrine in full for the first time. However, the rigid distinction between rebirth and baptism in the Spirit does not do justice to the unity of the work of the Spirit. Moreover this doctrine divides Christians into two classes: those who are only reborn, and those who in addition are at the same time said to be baptized with the Spirit. Finally, it seems the height of irony that in particular glossolalia, the gift which has so clearly manifested the playful character of Word and Spirit, has been made a legalistic 'proof' that one has received baptism with the Spirit. Out of dissatisfaction with this interpretation, theologians involved in the charismatic movement have gone in search of an approach which does more justice to scripture, tradition and the experiences of believers within this movement. This has resulted in a sacramental interpretation of baptism in the Spirit. Inspired by the early Syrian tradition, this links up with infant baptism, the sacrament in which baptism in the Spirit is potentially received. In the Eastern Orthodox chrism, Catholic confirmation or the Protestant confession, this baptism of the Spirit is then actualized or released. This notion fits in well with the existing church rituals and gives them more content (this applies above all to confirmation). Moreover the question is not whether the Spirit can work in this way but whether the Spirit is tied to the sacramental system. According to scripture and the tradition of charismatic movements (including the Pentecostal movement), that is certainly not the case. A one-sided emphasis on the sacramental interpretation makes the same mistake as the Pentecostal movement where it brings its two-phase structure (rebirth-baptism in the Spirit) into the established church by a liturgical door (infant baptism, confirmation/confession). It seems to do more justice to the Spirit as incomprehensible *ruach* not to fix this to a particular pattern and with Thomas Aquinas to begin from the fact that many surprising experiences (*innovationes*) are possible in Christian life with the Spirit.[3] So after the Pentecostal teaching and sacramental interpretation, recently above all in Europe a third approch is gaining ground which I call the critical-organic approach. In different ways it is shown here that baptism and the gifts of the Spirit form an organic part of Christian and church life. This avoids fixation on a closely defined pattern of experience and at the same time involves a criticism of a church doctrine and practice which have denied this dimension.

The three interpretations which I have mentioned seldom go clearly into the question to what human lack or existential situation baptism in the Spirit is really an answer. Usually the baptism with the Spirit is vaguely described as an added power to bear witness to Christ or a making conscious of what one has received in infant baptism. In my view this vagueness also explains why the relationship between the baptism of the Spirit and the gifts of the Spirit remains unclear. Often it is simply presupposed that the former is the condition or the source of the latter. However, why this is the case remains obscure.

In what follows I shall try briefly to develop a critical-organic interpretation of the baptism with the Spirit and the charisms which clears up these points and at the same time explains the markedly playful character of Pentecostalism.

Baptism with Word and Spirit before the Resurrection

(i) John, proclaimer of the fiery baptism of the Spirit

According to the Gospel of Luke, John the Baptism calls the coming Christ (in Hebrew, Messiah) someone who is 'stronger than I': 'I baptize you with water, but he... will baptize you with the Holy Spirit and with fire' (3.15-16). Just as baptism with water was characteristic of John, so baptism with Spirit and fire will characterize the ministry of Christ. Outside Luke, we find the addition 'and fire' only in Matthew 3.11. Here both evangelists are drawing on the same old tradition, a source (Q for short, after the German *Quelle*, source) which we know only from quotations in these two Gospels. This source, strongly coloured by the wisdom tradition, is older than the earliest Gospel (Mark).[4] What does it mean that the Messiah will baptize 'with the Spirit and fire'? In the first place this statement must not be understood as though there were two baptisms, one with the Spirit and one with fire. The Greek conjunction *en* (with, in) embraces other elements, so that there is one baptism with fiery spirit. In the second place John thought and spoke above all in the imagery of the First Testament. Secondly, during his stay 'in the wilderness' (Luke 1.80) he was very probably also influenced by the teaching and practice of the Qumran community.

> This community was founded by a group of pious Jews led by a mysterious 'Teacher of Righteousness' who had left Jerusalem in order to form together the one true Israel close to the place where according to Ezekiel 47 a brook from the temple would flow in to the Dead Sea and make this fresh. The Qumran community had a strikingly ascetic way of life, a marked eschatological expectation and a great emphasis on the study of the Torah. Their writings were only discovered in 1947 and became known to a wide public as the Dead Sea Scrolls. (My teacher at Claremont Graduate

School, one of the first translators, Dr William Brownlee, was still filled with amazement, thirty years later, when he thought back to the moment that he saw the scrolls for the first time.) What made this community special was that in a time of 'confusion of the Spirit' in traditional Judaism they felt that they were endowed with the Spirit of God. The members felt themselves called to make a way for God in the wilderness. This had to happen by the study of the Torah and a life of obedience through which they would vicariously bring about redemption for the whole of Israel (1QS 8.14-16; 9.3-5). This new way of life is expressly a gift of the Spirit, which enlightens them through the Torah with knowledge of God (1QH 4.30-33; 7.6-8; 12.11-12). This dovetailing of Word and Spirit was characteristic of the Qumran community; revelation by the Holy Spirit and study of the scriptures went hand in hand.[5] We also find in John the Baptist the eschatological expectation, the emphasis on the Spirit and on asceticism and the call to build a way for God by a pure life. John's baptismal practice was also very probably inspired by the ritual washings in Qumran, which were an expression of repentance and inward purification by the Spirit. Also through these washings (which are also practised today by the independent Zionists in South Africa) the Spirit put members in a position to live in accordance with their exposition of the Torah and thus to build up the community (1 QS 3.6-8).

In my view the fiery baptism which John expected can best be understood in the light of the working of God's Word and Spirit in the First Testament. This working is often indicated with the image of the storm.

(a) The storm as an image of the liberating God

The exegete Walter Eichrodt pointed out that in the First Testament the storm is the most important image of the theophany, the manifestation of God.[6] Thus the author of Psalm 18 describes in dramatic words how God, riding on the clouds, hastens close to judge and to save. God's voice resounds in the thunder; fiery bolts of lightning scatter the enemy; the blowing of God's wind dries up the beds of the threatening waters; and God 'came to me out of great waters' (vv.8-20). As in many other passages in scripture (including those which deal with rescue from the Babylonian exile), here an experience of liberation is interpreted with the aid of the motif of the exodus.

In the book of Exodus God redeems Israel from Egypt by leading them in cloud, wind, fire and thunder (God's 'voice') through the Sea of Reeds (13.1-4, 15-17, 21-22; 14.20-26). God's fiery anger consumed the enemy and the *ruach* of God's nostrils made them drown (15.7-10). This imagery probably derives from the Sinai tradition, where God speaks to Moses on the mountain in a resounding storm and gives the people of Israel the ten words of the covenant (19.16-20; 20.1-21).[7] The first commandment runs: 'I am the Lord your God who has brought you out of the land of Egypt, out of the house of slavery. You shall have no other gods than me.' For Israel, the experience of God's rule is an experience of liberation. Although in reality it was probably only individual tribes which escaped by night from the labour camps of Egypt, this sense is deeply rooted in Israel's soul. Just as the experience of beauty defined the ancient Greek vision of the divine, so for Israel God is the Lord of the Exodus, who redeems from slavery and idolatry. We shall see in due course that this liberation was later radicalized in Christian experience: 'Where the Spirit of the Lord is, there is freedom' (II Cor.3.17). In the Exodus God's column of cloud and fire leads the people on to Canaan (40.34-38). This happened in accordance with the covenant agreement that Israel would worship God as the only God and on the other hand that God would bring them to the promised land (34.11-14). The covenant expresses the bond between Israel and the Lord of the exodus and therefore means real freedom.

The dramatic picture of the storm combines three aspects of God's liberating rule: wind, fire and thunder. The wind brings clouds (of rain) which on the one hand stand for the glorious presence of God and the purification (washing) of the believers and on the other for new life (in the rains which make the parched land blossom). In scripture and also in Qumran the fire symbolizes the glow of God's love in judgment and purification. Finally the voice of God resounds in the thunder. Now the first two aspects are also associated with the Spirit. The clouds and rain is also echoed in the term *ruach* (wind). Hence the Spirit is often spoken of in 'fluid' terms: it is 'poured out' or 'shed'. On the other hand the aspect of washing or purification by water is synonymous with the purifying force of fire. Alongside water, therefore, in scripture fire is also an image of the Spirit. Now if water and fire both symbolize the Spirit, and thunder God's voice, it can be concluded that the image of the storm stands for the liberating work of God's Spirit and Word. This emerges more clearly in texts in which the 'stormy' aspects are toned down. The prophet Elijah, in flight from the idolatrous Jezebel, does not encounter God on Mount Horeb (i.e. Sinai) as Moses did, in a storm with thunderbolts which make the earth shake and with fire. No, he hears 'the voice [Word] of a gentle breeze [Spirit]' (I Kings 19.12). In the intertestamental period, moreover, it is Wisdom who, through Moses, redeems the people from Egypt and becomes 'a shelter to them by day and a starry flame through the night' (Wisdom 10.15-21). The storm stands for the Word and the Spirit (held together in Wisdom) by which God time and again liberates Israel on the way to the promised land and, by extension, for the sabbath play of God's kingdom.

(b) The expectation of the renewed covenant

As Israel constantly broke the covenant and chose idols above the only God, over the centuries after the entry into Canaan the prophetic expectation grew that in the future God would renew the covenant. It would no longer be limited to Israel, but extend 'to the ends of the earth' (Isa.46.9). Then, according to Isaiah, the survivors in Jerusalem would be called 'holy', for the Lord would wash away the dirt from then and purify the city from bloodstains by 'the Spirit of judgment and the Spirit of fire' (4.4). God's judgment does not annihilate people but purges them:[8] a purification which means liberation from pride and idolatry (3.16-22). So the 'Lord will make the land blossom, it will be an adornment and splendour' (4.2). The eschatological liberation is interpreted in terms of the exodus, complete with the presence of God in cloud and fire (4.5). This passage (which probably originally stood on its own) is followed by a passionate love song of God over unfaithful Israel (5.1-7). Undoubtedly John the Baptist was influenced by a text like this, but also by prophetic passages which speak more explicitly of a future 'outpouring' of the Spirit.

Compared with the present situation, the expectation was, God's Spirit and Word would then be present in abundance. In playful terms it is announced that nature will be renewed and justice and peace will blossom (Isa.32.15-20). The unfaithful and banished Israel will make a covenant of renewal by which it will belong wholly to the Lord, its liberator. According to the later anonymous prophet who is given the name Second Isaiah, then even non-Israelites will adopt the name Israel (Isa.44.3-5). And yet later Third Isaiah writes that in this covenant God's Spirit and Word will not depart from the people or from their children for ever (Isa.59.21). We also find in Joel (2.18-32) this vision of an outpouring of Spirit and Word which will renew nature and the people so that it speaks the word of God (prophecy). After the judgment, described with the imagery of a plague of locusts, God's Spirit will be poured out on 'every living creature', including women and slaves. Humankind will be liberated from the enslaving order which brings division and oppression, a liberation which will be accompanied by 'fire and smoke'. This is the prophecy which according to Luke is cited by Peter to explain what happens on the first day of Pentecost (Acts 2.17-21). What this renewal of the covenant means is probably most clearly expressed by Ezekiel (36.2-28), whose book opens with an impressive vision of the coming of God in cloud and fire, from which a voice speaks to him (1.4,28). God will prove that he is the holy One by renewing his people. This will not happen because of their own merits: like the Exodus, the future renewal of the covenant will be wholly the gratuitous work of God. Israel will be restored to her land and purified from her idols. Ezekiel, who was not only a prophet but also a priest, here uses the liturgical image of sprinkling with clean water, which was used later in the Qumran commuity to express the purification of life by the Spirit (1QS 4.21). God will give the Spirit in their innermost parts so that they are moved from within to obey the Torah. In the words of Jeremiah 31.33, the Torah (God's Word) will be written on their hearts. Also in Ezekiel the inward re-creation of God's people finds its counterpart in the renewal of nature (36.29-30, 33-35).

The conclusion is that John the Baptist with his announcement that Christ will baptize with fiery spirit was thinking of the liberating presence of God's Word and Spirit. In thundercloud and fire God led Israel out of Egypt, made a covenant with them on Sinai and brought them to the promised land. Time and again God rescued Israel from its enemies and aroused the people to keep the covenant by prophets inspired by the Word and Spirit (Zech.7.12). The ongoing lack of faithfulness to the covenant led to the expectation of a renewal of the covenant, an inward exodus and liberation from idols and a new life in accordance with the Torah. In the sabbath play of human beings, animals, plants and things this new life would mean a renewal (or consummation) of creation. Moreover, the preaching of John the Baptist is characterized not only by judgment and purification, as is often thought, but also by the promise of new life. His baptism with water was a 'baptism of conversion' for the forgiveness of (liberation from) sins (Mark 1.4).[9] The immersion in the waters of the Jordan and the subsequent rising again from them was a dramatized, penitential prayer for a new inward exodus. It was a preparation for the baptism with Word and Spirit of the coming Messiah through whom, according to the Gospel of Luke, 'the whole of humanity will see salvation' (3.6). In expectation of this the baptized must try to bring forth fruits to match their prayer: in other words, lead a life in righteousness according to the Torah (3.7-14). Those who with self-satisfaction appeal to the existing order ('we have Abraham as our father') are told that they have no more rights before God than a stone and only belong to God's people through God's creative power, 'for nothing' (3.8). Through the wind and fire of his Word and Spirit the Messiah will purge the people from the chaff that clings to them, so that they will come into their own as shining grains of wheat (3.17). In a Calvinist country like the Netherlands it is perhaps not superfluous to emphasize that the chaff and the wheat do not stand for two different groups of people, one of which is destined to judgment and the other to salvation. Just as grains and chaff in the first instance form a whole, so here one and the same people is indicated. God's verdict liberates people from all that hinders them, so that they come into their own and live in accord with the Torah. It is a judgment of purification. Finally, it is notable that John the Baptist was the first prophet explicitly to combine the Jewish expectation of a future outpouring of Word and Spirit with the Messiah.

(ii) Jesus, baptizer with Word-and-Spirit

Jesus was such a fascinating person that his disciples tried to do justice to the impact that he made on them by using a variety of terms and titles from the existing tradition (above all the Jewish tradition). Schillebeeckx has shown that he was first of all seen as the eschatological messianic prophet like Moses (and thus filled with the Spirit).[10] Instead of speaking through the direct 'voice of the Lord' and the 'great fire' of Sinai, God would speak to the people through this prophet (Deut.18.15-18). Through the Spirit the prophet would interpret the Torah in the right way. This designation of Jesus as the eschatological prophet was fertile enough to inspire later titles like Christ, Lord and Son of God. Already at a very early stage his life gave occasion to describe him as the Messianic Son of David: not, however, in the warlike, nationalistic sense but in the style of the wisdom tradition. The book the Wisdom of Solomon describes the righteous wise man as someone who knows God, a person who sees himself as a child of the Lord and calls God his Father. His way of life is not that of ordinary men, and through suffering he will establish his kingdom, which is not limited to Israel but has a universal scope (2.12-20; 3.8). Passages like these probably also inspired the connection made by the New Testament between the Messiah and the prophecies in the book of Isaiah which speak of the suffering servant of the Lord who gives his life for the sins of the world (42.1-4; 52.13-53.12).

(a) The new Moses

As the eschatological prophet who brings the kingdom of God near, Jesus is the new Moses, indeed the prophet greater than Moses. Moreover in the Gospels, as in the rest of the New Testament, his life and work are often interpreted with the help of motifs from the Exodus tradition.

Just as Israel went into Egypt and was led out again, so Jesus fled with his parents to Egypt and returned: 'Out of Egypt I have called my son' (Matt.2.15, a quotation from Hosea 11.1). Jesus did not wait for the day of Pentecost in Jerusalem to baptize with Word and Spirit, as is generally thought in Pentecostalism. Edward Irving already wrote that all Jesus' words and deeds were a manifestation of baptism with the Spirit.[11] His messianic task consisted in this. Like the column of cloud and fire of old, in his baptism with water he went through the water of the Jordan with 'all the people'. There he was confirmed by God's Word and Spirit as the Messiah (Luke 3.21-22). The Spirit descended on him in the form of a dove, and a voice from heaven which could have sounded to the bystanders like a thunderclap (cf.John 12.29) called him 'my beloved son'. As God once said to Moses, 'Israel is my firstborn son' (Ex.4.22). And just as Moses and Israel were tested in the wilderness after the exodus for forty years, so after going through the Jordan Jesus was tested in the wilderness for forty days (Luke 4.1-13). The Gospel of John also regards Jesus in many ways as the prophet greater than Moses. I have already remarked how much for this Gospel Jesus is the wisdom of God in whom the Word and the Spirit are present 'beyond measure'. After a reference to the testimony of John the Baptist about the one 'who comes after me', the Prologue says: 'And from his fullness we have all received grace upon grace; for the Torah was given by Moses, God's covenant of love came through Jesus Christ' (1.16-17: 'grace and truth' is the translation of the Hebrew *hesed we emet* in the First Testament, which indicates God's unconditional love and faithfulness to the covenant). There is no question of a devaluation of the Torah here. In this Gospel Jesus can indeed speak deprecatingly about 'your law', but by this he means the specific interpretation of the letter of the law by scribes who are hostile to his purposes (and those of his disciples). We saw earlier in connection with Colossians 1.19 that 'fullness' refers to the presence of God in the world through the Word and Spirit, especially in Jesus Christ. The grace of God's covenant love given in him surpasses the grace given in the Torah of Moses. Even Moses had never seen God (Ex.33.20), but Jesus has made God known to us. Just as Moses led the people out to the promised land, so Jesus brings us into 'the bosom of the Father', in other words, the kingdom of God (1.18).[12] Moses gave the Torah; Jesus *was* the Torah. Moses followed God's column of cloud and fire: Jesus *was* in the Word and the Spirit this column of cloud and fire in which he 'baptized' the people (cf. Ex.14.19-20; I Cor.10.2). Therefore he was greater than Moses.

As we saw, as an expression of God's being, the Word and the Spirit of God are the creation principle which creates the world and makes it blossom into the eternal sabbath play in 'the bosom of the Father'. To use one of Tillich's terms, the Word and the Spirit represent 'the power of being' which is creatively present in all that is and offers resistance to the 'nothingness' of chaos and death. In the Genesis story they create the world from darkness and the ocean, for Israel threatening symbols of the nothingness which will only disappear for good in the new Jerusalem (Revelation 21.1,23). The Word and the Spirit continue the creation in an evolutionary process and find their supreme expression in the conscious self of the human being who is created in the image of God. The slow evolution of nature has given place in human beings to the rapid development of culture – ending in the eternal sabbath. Consisting of an identity

(Word) which develops with the world in a playful interaction (Spirit), human beings grow into the image of God. Being fully human, God's Word and Spirit (Wisdom) made 'flesh' can be summed up according to the Torah in perfect love for God and the neighbour (Deut.6.5; Lev.19.18). This is confirmed by Jesus (Luke 10.26-28). The Torah is not a law but a way to life: the way of love. Moreover in the intertestamental book of Baruch (4.1), Wisdom is identified with the Torah. Jesus, the 'image of the invisible God' (Col.1.15), did not therefore come to abolish the Torah, but on the contrary to fulfil every jot and tittle of it in his own life. In the Word and the Spirit he was the meaning of the Torah – love – and thus the kingdom of God in person (Matt.5.17-18; Luke 16.16-17). According to developmental psychologists, too, the supreme form of humanity involves the supreme form of love, including a universal compassion and readiness to suffer for the sake of justice.[13]

Schoonenberg has rightly pointed out that God and human beings are not rivals.[14] The divine is not non-human. On the contrary, as is clear from Jesus, the divine reveals itself in what is authentically human. No one is as human as God, in whose image we are made. As Augustine says in his *Confessions*, God the other is at the same time 'more inward than my innermost being'. God is our deepest self, but also infinitely transcends us, so that incarnation is an infinite process of self-transcendence in which we constantly live from our true selves (the image of God). The true, eschatological person has a full part in God's self through the Word and Spirit and is therefore 'like God', is love. Moreover, following the fourth-century bishop Athanasius, the Eastern Orthodox tradition calls the perfecting of our humanity 'divinization' (*theosis*, see II Peter 1.4; I John 3.2). And the Byzantine theologian Maximus Confessor wrote around 600: 'Love makes man God and discloses and manifests God as man.' Hence too Jesus, as an already perfect human being, can say, 'Whoever has seen me has seen the Father' (John 14.9). The destiny of human beings is to be transparent to God, and this sheds light on Jesus' messianic work as baptizer with Word and Spirit.

(b) The new Exodus

Within the limits of our present existence God's self thus expressed itself fully in Jesus. It is striking that more than Moses or the other prophets before him, he did not address himself to Israel as a collective but above all to the individual. He comes to human beings personally as a herald of the time when he will be *in* them, liberating them through Word and Spirit for a life of love. Jesus is concerned with a change in the deepest human self, from which all evil ultimately comes (Mark 7.20-23).

Love is experienced as a judgment to the degree that it burns away whatever goes against its nature, and as new life to the degree that it opens up unsuspected sources in human beings. The fire of God's judgment is the fire of God's love (Song of Songs 8.6). Moreover Jesus can tell hypocritical Pharisees in one breath that they pass over 'God's love and judgment' (Luke 11.42). Jesus went through Israel like a purifying judgment. According to the Gospel of Mark he did his first miracle in Capernaum, where his 'teaching with authority' released a man from an unclean spirit (1.21-28). We have already seen that he healed the sick, cleansed lepers and forgave sinners. Through the Word and the Spirit he represented the presence of God and creation as this was intended. Moreover his miracles were not alien to this world, but on the contrary a guarantee of the consummation of the present creation. They do not make inroads in the natural order but are momentary concentrations of the universal, creative activity of God's Word and Spirit in which the rigid order of sickness, violence and death is overcome and creation comes into its own in the sabbath play in which people flourish.[15] According to Mark, Jesus' mission came to a climax in the cleansing of the Jerusalem temple, the religious but corrupted heart of Israel (11.15-19). This action was the direct occasion for his arrest and execution.

In the story of the Transfiguration, which is accompanied by light (fire?), a cloud and the voice of God, Jesus' death is anticipated in a conversation with Moses and Elijah (Luke 9.28-36). They talk of 'his exodus, which he was to fulfil in Jerusalem' (v.31). Moses and Elijah represent the Torah and the prophets (exponents and appliers of the Torah), and Jesus' 'exodus' refers to his death and resurrection.[16] A little later in the Gospel of Luke (12.49-50) Jesus utters the urgent words: 'I have come to cast fire on the earth, and how I wish that it were already kindled! I have a baptism to be baptized with, and how I am constrained until it is accomplished!' Here Jesus explicitly identifies himself with the expectation of John the Baptist that he would baptize with the fiery Spirit. As the messianic, eschatological prophet greater than Moses he represented the liberating presence of God in thundercloud and fire, in the Word and the Spirit. But his work had little effect. The fire of God's love did not spread, as emerges from the preceding passages. People were not willing to follow him consistently (9.57-62), and even accused him of being possessed by the devil, or mocked him (11.15-16). The opposition increased, whereupon Jesus encouraged his disciples and warned them to be watchful (11.37-12.38). He saw how the opposition to him would lead to division among people (12.51-53). God's love in Jesus is experienced by his audience above all as a judgment that they instinctively flee. They are alienated from their true selves, and Jesus' call to them become human provokes principally opposition and aggression. Jesus has already announced his suffering twice in this Gospel, realizing that his 'exodus' in Jerusalem is approaching. This is the 'baptism', going through the waters of chaos and death, with which he must be baptized. Without his 'baptism' in death the glow of love, the fire of God's Word and Spirit, cannot be kindled among people. In Mark 10.38 this 'baptism' is called a 'cup' which Jesus has to drink, the cup which he will pray to be spared in Gethsemane (14.36). In the background here is certainly the cup of God's judgment which in the First Testament often means death, an event of which God is seen as the active cause (Isa.51.17-20; Jer.25.15-19). As I have already remarked, God's judgment is, however, a judgment that is focussed on liberation and preservation, not on annihilation.

Certainly it is the case that those who turn from God thereby cut themselves off from the source of life and by definition take a course on which one is written off to death. This is the way of the false self. 'See, the hand of the Lord is not too short to save, nor his ear too weak to hear; but it is your injustice which brings division between you and your God' (Isa 59.1,2). And the book of Wisdom says, 'God did not make death'; God 'created all things so that they should abide'. It is human beings who 'attract death by the foolishness of [their] lives' (1.12-14). Influenced by this, in his letter to the Romans (1.18-32) Paul depicts God's anger as injured love which with pain in the heart must deliver over to their evil and fatal way those who, though knowing better, choose idols above 'the majesty of the incorruptible God'. 'The creation [is] worshipped and served above the Creator', which always leads to its corruption. Just as the Egyptians in the plagues were tormented by the very things with which they sinned (they worshipped frogs and flies idolatrously, Wisdom 11.15-20), so God must 'deliver over' those who follow their own idolatrous thought to their way which leads to nothingness.

It was not enough that Jesus during his life and work on earth baptized people with God's Word and Spirit. If the fire of God's love is really to be kindled, then the Word must be written by the Spirit on human hearts. For that, it is necessary for Jesus to drink the cup, be 'baptized' in death, and fulfil his exodus in Jerusalem. In and through him the exodus from Egypt is radicalized into an inner liberation of 'every living creature' (Acts 2.17). Only then will he be able to kindle the fire of God's love on earth; only then can the covenant be renewed. For his cross and resurrection will liberate people for a true relationship with the two extremes of their existence: God and death. This opens up the possibility of living wisely in union with God and the whole of creation.

2

Anxiety and Idolatry: The Spoiling of Life

Anxiety before God is expressed in a mythical way by the story of the first human beings in the garden of Eden. The serpent nurtures anxiety by presenting God as a potentate who does not give people any room to live: 'Did not God say that you may not eat of any tree in the garden?' (Gen.3.1). The consequence is that people begin to seize what God wants to give. Created in God's image, they nevertheless want to 'be like God' in their own power (1.27; 3.5-6). This is the striving of the false self, which wants to hold life in its own hand. Alienation develops: people cover themselves before the Creator in fig leaves and skins, while God calls out 'Where are you?' The loss of union with God means death, and thus a life which is regulated more by strict necessity than by light-footed play in the garden. A return to paradise and thus an exodus from the slavery of the false self and the lie that God is against human beings is possible only through the purifying fire of the flaming swords of the cherubs (3.24).

(i) A God of human beings

However, that God is on the side of all that is human emerges from the first freedom manifesto in written history (Exodus), in which God in thundercloud and fire rescues an insignificant slave people from the grasp of their powerful oppressors. God's Spirit later 'leapt' upon the judges and time and again redeemed Israel through these charismatic leaders. Prophets inspired by the Spirit like Amos and Hosea castigated with their judgment the rich who, lying on ivory divans, oppressed the poor for a pair of sandals. Only justice and grace, they said, can build up the people. So the liberation theologians rightly emphasize God's preferential option for the poor. Not because the poor are better people than the rich, but because in their suffering they confront the West with the truth. As victims of the economic behaviour of the West, only the poor are in a position to make the rich lands really aware of what they are doing. In a similar way, only those who (and that which) suffer from the poisoning of the environment can make clear to us the truth about our exploitation and pollution of nature. We ourselves in the West are too conditioned by the political and economic system for our interests to show the truth truthfully 'on the other side of the line'. This is simply a variant of the well-known principle that only in and through others can we get to know ourselves (including our thought and action) properly.[17]

God is a God of love and truth, and in the First Testament this is expressed above all in the expectation of the Messiah. From the condemned dynasty of David the Messiah will come, on whom 'the Spirit of the Lord will rest, the Spirit of wisdom and understanding, the spirit of counsel and strength, the spirit of knowledge and fear of the Lord' (Isa.11.1-5). Through these charisms the future king will be transparent to God's will in politics and legislation. In an unprejudiced way he will do justice for the oppressed. Through the Word and the Spirit ('the reed of his mouth and the breath of his lips') he will slay violent and evil men – a literary exaggeration to emphasize the seriousness with which the Messiah will judge evil. He will be clothed in righteousness and truth. In what is probably a later addition, this vision is extended to the whole earth (vv.6-10). The sabbath play of the perfected creation is described in the imagery of the wolf which lies down with the lamb and the panther which lies down with the hind. Lions will eat straw like oxen and a baby will be able to play safely on an adder's hole. Not only nature but all human society will be a 'game of peace' in which evil and corruption are banished. And as water covers the sea bed, so the earth 'shall be full of the knowledge of the Lord'.[18] This vision of the king anointed with the Spirit, who brings a paradisal peace, is strongly reminiscent of the prophecies of a future outpouring of the Spirit in which the wilderness becomes a pleasure garden and 'the fruit of justice shall be peace' (Isa.32.15-20).

In Isaiah 53 the Messiah not only stands up for the sufferers and the oppressed but even identifies with them. 'He has taken our sicknesses upon himself and borne our sorrows' (v.4). In the Messiah God takes evil upon himself, as God earlier cried to unfaithful Israel through the mouth of the prophet Hosea: 'How shall I give you up, Ephraim, or hand you over, Israel?... My heart turns in me, my mercy is fully awakened... For I am God and no man, the Holy One in your midst, and I shall not come in anger' (11.8-9). I have already pointed out how Luke makes Jesus' ministry begin in the synagogue at Nazareth, where he applies the messianic expectation (in the prophetic sense) to himself. So this evangelist already sums up Jesus' word and work at the beginning, including the positive and negative reactions which these arouse (4.14-30). Jesus has fulfilled the Torah completely. He has loved to the last. God in him (II Cor.5.19) has reconciled the world to itself by identifying himself with the sick, the oppressed, even with those who are 'far from God' in the godforsakenness of the crucifixion (Mark 15.34). Like Wisdom wandering through the streets, God in Jesus has sought out those who were most alienated from him and thus reconciled them with himself. Conversely, his identification with the victims and the abandoned means that these can identify with God in Jesus. In the tortured and rejected Messiah they recognize themselves, just as the sick in the monastery hospital of Isenheim (in Alsace) recognized their own drawn and dying limbs in the distorted body of the crucified Jesus painted by Grünewald. Their identification with God in Jesus gives hope to the despairing, and healing and new worth to the oppressed and downtrodden. This awareness of their bond with God in Christ (their true self) gave many charismatic movements in history an emancipatory power, just as Pentecostalism today speaks to the poor masses and opens up new possibilities in their hopeless existence.

If God's preferential option is for the poor and the victims, how are those who do evil then reconciled with God? One of the most disconcerting things that Jesus did was to forgive sins. In Jewish thought this was reserved for God (Luke 5.2-26). Sin is the denial of togetherness and destroys the sabbath play of Word and Spirit. The divine love overcomes the divine anger (which is injured love) and grants forgiveness by taking the consequence of sin and evil upon itself in identification with the victims. For this is what love does: it does not recompense evil with evil, which always leads to a spiral of violence from which no escape is possible. No, love takes sins upon itself, thus openly displaying and condemning them, and in so doing takes them away. This makes forgiveness and a new beginning for evildoers possible. The cross of Christ is the revelation in time of how God is in eternity: a God of love who wants to be associated with human beings, takes their sins upon himself and bears the pain in order to heal broken relationships.[19] This liberation from sin is as unconditional as the creation of the world and the rescue of Israel from Egypt. Only a God of love can keep liberating anew for a playful existence in communion with the whole of creation.

(ii) The dread of God

However, the dread of God makes a playful way of living impossible. Such dread is caused by an image of God which has now been definitively done away with by Christ. This image of God is a projection in which God is in many respects greater than, but in a few *other* than a human authority. Adam and Eve break down before these lies in the story of paradise. As is usual in the love between human beings, conditions are attached to God's love. No wonder that in reaction to this people cover themselves up before God and lose the freedom of the game. But God's love knows no preconditions: it is dynamic and creative, and through the Word and the Spirit shapes the human partners in the covenant in God's image. According to Jewish teaching a person can repent at any moment (the word is *shub*, which means not only inner repentance but a turning of the whole person), and be accepted by God. The exegete Arland Hultgren concludes in a detailed study that in the New Testament this is also the oldest interpretation of God's liberation in Christ.[20] This interpretation, by Paul and Mark, sees redemption in him as universal and unconditional. His action of righteousness resulted in a 'justification which brings life to all men' (Rom.5.18). God *has* reconciled the world to himself; through Christ the world *is* justified. This is the source of justification by faith. Faith is not the condition of our justification but our response to our already being justified in Christ, through which a righteous life becomes possible.

Certainly Paul and Mark also speak words of judgment (I Cor.1.18; Mark 3.29), but these are meant as warnings. Love lays down no conditions but rejoices in righteousness and truth. Hultgren distinguishes three later interpretations of redemption in Christ in the New Testament. The second is found in Matthew and the Lucan writings. Here the liberation in Christ is seen above all as future, but it can already be experienced in the forgiveness of sins. This presupposes a life of discipleship in the community: 'whoever perseveres to the end will be saved' (Matt.10.22). The third interpretation, which is typical of disciples of Paul (including

Colossians, Ephesians and Hebrews), I Peter and the Revelation of John, all stress that the final liberation in Christ will be universal. Here, however, Hebrews concentrates so much on the community that the question of the fate of people outside it does not arise. I Peter 4.17-18 has threatening words to say to those who are disobedient to the gospel, while Revelation, though ending with a universal vision of the new Jerusalem (22.1-5), announces annihilation for those whose names are not found in 'the book of life' (20.15). The latest interpretation of God's liberation in Christ is characteristic of the 'school' of John (the Gospel and the letters) and is the most exclusive. Here sin is not alienation from God in general but unbelief. The Gospel has a hard polemical tone in which unbelieving Jews are even called 'children of the devil' (8.44). God's universal love for the world is certainly emphasized, but the accent falls on the human response of faith or unbelief in place of the unconditional liberation by God in Christ. This attitude is also characteristic of that part of Pentecostalism which regards people who stand outside Christian faith as 'eternally lost'. Like the community in which the Gospel of John came into being, here we have groups which feel themselves in a state of siege from a threatening environment; that explains the black-and-white way in which they think. Finally, in the letters of John, the enemies are not the unbelieving Jews outside the community but people who make decisions within the community. They are condemned as representatives of the 'spirit of Antichrist' (I John 4.3). Hultgren concludes that the earliest interpretation (by Paul and Mark) does most justice to the unconditional love of Jesus. This also resonates with the universality of God's covenant as it already emerges within the First Testament, beginning with the promise to Abraham that through him all people on earth will be blessed (Gen.12.3). The other interpretations are developed in already established communities, the members of which have become aware of their own Christian identity in relation to their environment (Matthew, Luke) or are fighting the hostility of the synagogue (John) or the Roman emperor (Revelation). Their interpretations served to help to meet the challenges of a specific situation, and for this reason need not be condemned in a negative way. In the light of the First Testament and the life of Jesus, however, the theological priority lies with the earliest view of God's unconditional liberation in Christ.

The unconditional character of God's relationship with us at the same time means that a doctrine (also current in Pentecostalism) in which the 'sacrifice' of Christ's life to a God offended by our sins must give satisfaction has to be rejected out of hand as unbiblical. Here God's covenant love is degraded to a kind of 'to whom does what belong' contract. The idea of satisfaction is above all derived from mediaeval penitential practice in which forgiveness is made dependent on doing penance. The suffering of women in history is often regarded, along the same lines, as penance for the sin of Eve the seducer. Moreover, this Western doctrine of atonement (inspired by Anselm) begins from the assumption that God 'wants to see blood', namely the death of Jesus. But in God, source of love and life, there is no violence, as the unknown author of the Letter to Diognetus wrote around 100. This idea of a violent God of whom people must be afraid was also nurtured by the many 'holy wars' in the First Testament. But quite apart from the fact that the image of God of the writers of this time was imperfect (it was influenced, among other things, by the Baal cult), it must be emphasized that the First Testament is above all a liturgical book. The 'holy war' served in worship as a metaphor for God's liberating intervention on behalf of the small humiliated Israel.[21] In the war stories, moreover, any possible historical context often disappears behind all kinds of liturgical signals. Thus the story of the Exodus is marked by the celebration of a passover meal, the singing of a liturgical hymn and the celebration of the sabbath (Ex.12.15,16). War stories are 'sabbath reading' which tell of a different order from that of the violent powers, an order in which God stands up for the tiny and small – through thundercloud and fire, the Word and the Spirit.

Another frequent reason why violence is attributed to God is the view that God should be omnipotent, a notion which has emerged above all since the Renaissance. But the expression 'omnipotent God' does not occur in the Bible and moreover it denies God as creator. The Jewish philosopher Hans Jonas has pointed out that not only does this term only make God completely incomprehensible (for how can God here still be good *and* tolerate the present world?); the term 'omnipotent' has no content in itself.[22] Power is always relational: you have power over something or someone else. But absolute power is by definition not limited by anything, even by the existence of another thing or person. The presence of a stone, animal or human would already be a limitation of omnipotence. This can only exist in a vacuum, but in that case it no longer makes sense to speak of power. So an omnipotent God would be a God without a world – the exact opposite of the biblical Creator. But the Tenth Sunday of the Heidelberg Catechism (though with the best intentions and to oppose the Pope's claims to power) says that everything – good and evil, health and sickness – comes from God's fatherly hand. According to the Doctrinal Rules of the Synod of Dort (1618-1619), everything that happens is the result of the eternal counsel of God which is perfect and therefore (a Greek way of arguing) immutable. Free will and chance do not exist in this way of thinking. How widespread this view was is evident from its application, later in the same century, by the Amsterdam Jewish philosopher Spinoza (in his *Tractatus Theologico-Politicus*) to nature; this is ruled by God's eternal, immutable laws. That makes miracles impossible, because God would be contradicting himself in performing them. Such an omnipotent God by definition has two faces, one of which is benevolent and one of which is malicious, and you never know precisely which face is turned towards you.[23] Such an image of God leads to a defensive flight into a static, even fatalistic, attitude which is radically broken through by the struggle for a just society which is the concern of charismatic trends like the Quakers, the early Methodists and the Holiness Movement, and by the concern for healing in Pentecostalism.

It is not a biblical notion that creation is already perfect and God's liberating rule complete. Scripture gives a dynamic picture of God's creative activity by Word and Spirit. Chance is the space in which something surprisingly new can emerge, an evolutionary leap, or a moment in which you can be lucky, or a 'miracle' can happen – but also still the moment in which misfortune can strike. Any 'explanation' of suffering in fact tries to trivialize it. A protest movement already arose against this within the Wisdom tradition. Thus Job's friends explain his suffering by saying that he has done something wrong. The pious are rewarded with prosperity (4.7-11; 5.12-16). With this argument they show the impotence of a world order which can think only in terms of cause and effect. However, Job comes to the opposite conclusion: it is often the pious and righteous who have to suffer opposition (21.7-34). Suffering is 'sheer disaster'.[24] The eternal question is: Why? Then a fourth friend, Elihu (who was probably added later) makes an unexpected appearance. There is something 'charismatic' about this Elihu; he is full of Spirit and Word (32.6, 7, 18) and encounters God in dreams and visions. Unlike the first three friends, Job has a real encounter with him and mentions him by name. Elihu hardly argues, but lauds and praises the Creator. In this way he prepares the way for a healing encounter between Job and God himself (chs.33-37). When a divine answer finally comes from the storm (!), it points to God's creative activity (38-41). The author George Bernard Shaw did not find 'I can make a crocodile' an answer to the problem of suffering. That is true as long as one begins from a static picture of creation. But what the divine answer in fact conveys is a question about trust in the process of creation which has been set in motion by God (not to mention the element of play, 40.15, 24), that will ultimately overcome suffering and death. Moreover Job's reply also ends on this note of trust: 'I know that you can do everything and that nothing is impossible for you' (42.2). This trust is the consequence not of a logical argument but of an existential encounter with God: 'I knew you only from hearsay, but now I have seen you with my own eyes' (42.5). For Christians, this trust is all the more justified because in Jesus God himself has not avoided suffering and has broken the power of death. God's Word and Spirit are aimed at a consummation in which death, according to Paul, will be dethroned as the last enemy and God is 'all in all' (I Cor.15.26-28). Till then, Jews pray for the coming of the Messiah and Christians pray 'Your kingdom come'.

The New Testament nowhere sees the life and suffering of Jesus as an act performed in the name of humanity over against God. Far less do we find the notion that Christ turned away God's wrath by sacrificing himself. There is no split between God and Christ. It is not God who must be reconciled, but humankind: 'God was in Christ reconciling the world to himself' (II Cor.5.19). In different words we read that Christ 'died for our sins'. This does not mean that Christ as our representative bore God's punishment for our sins. Precisely the opposite: Christ is as it were God's representative because we see in his life the passion of God himself who suffers under our anxious, aggressive behaviour and nevertheless does not seek retribution for our evil but forgives it. God's relationship with us is visible not only when Jesus straightens a woman who is bowed down but also when he is impotent to help people because of their unbelief. Even on the cross Jesus prays for forgiveness for those who murder him. So what does it mean that he has died for our sins? In the first place he died 'for us' because in his innocence, defencelessness and readiness he gave concrete, visible form to both the greatness of God's love and our capacity to do evil. God's passion (*pathos*) in Jesus calls for our sym-pathetic response (as expressed in the prophetic appeal which resounds in the litany of Good Friday: 'O my people, what have I done to you? In what have I wearied you? Answer me' (Micah 6.3). Only this confrontation with God's pain and the recognition of God's greatness in it can lead to our conversion in the confession of both God's faithfulness and our lack of faith – a confession which brings liberation leading to a new way of life.[25] In the second place, Christ died for our sins because through his 'exodus' which he accomplished in Jerusalem he removed the main cause of sin. This cause is anxiety about death, which ultimately also underlies anxiety about God. His resurrection has in principle freed humankind here (a New Testament word for liberation or redemption like *apolutrosis* is 'exodus language').

(iii) The dread of death

Earlier I quoted Van Ruler's remark that the world has no reason and no ground and precisely because of that is open to both complete meaninglessness and the free play of the totally other God. The fact that our existence is not necessary and is thus a perfectly free gift on the one hand opens up at our feet the terrifying void of nothingness, death. And on the other hand it makes the joy of sabbath play possible. Death is both the definitive denial that we can find a basis for our existence in achievements and possessions and the definitive confirmation of the groundlessness of our life which is given to us as a free gift by God.

The dread of death results in our self being overgrown by a false self which seeks to ground itself and justify itself, and in order to do this escapes into the rigid order of structures and systems. For immutability maintains the illusion that time is not passing and that people are not mortal. At the same time, the false self strives to get life under control, if necessary at the expense of others, in order to be able to hold it fast. Driven by the dread of death into an inauthentic existence, the false self can only imagine a false image of God. Its God is a static, unchangeable God who has omnipotent control over life and death at the cost, if need be, of human beings. Thus the dread of death feeds a picture of God which inculcates anxiety.

By contrast, the true self is gratefully aware that existence is a free gift of God, and plays the creative game of Word and Spirit. Here human beings certainly remain mortal, but they are not ruled by the dread of death. For anyone who lives from the true self is aware of being in union with God, so that mortality is experienced as creatureliness. One trusts, in the words of Okke Jager, that friendship with the eternal Creator is an eternal friendship. However, that this trust is far from obvious is expressed in the lament of the Psalmist (88.11): 'Will you do a miracle for the dead; shall shadows rise up and praise you?' Herein lies the importance of Christ's resurrection, as I still hope to make clear. In the trust that I have mentioned, human finitude is not experienced as a threat but as precisely what makes a playful 'wise' existence possible. A game without limits is not a game. Imagine that a footballer scores a goal every time he has the ball. He does not need the other players, since from any place on the field he infallibly kicks the ball into his opponents' goal. After initial amazement, our attention would quickly slip, and we would complain that this was spoiling the game. We would regard the footballer as a freak, not as a good player. Paradoxically enough, complete success in a game destroys the game. Limitations (both in the rules of the game and in the players) are essential for a game and give it its challenge, tension and intensity. Only finite, limited beings can therefore play. In the concentrated attempt to extend their limits they experience the joy of their finitude.[26] Even when in the future the kingdom has fully broken through and God's Word and Spirit dwell completely in creation, human beings will remain finite creatures who are dependent for their existence on God 'who alone possesses immortality' (I Tim.6.16). Their unique, true self consists in the grace of its participation in God's self. On the other hand the infinite God can play only in and through finite creatures. We have already seen that this essential connection finds expression in scripture in the covenant between God and humankind. However, in the kingdom of God our finitude will be free of all that now spoils the sabbath play. It will be pure love which is wholly taken up in the play with creation. And because God's self, the source of the Word and the Spirit, is inexhaustible, this game will remain infinitely attractive by providing constantly new forms of surprise and joy and an ever-increasing capacity to extend our limits.

Psychological investigations above all in our century have made us aware how much people, out of the dread of death, only 'half live', as a Spanish proverb puts it. More seriously, their defensive way of living has a damaging influence on the life of others. Since the 1980s the German Eugen Drewermann has become widely known as someone who pays a good deal of attention in his theology to the part played by the dread of death in human existence. However, as early as 1973 the American anthropologist Ernest Becker published a famous book on this question. In it he shows how much the observations of the nineteenth-century Danish theologian Søren Kierkegaard anticipate the findings of modern clinical psychology (above all those of Otto Rank).[27] It is evident from Kierkegaard's whole work that for him the ideal person, i.e. the true self, consists in an optimal interplay between the subjective and the objective. These two poles can also be given all kinds of other names, like possibility and necessity, can and must, freedom and limitation. Too much freedom leads to chaos; too much limitation leads to suffocation. This corresponds with my view that the human self consists of an interplay between the Spirit (interaction with the world) and the Word (our limited, defined identity). Too great an emphasis on the Spirit leads to disorder. On the other hand too great an emphasis on the Word leads to fossilization. Both deviations, of which the latter occurs by far the most frequently, and even in its mild forms is regarded as normal, are caused by the dread of death and are characteristic of the false self. This existential anxiety arises whenever the ungroundedness and thus finitude of existence is not experienced as a free gift of God who challenges in order to play, but as pure necessity and meaningless fate. Freedom, the condition for playing, is then experienced as a terrifying void which leads to escapism.

As the story of paradise in the book of Genesis shows, human self-awareness ('knowledge of good and evil') contains the possibility of the dread of death which leads to a defensive way of life (3.3-8). Through the Word and Spirit, human beings consist both of a self that reaches to the stars and is aware of its divine origin and a body which will irrevocably return to dust with the animal world (3.19). Unlike the angels and animals, human beings therefore know existential anxiety about death. Angels have no mortal body, while the experiences of animals are limited by their instincts, through which they know the dread of death only in situations of acute danger. We do not have the same protection and know very well with the Psalmist that we have only seventy or eighty years to live, after which it is all over (Ps.90.10). And Ecclesiastes laments: 'For the fate of the sons of men and the fate of beasts is the same: as one dies, so dies the other... man has no advantage over the beasts. For all is vanity' (3.19). This thought is very difficult to bear. Certainly for modern men and women striving for autonomy death is a blatant scandal which puts a stop to their boast that they are their own creators. Everything in us protests against our absurd fate and tries to escape it. As I have already remarked, it is not our mortality in itself but our alienation from God and thus from the 'tree of life' which makes death terrifying. So our existence is dominated by the denial of death and our finitude. Instead of being a possibility for the play of love, it becomes the cause of evil.[28] According to the book of Wisdom (2.1-12), the wicked complain:

> Short and sorrowful is our life...
> Because we were born by mere chance,
> and hereafter we shall be as though we had never been...
> For our allotted time is the passing of a shadow
> and there is no return from our death...
> Come, therefore, let us enjoy the good things that exist.
> Let us oppress the righteous poor man,
> let us not spare the widow...
> But let our might be our law of right,
> for what is weak proves itself to be useless.
> Let us lie in wait for the righteous man,
> because he is inconvenient to us and opposes our actions.

Death has many different masks which stare at us the moment we are confronted with our 'unworthy' limitations and the fragility of our existence. The dread of death leads people to justify themselves and ground their own existence. Death says that we may *not* be, so that we constantly feel forced to prove the usefulness of our existence. So people want to stand out (beginning with sibling rivalry). They want to assert themselves and make their mark on the world. This effort leads to a tendency to proclaim one's own worth and to play down that of the other. However, the more people develop their unique individuality, motivated by the fear of death, the more anxiety about life increases. The more we come to stand alone as unique human beings, the more strongly we become aware of our fundamental 'nakedness' (vulnerability) and 'unworthiness'. The dread of death and anxiety about life are therefore interwoven. Anyone who

lives, risks death, and the more consciously people live, the greater
the threat of death. The result is that we lose courage and shrink
back from the freedom and possibilities that life offers. A powerful
longing arises to ground ourselves in something or someone greater
than we are, a 'god' outside ourselves which can give us a value that
transcends death. This conforming to something or someone greater
than ourselves removes anxiety and gives us peace. But this provokes
a conflict with the effort to be unique, 'special'. It is a conflict between
the wish to stand on one's own feet (autonomy) and the longing to
be fused with something or someone else (heteronomy). According
to Becker the way in which people resolve this conflict determines
the quality of their existence.[29]

(a) Stress and neuroses

People try to relieve the tension between autonomy and heteronomy
by transferring their dread of death and life to objects outside
themselves in which they ground themselves. This transfer functions
as a kind of artificial instinct, a human self-limitation in which harsh
reality is denied. For the moment anxiety can be controlled; we need
only to know how to deal with the object to which we have transferred
our anxiety. In relation to this we can then safely develop our unique
identity, as a child does in relation to its parents. We identify with the
transfer object and at the same time draw from this the strength we
need to stand on our own feet. However, the crucial problem is that
by definition we choose transfer objects which are too limited. For
the denial of death implies the denial that we are creatures, which in
turn implies the denial of the Creator. So we fall back on ourselves
and the world around us. We ground ourselves in finite, transitory
parts of creation which become idols. Since these are limited, they
also limit us. In his letter to the Galatians Paul calls this 'slavery' to
the 'elements of the world' (4.3, 9). These are parts of the creation
which are served as gods but 'in reality are not' (v.8). Even the Torah
can become an enslaving idol when it takes the place of God (v.5).
Christ has freed us from this slavery, a liberation which is realized in
personal life through the Spirit (vv.4-7). Without freedom, no playful
worthwhile human existence is possible. In his letter to the Romans
Paul sees slavery to idols as a cause of evil (1.18-32). Someone who
turns to an idol turns away from God. Idolatry is 'the beginning of
fornication' (Wisdom 14.12): the misuse of something which is good

in itself since it is created and ensouled by God's Word and Spirit. The dread of death corrupts our positive motives, like the longing to give and receive love, the struggle to banish evil and to be creative.

The denial of death by making a part of creation a transfer object of our existence (idolatry) thus implies a limitation of our freedom (slavery). This is what Kierkegaard called 'shut-upness' and psychology calls a neurosis, which is thus in the first instance not a sickness but a sin.[30] According to Becker, the neurotic symptom is the transfer object. As we saw, the true self brings the best play of Word and Spirit. But when the Spirit (the interplay with reality) is limited and the Word gets all the emphasis, people become rigid in a restrictively tiny existence to which they cling in despair. The most extreme form of this is clinical depression. The false self turns back on itself unmoved in order to avoid life, and thus the death which is inherent in existence. So in fleeing from death, ironically enough it ends up dead. On the other hand, when the Word (our concrete identity) is neglected and the Spirit predominates, this can degenerate into the symptom of the megalomania which becomes clearly evident in the mania 'I am Christ'. Here the false self floats free from the earth in a fantastic universe, in the illusion that it is not subject to decay and death. The death drive is also essentially a bold challenge to death, in the delusion that it can defeat death in this way. Bonhoeffer wrote: 'To clutch at everything or to cast away everything is the reaction of one who believes fanatically in death.'[31] These pathological images are a magnification of the 'spoiling of life' caused by the denial of death, which in a less striking way attacks everyone's existence (and is the reason why the mentally ill give us such uncomfortable feelings). What is neurotic is regarded as 'normal', in which case we have above all the first variant, the one-sided emphasis on the Word, on order and determination at the expense of the Spirit. As our survey of church history showed us, this is also the most dominant neurosis in the church, against which charismatic movements have protested time and again. Kierkegaard already observed acutely that the character or the lifestyle of a person is little more than a neurotic shield against reality. It is a lie which enables people to live, but at the cost of life itself. To be caught up in family life or a career helps us to forget intolerable reality. So people maintain the illusion that they are standing on their own feet and are *not* always embedded in a system that transcends them, whether this is the family, the cause, the action group or the university. With its roles and rules, society channels the human effort to justify existence and to develop one's own identity by bringing up children, studying or following a career. Cars, planes and other products of technology give us the fascinating feeling that we transcend our finitude as creatures. What we call a 'normal' character and a 'normal' society are in reality often denials of death, shields against reality which maintain the vain illusion that we are our own creators.

Out of anxiety about their finitude, people thus reduce reality to an idol in which they themselves are grounded, something which leads to the fossilization of character or culture. An idol cannot by definition change because gods need to be perfect and not subject to time, which implies transitoriness. But the opposite, anarchistic attitude, which consists in the grace of a constant attack on the prevailing order, is also an idol, which has to justify the existence of those concerned. A one-sided emphasis on the Spirit is as great a lie as too heavy a stress on the Word. Both attitudes distort reality and cause much suffering. Throughout history both normal, 'well adapted' people like Eichmann and individuals who, like Hitler, have succumbed to a Promethean madness, have plagued the world in an attempt to forget the truth of their own mortality. Dictators are notorious for their lack of a sense of humour and inability to relativize themselves, and also for their deliberate attempts to deny death. Thus the former Rumanian president Ceaucescu would not have his omnipresent portrait as a young, vital man replaced by a picture which corresponded more to reality. And the first emperor of all China banned talk about death in his palace and hoped that he would find support in his grave from six thousand man-sized terracotta soldiers.

Other people are the transfer objects which are best able to give us the feeling of security and meaning without which we cannot live. However, because they are as limited and vulnerable as we are, we ask too much of them if we promote them to be gods. When some worshipped pop idols die, they take fans with them, who in reaction to their death feel the ground dropping from under their feet and see no other way out than suicide. Another model is the romantic relationship in which the partner is divinized. This hampers the self-development of the 'worshipper' and can lead to all kinds of hidden aggression. Not only does the fear of losing 'my reason to exist' make people unreasonably jealous: any failing in the beloved is a threat to the 'worshipper', a proof that the partner is not God. This provokes all the dread of death and life in which the partner is seen as guilty, which can lead to adultery (as a revenge) or ill treatment. The pressure to fuse slavishly with the powerful people who give us the feeling that we count and are immortal explains the terrible cruelty and sadism of some groups. When the leader takes the responsibility, the members can safely and without restraint celebrate their urge to count without fear of the consequences (orders are orders). Human beings can be more cruel than animals because they are aware of their mortality. They constantly (and not just in moments of real danger of death) escape into defence mechanisms at the expense not only of themselves but of others. This last also applies to the 'other' when it is nature that is sacrificed to the efforts of human beings to justify their existence by incessant economic growth. Because through our corruptible body we ourselves are part of nature, any 'conquest' of nature gives the illusion of a conquest of our mortality. The most concrete evidence of this is the way in which for many people medical care seems to have taken the place of religion. Instead of accepting a life after death, people are now demanding that doctors should postpone death after life as long as possible, despite all the expense and problems involved.

The denial of death damages the bond with God, fellow human beings and nature, and condemns people to live in a derived sense, through an idol which hides a great deal of reality. So they become slaves to their own lies, or, in Kierkegaard's words, become 'inauthentic' people who are alienated from their true selves. They suppress their own uniqueness and allow themselves to be corrupted by drink and drugs, by the rhythm of pop music, by what is 'normal' and insignificant, and by what Pascal called the 'pleasures of diversion', as is evident from the immense popularity of the entertainment programmes on television. Only a crisis which brings down the idols can open their eyes to the truth, a process which has been described in a classic way by Leo Tolstoy in his story about the minor official in *The Death of Ivan Ilych*.

(b) Ideologies

However, the dethroning of an idol which shows the false self the vertiginous depth of nothingness opening under it can also lead to a panic flight into the corrupting arms of another idol. This explains the attraction of all kinds of ideology. An ideology is not perverse in itself. In it, reality is reduced to what corresponds to a central idea, which makes it possible to carry out this idea in practice. An ideology gives the necessary concentration which is the condition for concrete action and thus bridges the gap between thought and action. However, things go wrong when an ideology is absolutized and *a priori* excludes other ideologies. Then it becomes an idol. Van Gennep rightly remarks that a good ideology ultimately aims at universality, i.e. a world from which no one is excluded.[32]

But even a good ideology can become an idol and corrupt life. This has become evident in the great ideologies of the Enlightenment, capitalism and socialism. Here the longing to justify our own existence and transcend the limits of our finitude took the form of the struggle for the perfect society. Once the yoke of the church had been shaken off and science and technology had produced one dazzling result after another, the ideal society seemed within reach. But this great aim began to justify the means, and recently both the capitalist and the communist paradises have proved morally bankrupt. Idolized as they were, these ideologies with a universal orientation blinded people to reality. The disillusion has been great. There is a psychological parallel here to the relationship between feelings or inferiority and perfectionism.[33] Feelings of inferiority are the result of a mild megalomania, of an unrealistically attractive picture of oneself (often stimulated by advertising). Of course people cannot live up to this ideal and as a result constantly feel frustrated. In this way the unrealistic belief in human progress has led to disillusionment. Modern men and women are disappointed in themselves. But because many people still measure their right to exist by the achievement of goals, in order to avoid a new fiasco they have postponed their ambitions. In our 'postmodern' age people have become disillusioned with large-scale visions and world-embracing ideals. They anchor themselves more or less to the 'safe ground' of the *status quo*, however unsatisfying this may be from the perspective of justice, peace and the preservation of a healthy environment.

The situation in Eastern Europe and the former Soviet Union is more serious. More than capitalism in the West, Communism was the foundation which supported and determined everything. Since its fall the existential void greets the population everywhere, and the disappointment over their own deceived idealism is evident. In such a situation there is a great temptation to exchange one's own unworthy self for the new identity which all kinds of small, manageable ideologies have to offer. In contrast to the many more pretentious and therefore unrealizable aims of Communism, the effort of all kinds of religious and nationalistic ideologies seems manageable, and gives the false self peace. The supreme aim is now, for example, to give women veils, to make one's own language the national language or to persecute ethnic minorities. The false self stands or falls with the ideology which has to justify its existence, and this leads to absolute, violent statements. For 'the other' is experienced as a denial not only of one's own ideology, but also of one's own identity. The Jewish author Richard Rubinstein writes that in this way the Enlightenment dream of building the new Jerusalem can turn into the nightmare of a concentration camp.[34] In one sense the ovens of Auschwitz were fired by the wreckage of Western belief in human progress, a bankruptcy which made people vulnerable to the Nazi ideology with its attainable goal of the Final Solution, the extermination of the Jewish 'other'.

Along with politics and the economy, religion above all seems to be open to ideological idolatry. This is the most subtle way of presenting the false self as the true self, without needing to confront the dread of death. The Galatians had made themselves slaves to religious ceremonial, 'days, months, fixed times and years' (Gal.4.10). Thus the false self can also petrify a particular image of God, interpretation of faith or ethic (these are all interconnected) so that it becomes an idol whose absolute claims then have a sacral authority. There is no room for difference. As Kierkegaard wrote:

> A partisan of the most rigid orthodoxy knows it all, he bows down before the Holy, the truth is for him an ensemble of ceremonies, he talks about presenting himself before the throne of God, or knows how many times one must bow, he knows everything - the same way as does the pupil who is able to demonstrate a geometrical theorem with the letters A B C, but not when they are changed to D E F. He is therefore in dread whenever he hears something which is not arranged in the same order.[35]

Religious fundamentalism is notorious for its intolerance and capacity for violence and makes religious wars the bloodiest that there are. The legalism of some groups of Pharisees in the time of Jesus has also become proverbial. The Gospels make it clear (although this has been somewaht obscured by early Jewish-Christian polemic) that Jesus' confrontation occurred above all on this level. The freedom of his playful existence, in which he did justice to those who thought and lived differently, inevitably provoked the defensive violence of the false self of his religious opponents. But the false self of Pilate, who saw his political interests threatened (and interests are always based on anxiety, since they have to confirm the importance of a person's own existence), was equally responsible for the violence against Jesus (Mark 15.15).

The feminist theologian Valerie Goldstein has pointed out that in societies in which men are dominant, the false self predominantly manifests itself in arrogance and power. This has become the classic definition of sin. Among women, by contrast, this translates itself into excessive dependence and availability.[36] Both the strong ego of the male and the weak ego of the female are sinful, since they are expressions of the false self which enslaves itself to a transfer object – in the case of the male, for example, his career; in the case of the female, her status as an all-caring partner and mother. The same difference between strong and weak egos can also be seen in societies in which the rich dominate the poor or the whites the blacks. The tension which is characteristic of any healthy organism and system, between self-affirmation and integration, is lost whenever a person, through the dread of death, loses sight of one pole or the other. At the deepest level, the need for a transfer object is the symptom of a lack of courage. Seized with anxiety about nothingness, men and women cannot bear the freedom of gratuitous existence – a freedom which makes possible the play of the totally other God. The false self grounds itself in an idol which obscures the most essential characteristic of reality, namely that the world exists 'out of nothing'. So people live in a lie (which perhaps explains the resistance to a 'psychologizing' interpretation of scripture, because here the prophetic criticism of idols comes close to being unacceptable). The limitations characteristic of an idol lead to slavery and thus to the 'corruption of all life'. On the other hand, people cannot live without transfer. This is the only way of relieving the tension between the longing to be unique and the need to identify oneself with something or someone who is greater.

This incomplete (and necessarily somewhat one-sided) survey of the findings of Kierkegaard and modern psychoanalysis leads to the conclusion that human welfare requires a surrender to the least limited 'object' that can confirm one's uniqueness. Only from the perspective of someone or something which absolutely transcends people (God) can one speak of the ideal human character. Becker reacts to this conclusion (his own), by saying: 'Such a mixture of intensive clinical insight and pure Christian ideology is absolutely heady.'[37] Sin (*hamartia*, missing your mark) is the consequence of being without God. This is the main meaning of sin in Scripture and makes necessary an 'exodus' from the land of slavery to the freedom of paradise where the 'tree of life' blossoms.

3

Baptism with Word and Spirit after the Resurrection

Writing to a community which had to endure serious persecution and oppression, the author of Hebrews says that Christ partook of our flesh and blood, 'that through death he might destroy him who has the power of death, that is, the devil, and deliver all those who through fear of death were subject to lifelong bondage. For surely it is not angels that he takes by the hand, but... the descendants of Abraham' (2.14-16). The expression 'take by the hand' is the same as that used later by the author to describe the exodus from Egypt (8.9). Here we have a quotation from Jeremiah (31.31-34) which looks forward to the renewed covenant in which the Torah will be written on human hearts (8.8-12). The author's argument, expressed in 'temple language', is that Christ 'offered himself through the eternal Spirit as a spotless sacrifice to God' and thus became 'mediator of a new covenant'. For he underwent death 'to bring freedom from the transgressions under the first covenant' (disobedience to the Torah) and in order that 'those called may receive the promised eternal inheritance (the renewed or "better" covenant)' (9.14-15). The disobedience to the Torah involved above all a transgression of the first commandment and thus idolatry, which as we saw is a source of many evils. Moreover the prophecies in the First Testament about the future renewal of the covenant often explicitly mention liberation from idols (Isa.44.3-20; Ezek.36.25). The first commandment will then be fulfilled: not the idols, but 'I will be your God' (Jer.31.33).

(i) The resurrection power of God's Word and Spirit

The resurrection, as a fundamental breaking through of the rigid order of death, falls outside our finite conceptual framework but resonates with our deepest longing as this has found expression throughout human memory in the myths and sagas of immortal heroes and gods. Now perception is always interpreted perception. Just as, for example, an accident is 'seen' (i.e. interpreted) by different people in different ways, so too an experience of the risen Jesus is experienced and interpreted in different ways, all the more so since, unlike the accident, there was no precedent for a resurrection from dead. So it is not surprising that the stories about the resurrection are sometimes so different and here and there contradict one another.

However, the New Testament writers are agreed on one thing: 'God has raised Jesus from the dead' (perhaps the oldest Christian confession of faith), and this took place through God's Word and Spirit. Thus Paul cites the confession that Jesus 'was declared by the Spirit with power to be God's Son through his resurrection from the dead' (Rom.1.3). The verb 'declared' (or appointed, horizo) implies a verbal communication: the power of God's Word and Spirit raised Jesus from the dead, as confirmation that he is the Son of God. The Letter to the Hebrews also attributes Jesus' resurrection to a Word of God with a quotation from Psalm.2.7: 'You are my son, this day I have begotten you' (1.5). According to Luke, Paul understood this saying of the Psalm in the same way (Acts 13.32-33). The reason why the New Testament mentions the Word less explicitly than the Spirit (Rom.8.11; I Tim.3.16; I Peter 3.18) as a cause of the resurrection of Jesus will lie in the fact that I have already indicated, namely that for Jewish thought the Word resonates in the term Spirit (and vice versa). In the time of the New Testament the interpretation of the Torah had become 'spiritless', hence the many conflicts which Jesus and Paul had with the legalistic Pharisees: 'the letter kills, but the Spirit gives life' (II Cor.3.6). By this Paul means an approach in which the Torah becomes a static idol that throws people back on thmselves and their own claims, away from God. By contrast, this apostle and his followers are 'servants of a new covenant, not of the letter but of the Spirit'.[38] The New Testament is probably emphasizing the 'Spirit aspect' of God's Word and Spirit when it talks of the cause of the resurrection of Jesus so as not to be misunderstood, given the prevalent one-sided orientation on the Word.

Through the Word and Spirit God constantly creates the world for its consummation in the eternal sabbath play, the kingdom of God which was already present in Jesus. That does not mean that Jesus was a kind of invulnerable superman, removed from earthly cares, difficulties and pain. On the contrary, precisely because he was so completely loved, he suffered more than anyone else from lovelessness. And precisely because he was so free and one with God, he wrestled more than anyone else with the rigidity of death and with his godforsakenness on the cross. The more human one is, the more one suffers over inhumanity, as is abundantly clear from the Gethsemane story (see also Heb.4.17). God, who is on the way to becoming 'all in all' – which means that death is overcome (I Cor.15.16, 28) -, was already 'all' in Jesus. Therefore his crucifixion is God's definitive self-offering, in which God takes upon himself and forgives the evil caused by anxiety about death and idolatry and identifies with the victims in their 'godforsakenness'. On the other hand, for this reason the creative play of Word and Spirit – the 'love as strong as death' (Song of Songs 8.6) – could overcome death in Jesus. God cannot die.

The resurrection is the confirmation that the true self, which is bound through the Word and Spirit to God's being, cannot die. Driven as it is by the dread of death, the false self cannot imagine surviving death – and rightly so, since it does not. The false self is the 'perversion' of the true self, so that this often does not develop very much and is just about saved in death 'as through fire' (I Cor.3.15). The more someone is alienated from his or her true self, the less he or she will recognize it after death with Christ, as themselves. However, since God's Word and Spirit were already wholly expressed in Jesus' life, there was complete continuity with his risen self. He was recognized without difficulty by his disciples, also because he did not lack a body and therefore was no 'ghost' (Luke 24.36-43). This is the proclamation of the empty tomb: the whole of material reality will one day be completely indwelt, renewed and perfected by the Word and the Spirit. The Greek division between Spirit and matter is utterly alien to the Bible. Matter is created and made to blossom by God's Word and Spirit, as is already celebrated in the first chapter of Scripture (Gen.1.2,3,6). Thinking of the resurrection life, Paul could even speak quite naturally of a 'spiritual body' (I Cor.15.44). The opposite of Spirit is not matter, but sin, which breaks the link between creation and God.

(ii) Christ's Word and Spirit: overcoming anxiety

Through God's Word and Spirit Jesus rose from the dead, so that he has become the risen Lord. On the other hand, however, something also happened to the Word and the Spirit. Since the resurrection,

God's Spirit has also come to be called the 'Spirit of Christ' (Rom.8.9), the 'Spirit of Jesus' (Acts 16.7) or the 'Spirit of the Son [of God]' (Gal. 4.6). And God's Word is now also referred to as the 'Word of Christ' (Rom.10.17; Col.3.16). Moreover, a distinguished exegete and expert in Pentecostalism, the British James Dunn, concludes: 'As the Spirit [and, I would add, the Word] was the "divinity" of Jesus, so Jesus became the personality of the Spirit [and of the Word].'[39] God's Spirit and Word are now as it were stamped with Christ's life, cross and resurrection. This is the essence of Christian faith. Believers experience Christ as God's Word and Spirit, and God's Word and Spirit as Christ.

Moreover Paul can write that Christ became 'a life-giving Spirit' (I Cor.15.45).[40] This whole chapter is about the resurrection: 'If Christ is not risen, then your faith is vain and you are still in your sins' (v.1). Against some all too enthusiastic members of the community the apostle stresses that all is not yet subjected to God and death is still a reality (vv.21-28). We still live in the natural body of Adam. This comes first, and only afterwards, in the resurrection, shall we receive the spiritual body of Christ, 'the last Adam' (vv.45-46). But this last is not just 'pie in the sky'. Now already through his resurrection Christ has become a 'lifegiving Spirit', so that Paul (according to most manuscripts) exclaims: 'As we have borne the image of the early (Adam), so let us bear the image of the man from heaven' (v.49). We have already received a 'guaranteee' of the Spirit (II Cor.1.22; 5.5) through which Christ 'makes us live', so that our faith bears fruit and we are no longer trapped in our sins. This new life now already consists of conquest over the 'sting of death [the dread caused by death] which is sin [because it drives one to idolatry] and the power of sin is the Torah [since if it is made an idol this leads to sin, Rom.7.5]' (vv.56-57). On this basis, moreover, Paul can summon the Corinthians to a new way of life 'abounding in the work of the Lord' (v.58). So too I Peter (1.21-25) writes that through the truth of the resurrection of Jesus, 'sincere mutual love has become possible'. For although the believers are 'flesh' which perishes like grass, they are now 'reborn through the living and eternal word of God' – and this is the gospel. Hultgren stresses that from the beginning the followers of Jesus experienced his cross and resurrection as an integral, liberating event.[41] The cross was not overemphasized at the cost of the resurrection, as in some theories of the atonement with their morbid fascination with the wounds and the blood of Jesus. This attitude still has an influence in the sombre, static atmosphere of some Protestant celebrations of the eucharist. The fixation on the cross has often encouraged a passive acceptance of injustice and violence in history. By contrast, Jesus' first followers experienced in Christ's Word and Spirit that playful new life has already radically begun.

Kierkegaard wrote that if people want to be able to live authentically they must face their dread.[42] They must go through the 'school of dread' by which the false self with its concern for control and all its rigid idols is broken, and people can truly become themselves. This corresponds with the old idea that true spirituality always involves a form of dying. The false self must die so that a person can be reborn with his or her true self. Thus many Pentecostals bear witness that they had to go through a crisis before they arrived at a living faith. Only when people face their mortality and thus recognize that they are creatures do they discover that they are grounded in the unbounded Creator. Then in the Word and the Spirit they can become transparent to God who plays the game of love – following Jesus. We find such a notion in Ecclesiastes, who is far from being the doom and gloom merchant which many people make him. On the contrary, with him we already find the wisdom of the monks that 'remembering death' (*memento mori*) makes it possible to 'seize the day' (*carpe diem*). The great question posed by the Preacher is 'What is wisdom?'. Embarking on great enterprises? But they perish. Toiling and sweating? But that doesn't get you anywhere. Seeking fame? This always leads to disappointment. Saving money? The more you have, the more you can lose. Trying to be all too righteous? You will get no thanks for that. All the usual attempts by men and women to find a foundation fail in the perspective of the death which 'comes to all equally'. Being able to face this is, according to the Preacher, the secret of a 'wise' life, since only acceptance of one's own finitude makes it possible to enjoy the blessings of each new day. 'Go, eat your bread with enjoyment, and drink your wine with a merry heart; for God has already approved what you do. Let your garments be always white; let not oil be lacking on your head. Enjoy life...' (9.7-9). Kierkegaard calls such people free 'knights of the faith' who need no idols and do not saddle others with the consequence of their anxiety, but take their courage wholly from their Creator. This does not mean that they should make God a 'transfer object', which is always an idol. God is never object, but always intangible subject who through Christ's Word and Spirit gives us courage to die to our false self and 'to rise' as a true self which plays in God's presence. So transfer objects (idols) become superfluous. For God's Word and Spirit now have the quality of the cross and resurrection of Christ, through which believers experience that death is not the terrifying end that robs life of its meaning but, on the contrary, the beginning of a new life which is really meaningful. Now they share not only in God's self but in God's self *in and through Christ*, which puts them in a position constantly to go through 'the school of dread' (to crucify their false self). So the cross becomes a 'tree of life'. This is the new life of conquering anxiety and thus finding liberation from the idols: the Pentecost game of Word and Spirit which anticipates the eternal sabbath.

For this reason the New Testament also speaks in many ways about the 'power' (courage) that Christ's Word and Spirit give (Rom.1.16; 15.13; I Cor.1.18; 2.4). Luke begins his book on the history of the first Christian communities with the announcement by the risen Christ to his followers of 'the promise of the Father'. 'You shall receive power when the Holy Spirit comes upon you and you shall be my witnesses' (Acts.1.4,8). That means witnesses of the new, 'wise' life through Christ's baptism with Word and Spirit. The book of Acts describes the working of this 'baptism', which gave the Christians courage to 'die' to their anxious, false self and already play the crazy sabbath game which breaks down rigid barriers between people. Hence this experience is also called a 'baptism', a term which John the Baptist had probably derived from his own practice of immersing people in the waters of the Jordan. For the Israelites, water symbolized chaos and death, so that their immersion signified confrontation with it and thus their 'purification' from anxiety about death. Along with rising out of the water, as a 'rebirth' with the fullness of the true self, this ritual expressed the prayer for the new inward exodus in which the coming Messiah would liberate them. This takes place through the baptism with Christ's Word and Spirit which has become really effective through his cross and resurrection. If according to Luke this 'baptism' begins on the day of Pentecost in Jerusalem, the harvest festival at which around this time the giving of the Torah on Sinai was also celebrated, then he is depicting this, too, as a new Sinai event, complete with wind and fire (Acts 2.1-4). The Torah is no longer just carved on tablets of stone or written on parchment, but comes from the heart of believers in

playful glossolalic sounds in which the loveless division of Babylon
is overcome.

Pentecostalism is right when, differing from the practice in most
established churches, it emphasizes Pentecost as the consummation
and the crown of the events of Christmas and Easter. The end is more
than the beginning. The birth, death and resurrection of Jesus have
made possible the 'outpouring' of Christ's Word and Spirit on all
that lives, so that the purifying fire of God's love can now be kindled
all over the earth. The French philosopher La Rochefoucauld once
remarked that people cannot contemplate their own death very long,
any more than they can contemplate the sun. However, since the
resurrection of Christ, this capacity is no longer limited to some Old
Testament heroes who dared to contemplate their anxiety about
death without the encouraging experience of the conquest of death.
Now an intensification and 'democratization' of the play of Word
and Spirit has become possible, for Pentecost is the application,
world-wide and through time, of the event of Good Friday and
Easter. The self of the believer here experiences his or her bond with
the self of God that in Christ has overcome death. For God's self,
expressed in the Word and the Spirit, is now mediated through the
crucified and risen Christ. Thus the risen Lord of the sabbath
continues his messianic way as one who baptizes with Word and
Spirit and realizes the longing expressed in the old sigh attributed to
Moses: 'Would that all the Lord's people were prophets, that the
Lord would put his Spirit upon them!' (Num.11.29).

(a) The renewed covenant: life from the true self

God has always been a God of grace. This already emerges from the
first commandment, in which God unconditionally presents himself
to Israel as 'the Lord, *your* God who has brought you out of Egypt,
out of the land of slavery'. This grace is radicalized in Christ. As
mediator of God's Word and Spirit (Acts 2.33), he has become
mediator of the renewed covenant.

We already saw how for Paul the letter (the legalistically interpreted
Torah which has become an idol) kills, but the Spirit gives life (II
Cor.3.6). And so he has called the Corinthians his living letters of
commendation, 'which all can recognize and read'. In their new way
of life they prove to be 'a letter of Christ', written 'with the Spirit of
the living God, not on tables of stone but on tables of flesh in the

heart' (vv.2-3; see Ezek.36.26). After this he emphasizes that he and his fellow-workers are made fit by God 'to be ministers of a new covenant, not of the letter but of the Spirit' (v.6).

Then he contrasts the abiding glory of the ministry of the new covenant with the transitory glory of Moses' ministry (vv.7-11). In verses 12-13 he also contrasts his boldness and that of his fellow workers with the fear of Moses, who put a veil over his face. Moses could not appear boldly, because in contrast to the ministry of the apostle, his ministry had to fade away, as it was not capable of liberating the hardened Israelites from their sins. Associating with the word 'veil' in a rabbinic way, Paul concludes that 'a veil remains when the old covenant is read' which disappears only in Christ. So only in conversion to him ('the Lord') does the covenant come into its own; then 'the veil is taken away' (vv.14-16).

In v.17 Paul writes: 'Now the Lord is the Spirit, and where the Spirit of the Lord is, there is freedom'. This sentence is notorious for its exegetical problems, especially in connection with the title 'Lord'.[43] Does this refer to God or Christ? I think that this question *a priori* divides something which in which a distinction can indeed be made but which is essentially one. God's lordship points to the liberating dynamic of the Word and Spirit which has been made more radical by the conquest of death in Christ. So 'Lord' refers to God in Christ who takes away the veil from the covenant. So I would read the passage: 'Now God in Christ is the Spirit, and where the Spirit of God in Christ is, there is freedom.' In other words, freedom from the legalistic, idolatrous letter because the anxiety of death has been overcome and the covenant is written by the Spirit 'on tablets of flesh in the hearts'. This is the freedom which in a well known saying Augustine described succinctly as 'Love, and do what you want.' For Paul, too, love fulfils the Torah (Rom.13.8-10). This freedom is the freedom of the sabbath game, of the true self which is grounded only in God and lives 'wisely' in open interaction with the next person – respecting the 'otherness' of the other. In this interplay the identity of the believers grows, in and through Christ's Word and Spirit, into his image and thus into the image if God (II Cor.4.4).

The covenant 'written in the hearts' is thus life from the true self, a life in union with God and the creation. Moreover it is characteristic of the renewed covenant that it is within human beings. The Torah is the written objectivized expression of the play of Word and Spirit and thus both God's being and the true self of human beings. Driven by the dread of death, people often make the Torah an idol outside themselves – through legalism or by making Scripture a magical object which soothes their own anxieties but remains imprisoned in the false self. This often leads to a way of life which is the opposite of love. But now that God's Word and Spirit have also become Christ's Word and Spirit, the anxiety can be overcome and the Torah in them can come to life. People begin to live from their true selves, as Paul wrote to the Galatians: 'I [that is, the false self] am crucified with Christ, and yet I live; no longer my [false] self, but Christ [in Word and Spirit] dwells in me' (2.20). The same fundamental experience is put into words in the expression 'the Spirit dwells in me' (see Romans 8.9: I Cor.3.16), or 'the Word dwells in me' (see Col.3.16). The rhythm of 'dying' to the false self and rising with the true self gives an existential, analogous 'knowledge' of the death and resurrection of Jesus in the light of which discussions about the manner of his resurrection become theoretical. The awareness of not only the presence but also the indwelling of Christ's Word and Spirit is typical of Pentecostalism. Above all the Gospel of John and I John (by another author but from the same circle) go into this.

The Gospel of John was written late in the first century. This was a time at when Christians were increasingly concerned about the dying out of eye-witnesses of Jesus' life and work and about the delay in his return. So in Jesus' farewell words the 'Spirit of truth' (an expression that we encounter elsewhere only in the Qumran writings) is also called the 'Paraclete'.[44] The latter term denotes someone who is called to help, like an advocate. Some versions translate the word 'Comforter', but this limits the activity of the Paraclete one-sidedly to situations of failure or error. The translation 'Encourager' therefore seems better. Encouragement includes trust, but above all directs attention forwards, to the task of countering the hostility of the world and bearing witness to the new life in Christ (15.27; 16.8-11). If we investigate the nature of this encouragement, then it is that Jesus' 'going away' (his death and resurrection) is the condition for the coming of the Paraclete (16.7). The Paraclete is the fruit of Good Friday and Easter, and as 'another Jesus' (to use a phrase of R.E.Brown's, see 14.16), will not only remain with his followers but even be *in* them (14.17). Jesus announces that the Paraclete 'will take of mine and make it known to you. All that the Father has is mine'

(16.14-15). This last expression recalls 3.35, where it is said that the Father has given everything into Jesus's hands: we have seen that this denotes God's boundless gift of the Word and the Spirit to them. So the Paraclete is Christ's Word and Spirit which will be given to his followers. In and through the community, he will 'convince the world of sin and righteousness and judgment', and as an advocate convincingly defend the cause of Christ before the tribunal of that same world which executed him (16.8-11). For as 'Spirit of truth' the Paraclete makes it possible to live from the true self, revealed in Jesus. Moreover the remarks about the Paraclete are part of the repeated call to love (14.21-24, 28; 15.9-25). The Paraclete 'will teach all things and bring to mind' what Jesus has said (14.26), which implies an interiorization of the preaching (the Wisdom) of Jesus. Through the Paraclete his words will come to life in believers so that they can 'keep his commandments' and truly love (cf. Ezek.36.27; II Cor.3.1-18). What the disciples could not understand before Jesus 'went away' will become clear to them when, guided by the 'Spirit of truth', they take the way 'to all truth'. This means that in interaction with what comes their way in the future, they will increasingly learn to live from their true selves – through the Word and the Spirit (see 16.12-15). The Paraclete is as it were the inner counterpart of the Jewish methurgeman. This was someone who translated the scriptural reading and adapted it so that the hearers could live in accordance with the Torah in their current situation.[45] So the Paraclete is John's interpretation of the renewed covenant 'written' in the hearts which can take part in the game of love.

This play of Word and Spirit, summed up in the Gospel in the term Paraclete, is called an 'anointing' (*chrisma*) in the First Letter of John (2.20,27). We have already noted that Jesus owes his title Christ to such an anointing. Believers, too, have received this divine anointing, but it has been mediated by the crucified and risen Jesus: 'You have an anointing from the Holy One' (i.e. God, 2.20): 'the anointing which you have received from him (Christ)...' (2.27).[46] This anointing 'abides in (Greek *en*) you and you do not need anyone to instruct you' (v.27; see also 4.13-16). Like the Paraclete, the anointing functions as an inward teacher to interpret the apostolic preaching of Christ, which 'must abide in you' (v.24) and adapt it to counter the false teachers (v.26). Thus the anointing puts people in a position to unmask lies and live in truth, that is, in love: 'By this you can recognize the Spirit of God: [by the confession] that Jesus has come in the flesh' (4.2). The Gnostic false teachers denied this because of their antipathy to matter. They were disgusted by everything physical and therefore mortal, so that the later Gnostic Valentinus could claim that Jesus never relieved himself because he was above decay and corruption. This notion led to an abstract belief that attached little importance to the quality of everyday concrete life (see 2.15-17; 4.5). Over against this the writer constantly emphasizes that the concrete, 'fleshly' expression of God's love in Christ is the basis and norm of the new life (5.1). 'Anyone who does not love, abides in death' (i.e. is alienated from the true self, 3.15). Love proves that 'we have passed from death to life' (3.14), or have been 'born from God' through the Word and the Spirit (4.4; 5.1). This love inspired by the Spirit drives out the fear of death, for it gives courage in the face of the day of judgment, in which the guilty, false self will be 'punished' and disappear (4.16-18). Therefore the author can end with the remarkable statement: 'Anyone who is born of God [lives by the true self] does not sin' (5.18). But he also knows the character of Christ's Word and Spirit as pledge, so that his last line warns: 'Children, beware of idols'(5.22).

The baptism with Christ's Word and Spirit which makes possible the new life from the true self led Calvin to develop his doctrine of the indwelling testimony of the Spirit. There are several variants of this doctrine, but for Calvin the Spirit was the 'indwelling teacher' who aptly applies the word of Scripture to our heart so that our blind eyes and deaf ears are opened. This living witness of the Word and Spirit thus addresses not only the understanding but the whole person, which leads to our adoption as children of God. For Calvin this divine testimony, and not the Roman Catholic hierarchical order or Protestant dogma, was the highest authority for believers. Here he was in advance of modern thought which, above all since Kierke-gaard, has denied that truth is always personal. As long as Christ is outside us, Calvin writes, his liberation remains 'useless and worth-less' for us. He must come and dwell in us through his Word and Spirit, whose testimony we 'feel engraved like a seal upon our hearts'. This is the 'baptism in the Holy Spirit and fire' in which we are purified by faith and reborn to a new creation. The testimony of the Word and the Spirit is so convincing that the word 'faith' is often a synonym for trust and confidence. Moreover Calvin can write: 'It is a token of the most miserable blindness to charge with arrogance Christians, who dare to glory in the presence of the Holy Spirit, without which glorying Christianity does not exist.'[47]

(b) An experience with many names

Without experience (Spirit), information (Word) cannot be person-ally meaningful for us, far less encourage and change us. This was already emphasized in the East by Simeon the New Theologian, five hundred years before Calvin in the West.[48] He, too, was a reformer who, in a time when the Orthodox church had embraced the Byzantine political order and the faith of many people had become theoretical and abstract, was zealous for a new Pentecost for all believers. As well as water baptism, he wrote, a baptism in the Holy Spirit is necessary in which the believer becomes aware of the indwelling of Christ. To believe that this is the case is not enough: Christ's indwelling must be experienced personally. According to Simeon, no greater misery is conceivable for us than not to be aware of ourselves. Such individuals are indeed Christians by water baptism, but otherwise have to be compared with a corpse, which also does not feel anything. God in Christ is experienced as light and fire in which our 'I' is broken and we begin to live from God himself. In the Spirit God is experienced in our innermost parts as love, through which we can fulfil the commandments of Christ in life with our fellow human beings. According to Simeon, humility is the seed that bears fruit thirty, sixty, a hundred times in the charisms of the Holy Spirit.

That baptism with Christ's Word and Spirit is an experience is confirmed by many witnesses within Pentecostalism. So the Presbyter-ian preacher Dr Charles Price, who was initially very sceptical, wrote that when he visited a Pentecostal assembly 'something broke within my breast. An ocean of divine love flowed over my heart. This could not be explained by psychological actions and reactions. This was genuine.' And the Danish opera singer Anna Larsen Bjørrer described her baptism in the Spirit like this: 'My whole body shook; it was like waves of fire going through me, over and over again, and my whole being was as bathed in light.' Because of her crazy behaviour she was sent into a psychiatric hospital for observation, but was quickly released because, as the Director said in his report: 'You are the only sane person in this hospital, and all the rest of us are mad'.[49] James Dunn has sufficiently shown that baptism with Word and Spirit in the New Testament was in the first place an experience. He has also demonstrated that this experience did not necessarily coincide with water baptism (as was thought in the sacramental tradition), nor is it always a 'second blessing' which comes after that of conversion and rebirth (as many Pentecostals think). 'It is the gift of saving grace by which one enters into Christian experience and life, into the new covenant, into the church.'[50] The first Christians experienced that they were radically encountered by God in Christ, without any merits or achievements on their part. Moreover, in rapt exaltation Paul could attribute all the initiative to God, who had resolved beforehand (i.e. unconditionally) to make the whole creation blossom (Rom.8.28-30; 9.14-29). These passages were fossilized by Reformation thought, which was scholastic and poor in experience, into the doctrine of predestination. Where the apostle celebrated the many-coloured grandeur of God's grace, Calvinism restricted it to the black-and-white notion of a God who elects some people to life and others to eternal death.

Above all the charismatic renewal sees that the baptism with Word and Spirit can manifest itself both in moments of crisis and in gradual growth. We can say that this 'baptism' is the experiential dimension of faith which works itself out in numerous new experiences ('being filled', see Acts 2.4; 9.17; Eph.5.18). Without this experiential dimension faith remains abstract and powerless and the covenant a 'dead letter'. Here it is not something that is 'added' to people, as is often thought in the Pentecostal movement, where expressions like 'being filled with the Spirit' or 'indwelling of Christ' are taken quite literally. It is not that Something or Someone comes into us who is 'other than I'. On the contrary, the true human self exists to the degree that it is united with God's self, through the Word and Spirit. This self of God has taken on the 'colour' of the crucified and risen Christ, as a result of which we are freed from our anxious, false self. This is the baptism with Word and Spirit. It is experienced as a 'fiery baptism' because the infinite God burns away all our finite certainties (idols) with infinite passion. So in it we become more 'ourselves' (our true selves), just as in the still lifes of the painter Francisco de Zurbaran everyday subjects become more real than usual. Sometimes there is a renewal or intensification of the covenant relationship with God, above all at moments of a challenge or crisis in which anxiety increases and the false self firmly sticks up its head. So time and again a response of creative love becomes possible. The central experience of baptism with Word and Spirit is interpreted from different perspectives in the New Testament with various terms (in addition to 'baptism with the Spirit' and anointing') like 'receiving the Spirit', 'foretaste', 'promise', 'purification', 'rebirth' and 'renewal'.

The verb 'baptize (or be baptized) in/with the Holy Spirit (and fire)' occurs in Matt.3.11; Mark 1.8; Luke 3.16; John 1.33; Acts 1.33; 11.16 and I Cor. 12.13). Perhaps this experience is referred to in Heb.6.2 where there is mention of an elementary 'instruction on baptism' (*baptismoi*, water baptism and Spirit baptism). There is also mention in I Cor.10.2 of a baptism 'in the cloud [in the Spirit] and in the sea [in water]'. This central event is referred to in many other ways. The Spirit can be 'received' (Acts 1.8; 2.38; John 20.22); Paul writes to the Romans that they have received the Spirit of sonship (8.15). This experience is also called 'the promise of the Father' (Acts 2.16), which is 'sent' by Jesus to his followers (Luke 24.49; Acts 1.4). So too the Paraclete will be sent by him after his departure (John 14.15; 15.26). In Acts 15.8-9 Peter relates to the council in Jerusalem how God has given the Holy Spirit to the non-Jew Cornelius and his household 'as also to us' (i.e. on the day of Pentecost, see 11.16-17), 'purifying their heart through faith'. Similarly, Titus 3.5-6 says that God 'has saved us by the washing of regeneration and renewal in the Holy Spirit which he poured out (*ekcheo*, the word that denotes the Pentecost event, Acts 2.17,33) richly through Jesus Christ our Saviour'. So the baptism of the Spirit is a purification to rebirth or renewal of life (see Matt.3.12; Luke 3.17) and is therefore also implied in I Cor.6.11; 10.2-3). There is also reference to this experience as the 'promise of the Father' in Eph.1.13-14 (see also 4.30), where there is mention of people who when they came to faith were 'sealed' in Christ with 'the promised Holy Spirit, which is the guarantee of our inheritance until we acquire possession of it to liberation'. And II Cor.1.20-22 mentions the many promises of God which are 'yes' in Christ. These promises mean that God has 'anointed' (see I John 1.20,27) us, 'set his seal on our hearts and given us the Spirit in our hearts as a guarantee'.

Through the baptism with Christ's Word and Spirit people are saved, says Peter in his defence of the non-Jewish Cornelius and his household against some legalistic, Jewish-Christian Pharisees (Acts 15.5-11). And after the text from II Corinthians 3.1-18 that we have already discussed, Paul warns that those who do not accept the liberation of God in Christ 'who is Spirit' are 'lost', because they remain slaves of 'the God of this age', so that for them the gospel remains 'veiled' (4.3-4). By the 'god of this age' he means the 'so-called gods, whether in heaven or in earth': in short, all that is an 'idol' (I Cor.8.4-5).

Those who simply take note of the liberation through Christ's Word and Spirit (build on the foundation of Christ with hay and straw) remain imprisoned in the false self and have every reason to fear the day of judgment (I Cor.3.13-20). On that they will only be saved 'as through fire', which means that they will be purified from the many 'dead works' that they wrongly thought were part of their true identity. However, their true self, God's Word and Spirit which 'dwell' in them, will be saved. By virtue of this 'indwelling' the Corinthians are 'God's temple'. This was a revolutionary expression, for when the apostle wrote these words the temple in Jerusalem was still fully active. Through Christ's cross and resurrection, God's Word and Spirit can now dwell fully in all believers, so that they are 'holy'. This is foolishness 'in this age', but for God it is wisdom (v.18). Sanctification, as I have already remarked, is the often painful dying to the unfree false self which is unable to play, in a process of transformation acording to the image of Christ. The sanctified are 'a bit apart' since they have been set apart in the sense that they already have a share in the sabbath play of God's coming kingdom. This crazy play becomes most visible on their 'holy day' in the charismatic celebration (cf. I Cor.14). Moltmann points out that the terms making holy and making whole belong together linguistically.[51] Someone who is made holy becomes whole because through Christ's Word and Spirit he or she has a part in the Source of the existence from which they were alienated. The deadly anxiety which leads either to a flight into a rationalistic attitude at the expense of the body and the feelings or to an immersion in a sea of emotions and irrationality at the expense of the understanding is overcome. So a holy life is a spontaneous and holistic life: a 'wise' life in union with the whole creation. Therefore, Paul says, division between supporters of 'Paul, Apollos or Cephas' is of the evil one, since 'all things are yours:... whether the world or life or death or the present or the future, all are yours; and you are Christ's; and Christ is God's' (I Cor.3.21-23). Wesley (and, following him, the Holiness Movement) saw it as his task to spread 'sanctification over the land', which he also understood to include social reform. We saw that this holistic, 'Third World spirituality' is generally a prominent hallmark of Pentecostalism.

(c) The hallmark of modesty

We still have to answer the question why Pentecostals in particular, most of whom have experienced baptism with Christ's Word and Spirit, so often creep back into a legalistic order. We find this phenomenon in all the charismatic currents in history, beginning with the first Christian communities.

So according to Paul the community in Corinth did not fall short in any gifts of grace. In a typically rabbinic interpretation of the experience of Israel in the Exodus and the wilderness he warns them nevertheless not, as Israel did once, to succumb to idolatry and thus to all kinds of evil (I Cor.10.1-13). The Israelites were all baptized in Moses (an allegory of Christ), in the cloud (the Spirit) and in the sea (in water).[52] Israel was liberated from Egypt by God in Moses, in an exodus led by the column of cloud and fire, but it again lapsed into idolatry. The Corinthians, who have experienced a renewed inner exodus in Word and Spirit through God in Christ, must take this as a warning. 'Let him who thinks that he stands take heed lest he fall' (v.12). The point is that people in this life never studied in the 'school of anxiety'. In contrast to the moderate life of the established churches, which often 'have never heard that there is such a thing as an experience of the Spirit' (see Acts 19.2) and as a matter of course, with at most a nagging feeling of incompleteness, conform to the present order, Pentecostals have experienced the radical freedom of Christ's Word and Spirit. They are freed from the lies of the idols and have played the gratuitous game of the totally other God above the abyss of nothingness. However, after a while this existential experience can lead to an intensification of the fear of death and thus a reaction of flight into the 'wisdom of this world' with its rigid order. The psychologist Abraham Maslow gave such a reaction the appropriate name 'Jonah syndrome', by which he understood an avoidance of the full intensity of life.[53] This explains the legalism of many Pentecostals. It is further encouraged by the fact that so far they have no theology which really does justice to the baptism with

Christ's Word and Spirit and helps to keep this experience open. The more the experiences of this 'baptism' (i.e. the charisms, as I hope to show in the next chapter) are framed by the 'wisdom of this world', the more they lose that foolishness which changes life and the world. Having begun in the Spirit, one ends up like some Galatians in a life according to the 'flesh', mortal and ruled by the fear of death (Gal.3.3). This also explains why the first experience is often the most intense; at that time one was most receptive, and not yet so indoctrinated by fundamentalist interpretations or prejudiced by authoritarian precedents. Like the Corinthians or the often playful Kierkegaard, mentioned earlier, Pentecostals can live from their own true self as a matter of course. This comes about through the character of guarantee which the baptism with Christ's Word and Spirit as. Pentecostals, too, must be 'constantly filled with the Spirit' (Eph.5.18). For they, too, with the rest of God's people, constantly flock to the side of the Grand Inquisitor from Dostoievsky's *The Brothers Karamazov* in his rebuke to Christ that he brings too much freedom. Time and again believers lapse into the 'school of dread', which can make them increasingly aware of their constant need for Christ's liberating exodus in Word and Spirit. Moreover, a certain modesty ('humility', says Simeon the New Theologian) is the characteristic of the most authentic life possible in the present-day world.

To sum up, we can say that, as the prophet greater than Moses, the risen Christ accomplishes a renewed, inner exodus to the sabbath play of God's kingdom. Like the pillar of cloud and fire of old, his fiery baptism with Word and Spirit liberates from Egyptian slavery to idols and thus from many forms of evil. For in this 'baptism' we take part in the crucified and risen self of God in Christ. This redeems us from the dread of death which makes the human self a false self that seeks to ground itself in rigid structures or idolized persons. So the true self flourishes in the free play of love and is formed in God's image. The miracle of Christian faith is that in it the truth of one's own finitude, far from leading to the 'spoiling of life', is the essential condition for an authentic existence, namely the knowledge of the Creator. Christianity (above all in its 'Pentecostal' form) has always appealed to those who are most aware of their finitude and 'unworthiness': the prostitutes, tax collectors, those discriminated against and those who pick through the rubbish dumps. These are the ones who are most receptive to the power of Christ's Word and Spirit, so that the last in the present political and economic order are often the first to share in the crazy sabbath play of God's kingdom. This is evident from the massive attraction that Pentecostal meetings have for the poor. The charismatic experience in which existence is experienced as grace (*charis*), and thus as grounded in God alone, is therefore the positive element in the criticism made above all by feminist and liberation theology of the idols which discriminate against and oppress. Without the charismatic dimension these approaches critical of society can in turn degenerate into ideological idols which are served in a joyless way. On the other hand, Pentecostalism urgently needs these critical theological interpretations of reality to bring into its own the liberating power of the charismatic experience (which is also structural). Like Israel of old, the Pentecostals constantly lapse into 'safe' idols, like a literally inerrant Bible, a rigid opposition to the theory of evolution and blind deliverance to conservative 'reborn' politicians. Often enslaved to the *status quo*, they do not see signs of change as signs of hope but as apocalyptic signals which announce the threatening end of the world. Liberation theologians and feminist theologians often deal more playfully with scripture here, which they interpret in an interplay between text and context (their own situation). They usually approach the Bible more as an end in itself and less, as is often the case with the Pentecostals, as a 'proof text' for their own views. So Scripture can come to life in all its Spirit-surprising newness. Christians who do not recognize their own experience of God in the Pentecostal experience (usually because they do not see through the fundamentalist 'exterior') are therefore not without Christ's Word and Spirit. What distinguishes Pentecostals is that in teaching and preaching they put the emphasis on this dimension of experience, wait for the baptism with Word and Spirit in prayer, and above all make room for the charisms in which this 'baptism' is concretely experienced.

Before I go into these gifts of grace, I first want to investigate briefly to what extent the tradition of spirituality can clarify our understanding of the Pentecost experience, which according to Dunn is the 'beginning and principle' of Christian life.

4

The Pentecostal Experience in the Light
of Traditional Spirituality

Otger Steggink and Kees Waaijman, both connected with the Titus Brandsma Institute at Nijmegen, have developed a 'working hypothesis' by which spiritualities can be made visible and tested.[54] In it spirituality as an experience is seen as an interplay of five different elements. By means of this hypothesis I hope to clarify the Pentecost experience as this is experienced by Pentecostals. The elements are: the spirit of the time, the basic inspiration, the self, the initiation and mysticism.

(i) Elements of spiritual experience

1. The social and cultural context or spirit of the time also determines the spiritual experience. According to the Van Dale dictionary, the spirit of the time is the predominant way of thinking and acting in a particular historical period. Any human experience, including religious experience, is coloured by the time and situation in which one lives. So present-day Pentecostalism took shape above all among 'little folk' uprooted and alienated from their traditions, masses of whom migrated from the North American countryside into the great cities. They included numerous former slaves and children of slaves who were brutally rejected and discriminated against because of the colour of their skins. There were also many women among those who, at a time when the struggle for votes for women was gaining more and more suporters, were becoming painfully aware of their 'invisible' presence in a patriarchal society. Finally, rationalism emerged strongly in this period. Moreover from the beginning the Pentecostal experience was a democratic and holistic spirituality which is experienced as healing. In such a context of marginalization and urbanization Pentecostal spirituality is flourishing today in many countries in the Third World. The indigenous, non-white churches

are growing above all where under the influence of the modern mass media ancestral traditions have come to clash with Western culture. All this coincides with the observation that above all people who go through the 'school of anxiety', robbed as they are of their civil and religious certainties (which function as idols), seem to be able to arrive at an experience of God. So the charismatic renewal is often blazing out today in countries in which the familiar church communities and traditions are crumbling as a result of secularization. 'It is when wind and waves and darkness have taken over, when there is nothing but the abyss under our feet, that the Lord approaches.'[55]

2. The next element of spiritual experience is the basic inspiration. This is the fundamental animation which motivates people and groups and orientates them within their social and cultural context or in confrontation with it. Thus the basic inspiration transcends the changing spirit of the time, as for Pentecostals and Christians generally does in the revelation of the God of Israel in Jesus Christ. This basic inspiration is expressed in all kinds of leitmotifs. In addition to scripture and Jesus as baptizer with Word and Spirit, for Pentecostals this is above all the charismatic celebration as described in the First Letter to the Corinthians (12; 14). Here the character of Pentecostal spirituality as play is given its clearest form and outward manifestation in personal, diaconal help (see also Acts 2.42-47; 4.32-36).

3. The self is the third element in spiritual experience. By this is meant not the socialized identity of a person, like a role or function in society, but the uncontrollable part of the person which time and again bubbles up spontaneously and creatively. I have described this self, which is also called the human 'soul' or 'spirit', as the supreme dynamic expression of God's creative Word and Spirit. The self shares in the nature of God in Christ and manifests itself in the play of love in which people constantly transcend themselves. Being human is *becoming* human, and in this the self increasingly realizes itself in the self of the 'other'. The Pentecostal experience of faith has a markedly individualistic orientation, but it is not individualistic (as with Thomas à Kempis and his 'book in a corner'), since it is always also experienced and shared with like-minded people in celebrations, prayer circles and the like. However, as a result of experiences of rejection and fundamentalist influences there is little interaction with the broader society. The relationship with that is limited to a one-

way traffic: Pentecostals preach and bear witness, but seldom carry on a real dialogue with people with whom they do not feel spiritually akin. There is no real interaction (at most, in the charismatic renewal) with those who are 'different' in a religious and ethical respect, and this tends to retard the development of the Pentecostals' self.

4. The initiation is the training (ascesis) in which people adopt the basic inspiration. Thus it is the link between the basic inspiration from which people live and the self – within a given context or spirit of the time. In Pentecostalism there is concentration here both on the personal pattern of life and on the community. The adoption of a particular form of behaviour is expected, and interpreted as 'discipleship of Christ'. Often this amounts to a legalistic, culture-conditioned code of behaviour like not living together outside marriage, not smoking and bearing witness to your faith in many ways. I recall from my time as a student at a Pentecostal Bible school, where there was no drinking but you were allowed to play billiards, our bewilderment when a guest from a similar school in Spain unsuspectingly told us that they had their own vineyard, but billiards 'of course' was of the devil. In the non-white indigenous churches, including the charismatic base communities in Latin America, initiation also means a new evaluation and appropriation of one's own ancestral traditions. In addition, a training in group behaviour takes place in the celebration. So people make themselves at home in the oral 'charismatic etiquette': when and how you say a prayer, give a testimony or venture a dance. Then one learns to share the needs of the world and one's own needs, often in a dialogue prayer in which the person who prays links up with the lament or thanksgiving of the other. The 'sacred space' (interaction) which arises through the initiation between the basic inspiration (God in Christ) and the self is expressed in the play of words, images (including sacraments and rituals), stories and movements which is so characteristic of charismatic celebration, and 'builds up' the believers. An important criterion for a good meeting is for Pentecostals to be able to say after they have left, 'Something happened to me'.

5. The last element within the overall tension of spirituality is mysticism. The word 'mysticism' has all kinds of misleading associations, varying from alienation from the world to special phenomena which have little or nothing to do with authentic mysticism. As Hein Blommestijn, also connected with the Titus Brandsma Institute, once put it, the mystic is simply a man or woman who has

awoken from the illusion that he or she is their own creator. A distinction can be made between the mystical experience and the mystical way.

(a) A pre-mystical experience

According to Steggink and Waaijman, the mystical experience is an event which intervenes in life, an experience of breakthrough. In it the self begins to 'awaken' and one begins to live from a new basic inspiration or is radically affected by this for the first time. This is precisely how the baptism with Word and Spirit, in which people share in the crucified and risen self of God in Christ, is experienced in Pentecostalism. The persons concerned experience themselves and the world in a new way through an experience which comes 'from the other side' and is completely gratuitous. Certainly one can prepare for it with certain forms of initiation, as in the 'tarrying meetings' of the Pentecostal movement in which people 'wait on the Lord' with fasting, prayer and song, or (in the charismatic movement) through a seven-week training which issues in prayer for the baptism with Word and Spirit. But the experience itself cannot be organized, only received. However, in Pentecostalism this experience is often attached to a particular pattern (for example, one must follow different 'stages'), which, above all in the emotional sphere of a celebration, can lead to counterfeit experiences.

There is always mention in connection with mystical experience of a core of experience which is experienced as absolute, which will begin to determine the whole of life aes a (new) basic inspiration. For the classical mystics, for example, this was 'the Word' or 'the Spirit' or 'Fire'; for the Pentecostals it is 'Jesus'. Pentecostalism itself is so orientated on Jesus that God sometimes threatens to become a 'forgotten Father', as one Pentecostal writer, the Anglican Thomas Smail, once put it.

The mystical experience is also characterized by the direct influence of the core of experience on the mystic's self. This implies a transformation, in every respect, into love. Pentecostals experience themselves as temples of the Spirit and confess, 'Christ dwells in me'. Taking part in the crucified and risen self of God in Christ, they 'die' to their false self and 'rise' with their true self in which they become a gift. The experience of a 'night' or 'wilderness' is an important aspect of the mystical experience and this is known as a term, above all also in the Pentecostal movement. I have often heard sermons and Bible studies in which the believers are aroused to follow Jesus who, after his experience of Word and Spirit by the Jordan, was driven into the bleak wilderness by the same Spirit to be tested. However, here at the same time there is a crucial difference from the mystic, a reason why the Pentecostal experience ultimately remains a pre-mystical experience. Pentecostals see the wilderness period above all as a time in which the behaviour of the believer is changed, not so much his or her being. The reason for this is the scholastic distinction between nature and supernature which is used in a simplistic way within Pentecostalism. This distinction goes back to Augustine's notion that God's grace, of which love is the supreme form, is in no way a part or possession of creatures. However, Pentecostalism derives from this the notion that the 'supernatural' God can be experienced, but always in competition with 'natural' humanity. God works through people as through neutral 'channels' (a favourite expression), and through 'supernatural' gifts puts them in a position to do things which lie outside their own capacities. In this thought there is little room for an authentic interplay between God and human beings. For Pentecostals God rushes as it were through people like a car which leaves the landscape otherwise untouched, whereas for mystics God is the nurseryman who devotedly works on the garden of their selves. In Pentecostalism attention is paid less to the inward transformation than to the external manifestations of the Spirit, which also explains its pragmatic and activistic approach.

Finally, the mystical experience works through in the crazy and paradoxical use of language and the behaviour of the believer. The existing words fall short of giving expression to the divine reality. Moreover mystics are often linguistic innovators. Pentecostals are not usually part of the most developed part of humanity. One looks among them in vain for a poet like John of the Cross or storytellers like the Hasidic masters. Many Pentecostals discovered for the first time in charismatic celebration that they have something to say. Their language is 'brought out' by fellow believers who expected a word of insight or a prophecy from them. But they also know the pressure to give expression to their experience of baptism with Word and Spirit. They do this in the play of the charismatic celebration but also in glossolalia, in which they give expression to what (certainly with a limited command of language) can never be expressed adequately: the love of God in Christ. In a sense glossolalia is the democratic counterpart of a talent for poetry.[56] Glossolalia does not use an existing vocabulary, but it is not gobbledegook either. It is a playful way of communicating, comparable with abstract art or music. Glossolalia is a purposeless, unformed expression of the self in Word and Spirit, unhindered by rules of language and codes of behaviour; it is an expression of a bond with God and other people which transcends barriers (of language). Edward Irving observed that the gift of tongues is also an implicit criticism of any language which tries to 'capture' God, an insight which, however, is usually lacking among present-day Pentecostals - another reason why they are often stuck in clichés. In addition to language, Steggink and Waaijman write, the behaviour of the mystic also breaks codes and tabus. So the mystic is often seen as a fool. I have already commented on the foolishness of Pentecostalism, but here I also want to mention the foolishness of a radical change of life. Some Pentecostals have broken off their study or their career to go into mission, to become a minister or evangelist, to go and live in a charismatic community, or to work among the homeless and poor – in short, to 'serve the Lord' utterly and always. For, as the Flemish mystic Ruysbroeck wrote, such a person feels 'the need ceaselessly to flow out into all who need him, for his riches consist in the living source of the Holy Spirit which one can never exhaust'.[57] Certainly in Pentecostalism concern over the result of one's own efforts often remains great, and conditions are attached to the service of others (the expectation is that these 'are converted', 'begin to speak in tongues' or begin to follow a particular ethical code). The reason for this lies in the fact that Pentecostals do not take the mystical way to the end, so that the heart of the false self, which is concerned for confirmation of itself, remains untouched.

(b) A partly trodden mystical way

The mystical experience is what Steggink and Waaijman call the 'beginning and principle' of the mystical way, which is not a straight way but more like a mountain path with its hairpin bends. As one gets higher, one keeps criss-crossing the same side of the mountain. In the constant interplay of breakthrough, core experience, immediacy and assimilation of the mystical experience, ever deeper layers of the self keep being transformed in love. The number of phases that can be distinguished on this way varies. Starting from the classic work by Evelyn Underhill, Steggink and Waaijman mention four phases (she distinguishes five) which keep recurring at a higher level.[58] These phases are conversion, illumination, the dark night and union.

1. In conversion one becomes unexpectedly aware of the presence of God. This is experienced as space, light and joy. It is preceded by a period of restless searching and unease. Everything seems to have become flat and dull. One is on the look-out for existence and the conviction grows that only something new, 'I know not what' (as John of the Cross put it), can give peace and happiness. Following the evangelicals, the Pentecostal movement calls this first phase rebirth. That is the right term, because here the transition from the old existence (according to the false self) to the new life (from the true self) is experienced decisively for the first time, so that one has the feeling of having become a new person. This experience is also sometimes called a rebirth in the New Testament. However, the Pentecostal movement is wrong when it usually sees this phase as quite detached from the baptism with Word and Spirit. This is the experiential dimension of faith, and conversion is the moment at which someone becomes aware of it for the first time. It is the beginning of a lifelong process in which the believer will still have to be converted many times, 'die' to the false self and be 'reborn' as the true self. For while the orientation of life is now different, the peace and happiness do not last. After the joy follows a period of struggle and new seeking in which a person becomes aware of his or her own inability to offer resistance to the compulsion of the false self. The need for 'power' to lead the new life increases. It is no new observation that many members of the established churches get stuck at this stage (if they ever get as far). The most important reason is that they have simply never been taught that the way with God goes further. Indeed, anyone who wants 'more' of God will often be accused by a church fixated on order of a lack of faith or wanting to seek support in an experience.[59] Moreover I have often heard loyal church members who came into contact with the Pentecostal movement or the charismatic renewal and discovered that the way with God indeed goes further, exclaim, 'Why wasn't I told this before?'

2. The new quest ends, often in a flash, in an experience of illumination. A new peace and joy fill the believer. The longing for prayer increases. The mystic energetically sets to work doing all kinds of things in the sphere of guidance, giving help and so on. The mystic takes a full part in everyday activities, but at the same time moves in inner converse with God, the great Beloved. Moreover in this

phases 'paranormal' (literally alongside the normal) gifts manifest themselves: the mystic knows what others are thinking, has visions, performs cures which cannot be explained by medicine, and feels the presence of angels or demons. This phase, in short, is entirely typical of Pentecostalism. In general Pentecostals are very active in mission, evangelization, personal aid and founding and running all kinds of organizations. Praise and joy is characteristic of their experience of faith, while there is also great emphasis on personal converse with God in prayer. And of course their gifts include words of knowledge and prophecy, glossolalia, gifts of healing and exorcism. On the basis of these and other charisms, which can be seen as heralds of the last phase (union), the participants have a contribution to make to the play of celebration. This phase of illumination is often regarded in Pentecostalism as *the* baptism with Word and Spirit, and has been aptly compared by Schoonenberg with falling in love.[60] Pentecostals are in love with God in Christ, and this gives the whole of reality a new glow and opens up unsuspected sources of happiness and joy in life among believers. Moreover the most popular Pentecostal hymns are often like love songs. One only has to look at one of their hymn books to see this. The hymns are not great poetry, but the experience of being in love which they express is no less authentic. Pentecostalists regard only this phase as the baptism with Word and Spirit and thus as the end of the way with God. Nevertheless, the mystics teach, this being in love calls for maturing to love (though they need not go wholly into this).

3. This maturing to perfect love takes place in the period of dryness which is called 'night' or 'wilderness'. As I have said, the Pentecostal movement above all knows this experience in which the false self is still further broken. But the transformation in love is usually not radical. The being in love which forms an ideal picture of the Beloved and clings to that remains dominant. They avoid the bitter cold, the despair and the abandonment of the dark night. Pentecostals do not learn to know God as the one who is eternally evasive and who escapes all images. As the first commandment says, no absolute images can and may be made of God. The night or wilderness is the time in which people are weaned from their own image of God, while they have not got far enough to be able to try and evaluate the God without images. The God who fulfils our needs has gone, and God as God is in himself has not yet been reached. Wilderness periods are therefore essentially for the maturing of the true self, because only

through them does one really learn to know and respect God (and thus one's fellow human beings) as the Other and thus love radically. 'O night which brings love with love', sings John of the Cross. God's rule, which is liberation in an exodus experience from the false self and its idols, means that all images are constantly broken. Only then can God really be loved and served as an end in himself and the true human self fully blossom in the gratuitous play of the sabbath. However, in Pentecostalism such 'night' experiences are too rapidly covered over with an appeal to the caring love of God the Father, positive exclamations ('Praise the Lord'), and comforting hymns. People do not last out the night, and so seem to get stuck in cliché images of a God who satisfies our needs. Above all within the charismatic renewal, however, the sense of discontent and unease is growing, a sense of 'standing still' and not being able to make more spiritual progress. When this experience is not suppressed as being negative or regarded as something from which one must be redeemed through prayer (as often happens) but is accepted with all its loneliness and confusion, it can lead to the discovery of the classical mystics' higher school of love.

4. In the last phase, anyone who is radically purged in the 'night' or 'wilderness' of his or her false self orientated on the 'I' experiences union with God. This is the real mystical experience. Any mediating picture of God has gone, and God as the core experience now works directly on the self of the mystic and breaks down all he or she has still held on to. A change of perspective takes place which leads to an 'active passiveness'. The initiative no longer lies with the mystic but with God: it is not that the mystic goes God's way but God's way goes with her; it is not the mystic who prays, but God who pray in him. It is like musicians who begin by studying a piece and are aware that they are the ones who are playing it, but find that at a later stage the music takes over, so that although they are playing it, they are caught up in it. So too mystics cease to be aware of their love for God but are carried along by God's love. They live radically from God without a sense of 'I': 'not I, but Christ dwells in me'. Here the false self of the mystic has disappeared; the self of the mystic has become perfectly true and transparent – in other words, one with God. There is no longer any fear of death, so that the mystic is ready to die a thousand times to the false self. The wound of love which God inflicts on the self is painful and sweet at the same time, for now one lives completely from the true self that is bound up with the self

of God in Christ. From this fullness the mystic returns to the world in order there, as God's covenant partner, to play his or her crazy game of self-forgetting goodness and open surrender in radical commitment.

But even this last phase is not the end of the mystical way. The mountain path keeps twisting in a new direction, illumination, night and union, in which constantly deeper levels of the self are liberated and transformed in love. This mystical experience is not typical of Pentecostalism (but that does not mean that some Pentecostals do not know it). Because the false self has not been broken radically enough in the 'night' or 'wilderness' from its tendency to ground and justify itself, Pentecostals generally do not get further than half-way up the first spiral on the mystical mountain path. The experience of faith remains too much what Levinas has called 'the prayer, piety and gratitude of the hungry stomach'. Pentecostalism is stuck at the phase of being in love, the illumination in which God comes to be consciously experienced by the believer. The individual generally remains in control and is therefore profoundly lonely. The moments of transportation and surrender which are experienced in celebration above all touch the emotional level, and only to a limited degree penetrate critically to the believer's self.

The conclusion is that the New Testament baptism with Christ's Word and Spirit corresponds with the mystical experience, but for Pentecostals generally it remains a pre-mystical experience. In addition to their defensive attitude and inadequate theology, it is also a fact that the mystics speak so inexplicitly about the Spirit that they are not very accessible to Pentecostals. It is remarkable that, on the other hand, theorists in the sphere of mysticism are so often negative about Pentecostalism. One of the few exceptions was the important Roman Catholic theologian Karl Rahner, who has described Pentecostalism as an 'everyday mysticism'.[61] It seems to me that specialist attention should be paid to the Pentecostal experience. In present-day Pentecostalism the dream of the great mystics that everyone should share in their experience seems nearer to realization than at any other moment in history.

Part Five: The Gifts of Grace

The Pentecostal movement and a large part of charismatic renewal regard the gifts of the Spirit as supernatural. They have little or nothing to do with ordinary human talents and nothing at all to do with so-called paranormal gifts (these are rejected as a demonic imitation). To use a well-known term of Barth's, the charisms in this view come 'vertically from above'. The sense, which is important in itself, that God's Word and Spirit are effective in our life thus leads to a reduction of the person concerned, who is simply a 'channel' of God's grace. I have already pointed out how much this approach hinders the process of personal formation (though the practice is often better than the doctrine). In general Pentecostalism regards only the gifts which in the New Testament are explicitly called charisms as gifts of the Spirit; moreover there is a concentration on the nine gifts of I Corinthians 12.8-11. Because these gifts function above all in celebration (Paul's argument in I Cor.12-14 is predominantly about worship), this has led to an underestimation of the dynamic of the Word and the Spirit in the political and social spheres and outside the church generally. A minority in Pentecostalism, aware of the limitations of the Western anthropological model (for example, exorcisms and glossolalia are a normal phenomenon in a number of non-Christian cultures in the Third World), rejects this mediaeval, scholastic division between nature and supernature. There is an emphasis on the fact that scripture does not know this division and that the gifts of the Spirit are aspects of human life which are hallowed and mobilized in the service of Christ.[1] Nor is there any agreement over the relationship between the gifts of the Spirit and the fruit of the Spirit (sanctification). Somtimes they are identified; however, others see no connection between them. The whole early Pentecostal movement regarded a sanctified life as a condition for the reception of the charisms. Catholic theologians in the charismatic renewal often still make the traditional distinction between gifts which make the recipient holy (*gratia gratum faciens*) and gifts which serve to put the recipient in a position to serve others (*gratia gratis data*). However, it is difficult to imagine how people who are transformed (sanctified) can be detached from their interaction with the neighbour and how, conversely, one person can really serve another without being shaped by so doing.

The confusion over the relationship between the charisms and sanctification is to be derived from the tendency of Pentecostalism to fixate itself on the 'outside' of the gifts of grace, a tendency which increases, the more unusual the gifts are. There is an investigation of glossolalic sounds or a prophetic word without asking what the common nucleus of these different expressions is that makes them a charism. However, the issue is not the external manifestations but God, as Bill Seymour already wrote at the beginning of our century.[2] Both also explain why the formally less unusual gifts like the charisms of service, instruction or guidance (Rom. 12.7-8) are usually neglected in Pentecostalism. At the same time the connection with baptism with Word and Spirit remains obscure.

In this part I want to demonstrate that a charism is a concrete expression of Christ's baptism with Word and Spirit. In it we are freed truly to encounter the other and thus God as the Other. This is the dynamic secret of the church as a charismatic community. Any encounter involves an interaction of giving and receiving in which we are reshaped as human beings and enriched ('built up'). This has consequences for our actions and life in the world.

I

Life by Grace (Faith) Alone

Until half way through our century the word charism barely occurred in European dictionaries. Even theologians within the charismatic renewal usually do not realize sufficiently how essential the gifts are for the New Testament view of Christian life. This is already evident from the fact that the word charism is derived from the Greek *charis* (grace), a fundamental concept in scripture.

(i) A power which justifies

For Paul, the terms 'grace', 'Spirit', and 'Word' are all closely connected. They denote the unmerited, liberating power of God in Christ, a power which inspires and determines the life of believers in the midst of their everyday existence.[3] Moreover this power is a clear experience.

So Paul can begin from the fact that the Galatians remember when they received the Spirit (Gal.3.2), and elsewhere see the grace of God as a verifiable event (II Cor.8.1). Moreover the letter to the Colossians (3.16) regards the indwelling of the Word of Christ as an almost tangible reality which among other things inspires people to teach in all wisdom and glossolalic song ('spiritual songs'). And the author of the letter to the Ephesians can argue for the greatness of God on the basis of the 'power which is at work in us' (3.20), which is already well known to his readers, a power which makes possible the charismatic unity in difference (4.1-16). Over against the intoxicating inspiration of wine he sets the equally concrete folly of being constantly filled with the Spirit which, like the indwelling Word of Colossians, inspires Christians to give praise in psalms, hymns, glossolalic song and a life of service to the other in awe of Christ (5.18-21). These experiences of God's grace are not alien to our human existence but make it come into its own even more. It is a matter of being aware of God's power in Christ's Word and Spirit, with and beneath the experiences of life which assure us of God's solidarity with us.[4] The baptism with Word and Spirit is another term for this experience, the radicalized power of God's grace.

The word charism means expression of grace, so that 'gift of grace' is the best translation. The term occurs only in the apostle Paul (apart from I Peter 4.10, but this is a passage which clearly betrays Paul's influence). He himself gives the word a new significance. We can really say this of no other term in his letters, so that already indicates the importance of charisms for his theology. He opens his letter to the Romans with the thematic statement that the gospel is 'the power of God for salvation to everyone who has faith' (1.16-17). Faith is the human side of God's grace; so this is a matter of surrender to God alone. The power of God's grace (i.e. of the Word and the Spirit) leads to a life in faith, which means freedom from the anxiety that drives us to pseudo-certainties (idols, see 1.18-32). God's covenant love is unconditional and therefore does not depend on any achievement or merit (being Jew or Greek). So people no longer need to justify their own existence, and come into their own as God's fellow players in union with creation: 'He who is justified by faith shall live'. According to scripture, those who are justified by faith can also do justice to others. In Hebrew the same word (*tsedaqa*) means both divine justification by grace and human justice. The *tsedaqa* of God and the liberation of human beings are therefore parallel terms (Isa.46.13).[5] According to Paul this new life stands in abrupt contrast to the life of the old Adam (the false self), through whose sin 'death ruled as king' (Rom.5.14). Death is the compulsive power behind the need to justify our existence, as a result of which even the Torah becomes an enslaving idol. In Jesus Christ, who was 'raised for our justification' (4.25), by contrast the new life has come in abundance; this is indicated by Paul in one sentence by the terms *charisma*, *charis* and *dorea* (gift, 5.15). These terms are in practice synonymous. This is confirmed in the next chapter, where the apostle, as the conclusion to an argument about the new way of life, writes: 'the charism of God is eternal life in Christ Jesus, our Lord' (6.23). The crucified and risen Lord is the primal charism, the source and measure of all charisms. These gifts of grace are concrete expressions of the new ('eternal') life which overcomes death. This is the life of God's kingdom, and therefore of the eternal sabbath play. Without gifts of grace there is no grace and no pledge of this new life.

In other words, in every gift of grace, as the one who baptizes with Word and Spirit Christ manifests his rule in a liberating exodus from the false self which justifies itself, to the life in grace of the true self. This plays the wise game of the totally other God. As Moltmann writes: 'The charismata of the Spirit are present wherever faith in God drives out the fears from life and whenever the hope of the resurrection overcomes the fear of death.'[6] And the exegete Ernst Käsemann concludes that Paul's remarks about the gifts of grace are the consequence of his central doctrine of justification by faith, and, conversely, indicate the enormous breadth of this doctrine.[7] So in practice Pentecostalism takes the line which was again laid down clearly by the Reformation with its 'faith alone, grace alone' (*sola fide, sola gratia*). The life of faith is expressed in numerous gifts of grace, moments in which one is liberated from the false self and the Torah is fulfilled in love.

This also emerges from Paul's introduction to the gifts of grace in I Corinthians 12, in which he directly contrasts these with the ecstatic expressions characteristic of the worship of idols in which the members of the community had been involved in the past (vv.1-3). The gifts of grace contrast with these idols that make people blind to their true selves and thus condemn them to a deadly existence (the word translated 'led astray' in fact denotes the dragging of sacrificial animals to the altar). The charisms make it possible to lead the new life in love which found its complete bodily expression in Jesus of Nazareth. Therefore the believer confesses through Word and Spirit that 'Jesus is Lord'. By contrast, the exclamation 'Cursed be Jesus' implies the Gnostic denial that God's Word and Spirit were fully revealed in the earthly Jesus (the Gnostics worshipped only a 'heavenly' Christ). This also meant a contempt for concrete life in love through the charisms (see also the selfishness at the Lord's table in 11.18-22; cf. I John 4.2-3).

(ii) Many gifts of grace, one significance

Paul, the New Testament author who has most to say about Christian life, gives preference to the word charism because it most clearly expresses his meaning, but he is not consistent here. As well as 'expression of grace' (*charisma*) he also uses 'expression of the Spirit' (*pneumatikon*), and we have already seen that he can also use a word like 'gift' (*dorea*). Yet other terms occur, above all service and work (I Cor.12.5-6), reflecting a diversity which is already characteristic of the use of the term charism itself.

For the use of this word is not limited to the well-known lists of gifts (I Cor.12.8-10, 28; Rom.12.6-8). Encouragement (Rom.1.11-12), an answer to prayer (II Cor.1.11) and celibacy (and, by implication, marriage, I Cor.7.7) are also called charisms by Paul. Furthermore the terms 'calling from God' and charism are closely connected (Rom.11.29), while the formula 'as God assigns to each in particular' typically ends up in gifts of grace (I Cor.12.11; Rom.12.3b; Eph.4.7). Moreover the appeal in I Cor.7.17 has a charismatic application: 'Let everyone live as the Lord has called him.'[8] Human life is always concrete and specific, and precisely in that can become a charism: as celibate or married, but also as circumcised or uncircumcised, as slave or as free (vv.17-24). The Jew who is justified by faith need not become a Greek, nor the Greek a Jew (see Rom.1.16). In their specific Jewishness or Greekness believers are called to become a gift, i.e. a concrete expression of God's grace in Christ. This also applies to being a man or a woman (Gal.3.26-28), being vegetarian or eating meat, out of piety observing particular days or regarding them as all alike (Rom.14.1-6). In short, each person can be a gift of grace in his or her unique identity and situation. So it is not the form that is essential for defining what a gift of grace is. This is simply the variable 'outside' of a charism. Even speaking in glossolalic sounds, prophecy and the exercising of a healing influence are general human possibilities which also occur outside Christianity in people with intuition. That they are unusual in our Western culture is still no reason for calling them supernatural, as Pentecostals often do. In fact in so doing they adopt the same rationalistic attitude that they in fact so fiercely dispute; the degree to which something is incomprehensible to our understanding is defined by its divine, 'supernatural' status. The understanding remains the measure of all things. However, the fact that a phenomenon is not unusual in a particular culture does not help to answer the question whether it is a gift of grace. This already emerges from Paul's summaries, which naturally put the charisms of readiness to help and give to guidance between the gifts of healing and glossolalia (I Cor.12.28). It is also worth noting that in this verse he can speak alternately of gifted people (prophets, teachers) and gifts. Ephesians 4.7-11 also interprets the 'gifts to men' as apostles, prophets, pastors and teachers. To have a gift is to be a gift. It is not *what* is given (which can be very different) but *the way in which* one gives that defines whether a gift of grace. As expressions of the liberating power of God's grace in Christ these charisms make possible a life of love. Here the bond of God with all men and women is realized. For the gifts realize the bond of community. So Paul can write that God does not break the covenant with Israel because the gifts of grace are irrevocable (Rom.11.29). And perhaps nothing is so unusual as this bond of love.[9]

(iii) Gift, surrender and task

Jurjen Beumer, the pastor of a base community, writes that between the gift (God's grace, expressed in teaching) and the task (a holy life) there must be the surrender of mysticism. If that is not the case, then faith can float loosely through the world without social relevance, or degenerate into a legalistic and cramped commitment.[10]

It is notable that large parts of the New Testament letters in which the charisms are discussed at length have this structure of gift-surrender-task. The gifts of grace are the hinge between God's gift and the human task. So in his letter to the Romans Paul begins with an extended discussion of God's grace in Christ which justifies both Jews and Greeks through faith (1-11). After that he goes into the charisms (12), to end with specific applications of the love which fulfils the Torah (12-15). This letter is the most systematic in construction, not least because Paul did not know the community in Rome personally. By contrast, the First Letter to the Corinthians is from beginning to end interspersed with references to problems in the community and is therefore much more a practical pastoral letter than a systematic sermon. But here too we find roughly the same structure as in the Letter to the Romans. His most important discussion about the gifts of grace in this letter (12) is preceded by instruction on God's gift of apostleship and the Lord's table (9-11), and followed by a call to love and its specific application in celebration (13-14). His argument about the resurrection body is an extension of this. In contrast to the Gnostics with their contempt for the world, here he wants to maintain the concrete, physical expression of life in the Spirit so that people will 'abound in the work of the Lord' (15.58). Finally we find the same construction in the letter to the Ephesians, which is influenced by Paul. This begins with a lofty argument about God's grace in Christ, realized in the community in which the dividing

wall between Jew and non-Jew is torn down (1-3); it is followed by
an account of the gifts (4.1-16), and ends with a call to the new way
of life in love (4-6). So the doctrine of grace comes to life in the
charism, while on the other hand the play of love is made possible by
the gift of grace. In a charism the gift of God's grace and the dedication
to the new life coincide, in surrender to the liberating lordship of
Christ. Therefore it is no wonder that in a church which denies its
charismatic essence and structure the doctrine and the practice can
so often drift so far apart.

Although the form seems so charismatic in glossolalic sounds,
prophetic expressions, or even the giving of body and goods, without
love it is not a gift of grace; it is 'nothing' (I Cor.1-3). In this hymn of
praise to love (perhaps an already existing text worked over by Paul),
the apostle sketches out as it were the person of Jesus in whom God's
Word and Spirit came to full expression (vv.4-7). The charisms are a
guarantee of the eternal sabbath play, moments in which the justifying
power of God's grace liberates us from our false self so that we can
live from our true self. When God's kingdom has finally dawned, the
gifts will be 'abolished' (v.8). This does not imply any relativizing of
the gifts of grace, as some commentators think. For Paul, God's grace
is all and everything. No, when God's Word and Spirit come to dwell
fully in creation and death is therefore definitively overcome, we
shall be redeemed from our false selves for good. Once God's kingdom
has fully come, we can no longer speak of separate gifts of grace.
Everything will then be of grace, and grace everything (God 'all in
all'). Far from relativizing the gifts of grace, here the apostle is
pointing to their fulfilment and consummation in the kingdom of
God. So in a gift of grace people now already experience something
of their eschatological identity – as disciples of Jesus who was already
utterly and completely the eschatological man. Now they only touch
incidentally and fragmentarily on our existence, which is dominated
by the false self. Now 'our knowledge is imperfect and our prophecy
is imperfect', but then 'I shall know fully as I myself am known' (vv.9,
12). Hence all gifts must also be tested to see whether they are real
charisms. We can only become a gift of grace 'according to the
measure of our faith' (Rom.12.3), which now is still incomplete. The
false self which justifies itself constantly grows over our true self.
Thus marriage can in reality be the dependence on a partner who is
served as an idol, and concern for the weak can be a confirmation of

one's own importance. Any charism is a conquest (an important conquest) of the false self by the true self.

Paul works out this tension between the true self and the false self above all in terms of a struggle between the Spirit and the flesh. After his concluding statement that the new life is God's charism in Christ (Rom.6.23), he goes on with a long argument about life according to the Spirit and life according to the 'flesh' (7-8). One common idea which is also popular in Pentecostalism is that Romans 7 is meant to describe the miserable life of the unbeliever (or that of Christians who are not yet baptized with the Spirit) and Romans 8 describes the conquering life of the believer (or of those received into the Pentecostal movement). However, it is much more probable that, as the later Augustine, Luther and Calvin thought, both chapters describe the same Christian experience.[11] Our weak, mortal 'flesh' (*sarx*) is ruled by the fear of death and is constantly concerned for self-preservation, as a result of which even the Torah becomes an idol, a 'law of sin and death' (8.2). Modern translations write 'sinful nature' here for flesh, but as a result of that the crucial aspect of mortality disappears. Only with the coming of Christ's Spirit (and Word) does one become aware of the true self and does a dispute break out with the false self, which as a slave is 'sold under sin' (7.14). This charismatic tension between the 'now already' of our eschatological identity in the Word and the Spirit (the true self) and the 'not yet' of our present 'flesh' ruled by anxiety (the false self) is generally seen as characteristic of Paul's thought. The division between the true and the false self goes right through the human 'I'. The Spirit bears witness that we are children of God, and thus to the unconditional righteousness of our existence (there is no way in which anyone can become a child by his or her own achievement). Thus the freedom of God's Spirit is distinct from the 'Spirit of slavery' which is characteristic of the sorry 'flesh' that justifies itself (8.15). Life in the Spirit contrasts with life in the 'flesh', as the orientation on the other in love contrasts with an obsession with one's own self-preservation in which the neighbour is made subordinate, or as 'fruit' contrasts with 'works' (Gal.5.13-26). The moments when the power of God's grace in our lives wins and we live from our true self thus manifest themselves as charisms. This is the unambiguous life which according to Tillich is expressed in different ways by the terms Spirit, kingdom of God, eternal life and love (*agape*).[12] That is also why for Paul the perfect life from the true self in the kingdom of God must involve a 'spiritual body' (I Cor. 15.44), a body which is thus free of the mortal 'flesh'.

The gifts of grace are relational terms in the New Testament. So they cannot be detached from the relationship with the other, and they encourage the 'building up' of the community (I Cor. 14.12). In my view Buber's thought about encounter can also shed light on the charismatic element.

2

The Encounter with God and Human Beings

Human beings are most deeply social beings. We live not only for others (as the Christian tradition emphasizes in a somewhat one-sided way) but also through others. That already emerges from the fact that every person is dependent for his or her biological existence on two other people, and we can only develop psychologically in interaction with our fellow human beings. Human beings are not their own autonomous creators, but flourish in an interplay which also involves nature. This essential bond between all things finds expression in scripture in God's covenant with 'every living creature on earth' (Gen.9.16), which will find its consummation in the eternal sabbath play. Now already the play of Word (identity) and Spirit (interplay with the other) makes authentic relations possible. But because this play is an expression of God's being, it means, as we shall see, that every authentic encounter is at the same time an encounter with God. Few have analysed the interweaving of the encounter with God with that with our fellow human beings (and with the non-human creation) as closely as Martin Buber in his book *I and Thou*, which appeared in 1923.[13] This work breathes the atmosphere of spiritual learning with sparks from Hasidic mysticism.

(i) An unbreakable bond

For Buber, the creation of true community is the main purpose of Jewish faith. Religion is not something which falls outside ordinary existence, but embraces the whole of life. He emphasizes that God is not 'obtainable separately'. The relationship with God coincides with the relationship with one's fellow human beings – although God always also transcends this.

This gives the encounter with God a concreteness which Pentecostalism, for all its emphasis on this, often misses. Here the much-used distinction between nature and supernature devalues the 'natural person' as a mediator of God. The 'supernatural' God works only 'through' (one should almost say 'despite') an individual, detached from his or her encounter with the neighbour. The giver prays for the working of the Spirit and is actively obedient to this, but only as an instrument or object of God's guidance. So human beings are neutral channels through which God's gifts slip into the community as through a pneumatic tube. Thus the charismatic experience begins in theory as a strictly individual event in which only secondarily does the other become the object of the gift. This results in an unequal relationship between the giver and the recipient. For Buber, however, the neighbour is wholly involved in the encounter with God from the beginning, in a mutual relationship of giving and receiving. The neighbour does not become an object (an 'it'), but mediates God to me as subject (as a 'you': the Buber translation uses the old-fashioned 'thou', but it makes for easier reading if we modernize it), so that I myself grow as a subject: 'through the "you" one becomes "I"'.[14] So this does not correspond with the theory of Pentecostalism, though it does with its practice. For although people do not often realize it, Pentecostals always give a gift, like a word of wisdom, an encouragement, a prophecy or other glossolalic prayer in response to the need of a fellow human being (which is felt intuitively). The gifts, and thus the experience of God, do not 'drop from the sky', but are mediated by the other. God is not an object that could be localized somewhere in space, or that one could count in the creation. In the Word and Spirit God is the Other who addresses us and encounters us in persons and things, and represents their deepest being – without our ever being able to get a grip on it.

In Buber's thought the social dimension of the encounter with God is given its full weight, so that his analysis can contribute to a correct understanding of the gifts of grace. Moreover we also find his view that the encounter with God and with fellow human beings are unbreakably connected in the New Testament, as in the judgment of the 'sheep' and the 'goats' (Matt.25.31-46). Anyone who has been a gift for the suffering other, whether this other was hungry, thirsty, a stranger, naked, sick or in prison, has been a gift for Christ himself. God in Christ is encountered in the neighbour.

This is the criterion of Jesus' judgment. Those who have had a concern for the other are worthy of the kingdom, for this will be the perfect continuation of the encounter with God who in Christ identifies himself with the neighbour. On the other hand those who have denied their fellow human beings in their suffering (the 'goats') have rejected God in Christ; so this is a choice in which they will be confirmed in the judgment: 'Depart from me' (v.41). The 'eternal fire' to which they go can best be understood as a purifying judgment which endures 'to the end' (*aionion*), that is to say, until there is nothing more to purify. In Palestine sheep and goats are separated only during the night, and brought together again as a flock the next day. It is also striking that here Christ does not identify with the giver but with the recipient of the gifts, a confirmation of my view that a charism is not one-sidedly about the giving of 'something' (the form) but about the whole event of encounter (a mutual giving and receiving in love). Finally, it is remarkable that 'all the nations' (v.32) and not just Christians are judged according to the same criterion: 'What you did for one of these least you did for me' (v.40). The decisive criterion is not correct doctrine but the right way of life. This relativizes not only the disputes about sound doctrine which also occur often in Pentecostalism, but also the differences between the churches, the religions, and even between believers and unbelievers. The atheist who loves her neighbour as herself and thus was a gift for her will be found worthy to enter the kingdom of God; by contrast the dogmatic Christian who did not regard those who thought differently as equals will first have to go through the night of purification as a 'goat'.

Jesus further says that love of God and love of neighbour need to be mentioned in the same breath (Luke 10.27). And the author of the First Letter of John even exclaims: 'Anyone who does not love his brother whom he has seen cannot love God whom he has not seen' (4.20).

(a) A playful interaction

Buber tells how as a child he made friends with a horse on his grandfather's estate.[15] Whenever he stroked the large animal and felt the warm body quiver under his hand, he was aware how much this being differed from himself. But the horse let him come close and became accustomed to his hand. However, one day the young

Buber became aware of his own stroking and realized how much pleasure this gave him. The contact went on in the same way as before, but something had changed. The horse no longer raised his head when he came near and Buber felt judged. The relationship in which he respected and encountered the horse in all his unique otherness as an end in itself (a 'you') had turned into an approach in which he now took something from the animal in order to satisfy his needs. The horse had thus become a means to an end, an object (an 'it'). This distinction between an I-it and an I-you relationship (which perhaps he made too strong) became fundamental for Buber. It corresponds to his distinction, mentioned earlier, between civiliz-ation, society, orientated on order and utility, and playful creative culture, community and religious feeling.

One can have both relations with nature and with the products of the arts and sciences. For example in the I-it relationship I see a tree or a painting as a useful valuable object that I can buy or sell. In the I-you relationship, however, these objects evoke wonder and become as it were the true subject, something 'over against' that touches one. The modern misuse of the environment and the exorbitant prices that are paid for some pictures show how much the I-it relationship now dominates society. However, the response of a tree or a painting in the I-you relationship remains below the threshold of language. Trees and paintings do not speak. Therefore the I-you relationship with fellow human beings is the main way to the encounter with God. Here a true dialogue is possible. In the I-you relationship the partners approach one another in playful interaction as an end in itself. Thus there comes into being a relationship which Waaijman terms 'mutually inward' (he coins a single Dutch word, *tegeninnig*).[16] Here the inwardness of the relationship is echoed, but also the dynamic 'towards each other' movement of the 'I' and the 'you'. The partners are active and passive at the same time: I receive the influence of the other on me (passive) and respond to the other by my being touched (active). This answer is my becoming a self: 'Through the "you" I become "I"'. This interaction creates a space between the two partners, a space which Buber calls love or also the Spirit. This corresponds to the Hebrew word for spirit (*ruach*), which is probably akin to the word for breadth or space (*rewach*). The Spirit is the sphere of play in which our identity (Word) blossoms. The whole of my existence is involved in this play: we are not looking for something in each other (like comfort, information or some talent or other).

The other gives himself wholly to me and I give myself wholly to the other. So the encounter has the power to make whole. Moved by the other who appears, I receive his or her influence to the depth of my being, as a result of which all separate actions (like thought, seeing and hearing) and perceptions (for example of pain and pleasure) are combined in me in one response to the other.[17] Thus the other is 'everything' for me, not in the sense that everything else is excluded; rather, this now appears in the light of my 'you'. Then I experience that everything is interconnected, and that gives meaning to my existence. Only the fox in Antoine de Saint-Exupéry's well-known book *The Little Prince* sees in the yellow cornfields the golden hair of the princess he loves, through which they become heavy with significance for him.

According to Buber, the relationship with God, the eternal 'You', is an extension of any I-you relationship. By the contact of any 'you' a breath of the eternal 'You' touches me. 'When a man loves a woman and brings her life to present realization in his, the "you" of her eyes shows him the radiance of the eternal "You".'[18] In this encounter with God I did not primarily receive 'something', like a religious feeling or the like, but a 'presence as power', I am touched and changed in my deepest self. I know that I am both dependent and free. The received 'presence as power' is a liberation and I cannot do other than express this in my unique identity and situation. This is my task and mission. It seems to me clear that Jesus, through the intense play of Word and Spirit in his life, was more than anyone else a 'you' for many – precisely also for those who felt used as an 'it' or rejected by the social order. In him they encountered God and knew that they were healed and liberated. At the same time they were given a mission, like the one who had once been possessed and who proclaimed throughout the city that Jesus had liberated him (Luke 8.39), or the Samaritan woman who told her fellow citizens that she had been accepted by him (John 4.28-30, 39).

(ii) The I-it relationship

So the I-it relationship is fundamentally different from the I-you relationship. Here there is no question of a playful interaction. The other is not an end in himself or herself but a means to an end and is objectivized and used. I want 'something' from the other, not his or her whole being. The drive to self-preservation has no interest in the unique 'you' but only in a useful part of the other. Whereas the 'I' of the I-you relationship is a person who is aware of being bound to others, the 'I' of the I-it relationship is an ego which is bent back on itself and opposes the other, of whom it wants to take possession. The first 'I' is wholly itself and says 'I am'; by contrast the second 'I' identifies itself with 'something' – like race, gender or nationality – and says 'I am this' or 'I am that'. The first 'I' is playful and dynamic; the second 'I' emphasizes his or her 'being such-and-such ' (Kierkegaard's lie of the character) and is static. The first 'I' encounters the other in the now which is always open and unpredictable; the second 'I' imprisons the other in a picture which it has formed from other experiences. So the neighbour is not really encountered, since the picture from the past stands as a screen between the two of them. Thus no justice is done to the other. As Max Frisch makes Julika say to Stiller in his novel *Stiller* (end of Book Two):

> 'So look at me,' said Julika. 'You've formed a picture of me that I'm well aware of, a finished and final picture, and that's that. You simply don't want to see me other than in that way – I'm well aware of that. There is good reason for the commandment "You shall not make any image". Any image is a sin. It's precisely the opposite of love, you see, what you're now doing with such words... If you love someone, then you leave all possibilities open for him and despite all the memories you're ready to be surprised, constantly to be surprised how different he is, how different and not just a finished and final picture like the one that you've now made of your Julika.'

The I of the I-it relationship brings to life rigid idols which do not do justice to reality. It does not help to replace these idols with God. That will only lead to making God, too, an object and thus an idol. So it is crucial for the I-it atittude to turn into an I-you relationship.

To make things quite clear, Buber emphasizes that the I-it relationship is not bad in itself and to a certain degree is even inevitable. The I-it relationship comes first in our natural needs and gives stability and a certain predictability to existence. Only 'it' can be organized in institutions, in a civilization, society and religion. Human beings cannot live constantly in this world in an I-you relationship. Nor do I want to give myself all the time. It can already be satisfying enough if I can respond to the wish of another for 'something' of myself – as someone to show the way, sell an article or repair something. Here already through my response in interaction with the other I become aware or him or her as *this* particular 'you' – a person with a known personality and with good or bad characteristics – as a result of which this person again becomes an 'it'. However, things go wrong if this I-it attitude and its organized world are made absolute. To remain meaningful and human it must always be crossed and renewed by the playful I-you order of God's world. 'Without "it" one cannot live. But he who lives with "it" alone, is not human.'[19] Buber's great concern was that the steadily extending modern it-world, the sphere of necessity and rigid order, threatens to overcome human beings – a danger that has in fact increased in our technocratic society. Because there is no real relationship, but only the I-it relationsihp in which the 'I' remains bent back on itself, the gulf between the 'I' and the other (the world and God) becomes ever greater. It is not the world but the it-world which separates human beings from God. The bending back of the 'I' on itself leads to an impossible situation in which the 'I' enters into a relationship with itself instead of with a 'you'. So the 'I' pursues itself endlessly in an empty circle. This can lead to all kinds of esoteric and pseudo-religious experiences which are no more than an empty echo of the 'I' (and even Pentecostalism is not free of this, any more than are trends like the New Age and the Goddess movement). Through the growing gaping void which comes into being between the 'I' and the world, the solitude and fear of the 'I' also increases, thus increasing the need for a conversion. This conversion involves a new orientation to the 'you' – and thus to the eternal 'You' – in which the 'I' is liberated. The new I-you relationship which comes into being is, as I have said, not permanent but afterwards remains latently present in the 'I', as an expectation of and orientation on the next 'I-you' encounter. This avoids the it-world being absolutized again. For through the sending of this 'I' a 'presence as power' streams into the world through which it is changed into the you-world of God (which I call the eternal play of the sabbath).

(a) The relationship with death

Like the Word, for Buber the Spirit expresses the living relationship with human beings and their world emanating from God, and the relationship of the latter to God. The Spirit is not enclosed in human

beings like the blood circulation, but is like the air between people
which is breathed by them. The Spirit is in the 'in-between' which
embraces 'I' and 'you', the playful interaction in which people grow
towards one another and encounter the eternal 'You' in the other.
Living in the Spirit is therefore an answer to the 'you'. In this answer
the Word expresses itself, but after that takes form in the I-it
relationship. In my concern for the 'you' (and thus for the eternal
'You') my existence is touched and liberated: in turning away from
the 'you' (which thus becomes an 'it') I return to the world and fulfil
my task and mission. For Buber this rhythm of turning towards
God (liberation) and turning towards the world (task) is the basic
movement of creation.[20]

The notion that the Spirit represents the 'inwardly mutual' relationship between the 'I' and the 'you' and the Word the 'I' that says 'you'
(or 'it') agrees with my view of the true self as consisting of an
interaction between the world (Spirit) and one's own identity (Word).
The Word defines my identity: the Spirit creates community with
others. As Word I exist; as Spirit I grow. However, whereas the true
self is a person and knows itself to be bound up with the world, it
often becomes overgrown with the false self which, as ego, is turned
back on itself and makes the world an object. The true self manifests
itself in the I-you relationship and the false self in the absolutized I-it
attitude. In the latter the dynamic Spirit as interaction with the world
is muted, and the Word as distinctive identity is rigidified so that it
becomes a 'being such-and-such'. The false self does not grow
towards the other but is fixed in a neurotic existence which is obsessed
with order. For Buber, the only liberation from this absolutized it-
attitude lies in conversion to the 'you', which is an interplay of God's
grace and human will.

The gift of grace, I think, represents precisely this element of
conversion. However, to understand it properly we need first to be
clear why it is that we absolutize the it-world. Buber does not go
explicitly into this, though he does mention the drive towards self-
preservation. This drive is by definition the instinct that self-loss,
i.e. death, will occur. Another Jewish philosopher, the Frenchman
Emmanuel Levinas, can help us further here. Whereas Buber felt akin
to the Hasidim, Levinas belongs to the Lithuanian Mitnagdim, the
'opponents' of Hasidism. Although his thought about the relationship
between God and man is akin to that of Buber (like the interweaving
of the encounter of God with the concrete encounter with the

neighbour) there are also essential differences. However, some of his notions about the relationship with death as a condition for the relationship with the neighbour can serve as a supplement to Buber.[21] Nothing, says Levinas, is experienced as being so radically different from ourselves as death. We have no control at all over death: it comes to us unpredictably as the great unknown. Death is not like us in any way and cannot be fitted into our existence. Moreover our relationship with our own death is a relationship with something that is really completely 'different'. Precisely in its intractability death is healthy, because it liberates us from being bent back on ourselves. On the other hand, however, it appears as disaster because death means the annihilation of our existence. The question then arises whether there is a relationship in which this liberating otherness can be experienced without it obliterating us. Levinas finds this in the relationship with the unique fellow human being whose face cannot in any way be reduced to myself.

Now it seems to me that a relationship which truly respects the otherness of the neighbour is by definition a relationship in which anxiety at death is overcome. Death is the great spell-breaker, because it says that we may not be. This compels us to justify ourselves, to achieve which the world (including our fellow human beings) is reduced to an 'it'. We experience the real 'other' of the neighbour as a denial of our own existence, a herald of the death over which we have no control at all. Therefore we harden this into an image that we can put in its proper place, an existing event over which we have power and which we can manipulate: 'he is like that'. The dread of death produces rigid idols which disguise the risky dynamic world and enable us to survey it. Hence, too, the stubbornness of the stereotyped images of people who in a specific social order are experienced as 'other', like blacks, gipsies, Jews and, in patriarchal societies, 'women'. 'They're like that': inferior, untrustworthy, stingy, saints or whores. People who are different are displaced to the it-world over which one has some control. This involves an objectification as a result of which in extreme situations, in which the threat of death increases, they can easily be made scapegoats. For the anxiety that their otherness evokes is essentially the same anxiety as that caused by a split in the ordering of the world (an economic depression or a war). Here we also experience the chill touch which reaches us here as an announcement of death. The solution of a social problem can then easily be translated into doing away with the 'other'. I have already indicated the role that ideologies play in this. Only if anxiety about death is overcome is real union possible. Then the neighbour can really be described as the 'other', as a 'you' who must be respected and encountered.

(iii) The charismatic encounter

We saw that those who are dominated by the fear of death try to justify themselves and reduce threatening reality to an inauthentic existence by means of idols. Necessity and order are emphasized at the cost of the possibilities which life offers. Such people cover themselves and cannot transcend themselves in an authentic gift. They respond to the expectations of society and simply give themselves to a certain degree to their work or care for their families. If they attempt anything in the sphere of art, the result is kitsch. Living in a lie, they cannot produce a work in which there is truth. The Czech Milan Kundera noted in his novel *The Unbearable Lightness of Being* (ch.6) that the inauthentic character of art and culture in atheistic, totalitarian states is caused by the fact that they have no answer to the problem of death. Kitsch, Kundera writes, serves as a screen to conceal death. By contrast, real artists are open to reality. Moreover they do not fit into the neurotic social order, which regards them as crazy (but when this craziness is imitated by pseudo-artists there is again a fossilization in the lies of the 'being like that'). True artists allow themselves to be touched by the craziness and fear of life and death and give themselves in works of art which express the truth and therefore have abiding value.[22] Whereas the producer of kitsch reduces reality to a self-confirming predictable 'it', the artist encounters the world boldly as a 'you' and becomes an authentic gift in a world who can liberate us from our reductive look at reality and evoke wonderment.

The German philosopher Hans-Georg Gadamer has pointed out that play (including the play of art) puts people in a position to surpass themselves to a degree that normally lies outside their reach. He compares this self-transcendence with an experience of God.[23] Where there is a transcending of the false self, in my view one can talk of a gift of grace. Love is the encounter with the other as a 'you', an encounter which transcends boundaries. This is the nature of a charism. Hence the discussions of gifts in the New Testament always end up in practical applications to live in love. Paul writes to the

Romans that he requires them to see 'that I may impart to you some charism to strengthen you, that is, that we may be mutually encouraged by each other's faith, both yours and mine' (1.11-12). And we saw that he calls the love which is now already possible through the gifts (though still incomplete) a knowing 'as I myself am known' (I Cor.13.12). So a gift of grace is not a situation in which one gives and the other receives, but is a mutual giving and receiving (a 'mutually inward' movement). As an expression of grace, the play of Word (identity) and Spirit (interaction) manifests itself in the encounter with the other, and thus with the Other. As part of the phase of illumination on the mystical way, the gifts are foretastes of union with God. For a charism is a moment when the other becomes transparent to God. This does not mean that the other as it were disappears to make room for God. It is like the difference between looking *at* a window and looking *through* a window (remember George Herbert!), in which the window itself remains of essential importance. In receiving the self of the other I receive the self of God in Christ which has overcome death. So the other becomes an encouraging 'paraclete', a 'Christ' for me. For this encounter with the eternal 'You' gives me courage to go through the 'school of dread' and thus to die to the false self that escapes into a rigid it-world and remains bent back on itself. This is a liberating event in which my true self, in the Word and Spirit, can encounter the other in a 'mutually inward' movement as a 'you'. This ecstasy (*ex-stasis*, literally standing outside) in which people go outside themselves to God in the other is characteristic not only of true humanity but also of the charismatic movement. Because in Pentecostal thought the experience of God is usually detached from the neighbour, however, this ecstatic movement is not directed to the concrete other and disappears 'into the blue', so that dialogue never gets going. In a gift of grace one thus loses the false self in order to gain the true self. Living from the true self *is* the conquest of the false self by knowing in the encounter with the other/Other that one is justified 'for nothing'. This is splendidly expressed in Luke's story about the road to Emmaus (Luke 24.13-35) in which he sums up the experience of the early community with the Lord. In the encounter of two disciples their anxiety and despair is overcome because they experience the risen Christ in Word and Spirit: 'Did not our hearts burn within us when he spoke with us on the way and revealed the Scripture to us' (v.32). In this charismatic community (see also Acts 2.43-47) the truth of the preaching of the apostles is experienced that 'the Lord is risen' (vv.34-35).

So such a charismatic moment does not seem to drop from the sky. It is a gradual event. The moment when the other becomes a 'you' instead of an 'it' *is* the liberation from my false self in the encounter with God in Christ as the eternal 'you'. In the playful action between 'I' and 'you' we give ourselves wholly to each other. Because this receiving of the other is thus at the same time the receiving of God in Christ, I experience that I am a temple of the Spirit: 'Christ lives in me'. On the other hand, in my turn I myself am received by the other/Other and experience that I am 'in the Spirit' or 'in Christ'. We are touched in our deepest being, an integrating event which is experienced in Pentecostalism as healing. For anxiety about the body and the feeling of vulnerability closely associated with it that makes for pain and death is overcome, something that the holistic 'Third World' spirituality makes possible. So people grow towards one another. In other words, they become a gift for one another, and thus a gift for God and the world. It is now clear why in our individualized age – which is therefore poor in relationships – people experience God as far away or lapse into all kinds of subjective illusions like esoteric phenomena. Moreover, the rise of the charismatic renewal in our 'postmodern' Western world can also be explained by the fact that there is no all-embracing binding ideology in which people can encounter and know one another. The one world has fallen apart into all kinds of partial worlds with their own language and own forms of meaning. This means that people have less community; they have become more 'the other' and thus it is more difficult for them to reach one another. This increases the need for the power of encounter (the charism). In this sense too the charismatic renewal is a new Pentecost event in which the boundaries between people in their separate partial worlds are broken down.

The charismatic experience of union, of unity in difference, corresponds with the two poles in the mystical experience: union with God (and creation) and the acute sense of being encountered by the totally Other. In a charism the otherness of the neighbour is experienced at the same time as a judgment and as a gift. As a judgment, because it painfully purifies me from my false self which seeks to make the other of my neighbour innocuous by incorporating it. The unique 'you' is thus reduced to a copy of myself, which explains the boredom so characteristic of inauthentic existence.

Everywhere I meet only myself. Knowledge of the truth and conversion always go together. In a gift of grace the unique 'you' is then experienced as a gift, a source of joy and enjoyment. This is by definition other than myself and therefore always surprising, fresh and new. Levinas emphasizes that this healing is essential for human beings, a view that we also already encounter in John of the Cross. For him the Spirit, as the 'living flame of love' scorches our self-directed way.[24] There is no other way of becoming open to the other – and thus to God), because in any conscious attempt to achieve this in our own strength (as in asceticism) we still remain preoccupied with ourselves. This stripping away of our egocentric attitude is painful but at the same time a 'sweet' wound. For the deeper the wound becomes, in other words the more clearly the neighbour really becomes 'the other' for me, the more I learn to know myself as the other. In other words, the more I die in the firestorm of Christ's Word and Spirit to the 'practice of the old life' in which everything was focussed on the satisfaction of my own needs (you must 'be broken', says the Pentecostal movement), the more I can enjoy the 'sweet-smelling plants and flowers' of the other who is my neighbour. The charism is the 'power in weakness' of which Paul is so fond of boasting. Any charismatic encounter is an exodus from my own, self-confirming presuppositions and thus literally becomes a 'revelation' (See I Cor.12.7). Herein lies the source of the joy which is so characteristic of Pentecostalism. The gifts of grace put people in a position to receive in wonderment the totally other in the neighbour, and thus in Christ. In the unique 'you' I encounter the eternal 'You' who is the foundation of originality and wonderment. However, where the initial power of the gifts of the Spirit diminishes in Pentecostalism through a flight into order, an attempt is often made to experience this joy again in a forced way. Few things are at the same time so sad and so repugnant as such a happy-clappy attitude. Here, too, the only way out is a conversion to the 'you' which begins with the silencing of any activism and of all attempts at self-justification. Even the charismatic renewal must constantly be renewed.

In this total acceptance of the other I can discover in him or her feelings and thoughts of which he or she was hardly, if at all, aware. It is no chance that the Hebrew word for love (*yada*) also means know. The liberation of anxiety in a charism opens us up to the other as the other is in herself or himself. We do not filter the 'otherness'

out of the other. And because we are redeemed from anxious, rational
control over our feelings and bodies, 'paranormal' gifts can occur.
So my knowledge of the other can, for example, lead to sympathetic
prayer or healing, the expression of an insight into a suppressed
traumatic experience (word of knowledge), or the indication of a
possible direction to take (prophecy). This is my answer, which I give
to the other with my whole being. In the gifts of grace, gift (God's
grace in Christ's Word and Spirit, mediated through the other who
becomes a 'you') and task (my answer to the 'you') are combined in
my surrender to the other/Other. Both I and the other are 'built up'
through the encounter and receive a presence as power which seeks
to work itself out in our unique identity and place in the world. So
this involves a transformation. We also find this in Pentecostalism,
with its call to serve 'as before the Lord' (though this often has a
moralistic content) and accent on sanctification and mission. At any
time, in a new charismatic moment, the I-it relationship can be
renewed to become an I-you relationship. However, we have no
control over this, although prayer, meditation and the liturgy generally help us to stop our constantly wandering thoughts and become
open to the presence of the other/Other in the now. Pentecostals often
live in the prayerful expectation that the charisms will function in
their existence. The life in faith can find expression in any moment
in a gift of grace, which can renew the prevailing order critically. ·
Thus the baptism with Word and Spirit that orientated the North
American Holiness movement was concerned with the other as a
unique 'I' and inspired a renewal from the oppressive it-world in
which slavery and child labour were abolished, and blacks and
women could become preachers and get the vote. As in present-day
Pentecostalism, women play a prominent role in this movement. This
perhaps confirms the view of Mary Grey that above all women are
open to God as the source of liberating union with all human beings.[25]

(a) Partial gifts of grace

The term charism as a source of social and political renewal has
become known above all through the sociologist Max Weber, who
took it via the theologian Rudolf Sohm from the apostle Paul. Unlike
bureaucratic or patriarchal authorities, 'charismatic' leaders have a
spontanous authority that inspires people and motivates them to
follow. They are regarded by the people as liberators. Jesus was

regarded as such a leader, and so were Moses and the judges from the First Testament, as were Gandhi, Martin Luther King and John Paul II. They also include people whom we could call partially charismatic, like Mao and Castro. Buber (without using the term) mentioned Napoleon as an example.[26] These last leaders were a 'you' for masses of people, but conversely they regarded their supporters as an 'it'. They reduced people to a means of achieving their end. Their original creative élan fossilized into a new order of slavery. This was inevitable because as a result of the lack of interaction with the 'you' of their supporters they themselves fossilized into the lie of a 'being such-and-such'. On the other hand, for those who followed them, the fascinating splendour in their leader changed from the eternal 'You' to the gold plating of an idol. The original charism gave place to disillusioning slavery to a dictator. Only in leaders who remain true to their calling does the charism come completely into its own. Their leadership remains creative and makes people flourish. This happens because they themslves are constantly being formed, for they continue to see and encounter their followers as a 'you'. Both this and the partial form of charismatic leadership can be found in Pentecostalism among presidents, evangelists, television preachers and people with a great talent for healing.

I am aware that in Pentecostal thought the encounter with God is detached from relations with the neighbour. This heightens the danger that something which is seen as an experience of God is in reality no more than an echo of a person's own 'I'. Pentecostals are well aware that not a few expressions among their members are 'fleshly', in other word eruptions of the false self. Their attempts to disitnguish these from the authentic gifts of grace by testing them by all kinds of criteria including the purity of the doctrine or way of life of the giver do not get to the heart of the problem. This only happens when the relationship with God is thought of consistently with the relationship with the neighbour. A charismatic moment *is* a concrete I-you relationship in which the true self emerges from the false self that absolutizes the it-attitude. Moreover an authentic gift of grace encourages the building up of those involved. A second problem connected with this is that Pentecostals are often fixated on a particular experience, on 'something' of the neighbour or God. This prevents an encounter with the 'you'.[27] Thus for example the other is reduced to his or her problem, to a 'being such-and-such'; the other is 'the sick person', 'the one who is emotionally hurt' or 'the seeker'. So people do not get into a relationship with the unique other, but with an aspect of the neighbour that he or she has in common with many others. There are numerous sick, traumatized people or seekers. This fixation on one aspect makes the other an object of help. In itself this can be legitimate, although for example in the medical world the limitations of this approach are becoming increasingly clear. But giving help is still no charism, and the community is not a hospital. Where this happens in Pentecostalism, people are still constantly trapped in the strategy of the false self that cannot bear the 'otherness' of the other and therefore reduces him or her to a general aspect, 'to which something must be done'. As the relationship with the neighbour is interwoven with that with God, it is not surprising that the encounter with God is similarly reduced to a particular aspect or specific experience. We have seen that above all the Pentecostal movement has the tendency to fix the experience of God in a particular pattern. For example, the reception of the baptism with Word and Spirit must be accompanied by the utterance of glossolalic sounds. So the charism does not really flourish as the sphere in which one encounters the other as 'you' and thus God as the eternal 'You'. The neighbour remains an 'it' which is in need and God an 'it' which satisfies needs. For these reasons the classical mystics were already sometimes critical of the gifts of grace and saw them as an obstacle to arriving at a real encounter ('union'). However, the cause of this does not lie in the charism itself but in the fact that this cannot completely come out (above all also because the gifts of grace are never adequately integrated into theological thought and church life). Just as the baptism with Word and Spirit in Pentecostalism generally stops at the phase of illumination and remains a pre-mystical experience, so the charism mostly remains a partial gift of grace. The conversion is not radical enough, so that the false self and thus the ordering it-world continue to be influential.

Nevertheless, the gifts of grace often still function perfectly in Pentecostalism to bring about a revolutionary acceptance of the fellow human being who is 'other'. This explains why people denied by the social order often make an equal contribution to the celebration. We have seen that this also applied to other charismatic currents in the past, beginning with the first Christian communities. Without the gifts of grace it is also impossible to explain how the present-day charismatic renewal could come about, with a spontaneous ecumenical élan without precedent in church history. Here the one who is 'other' in respect of the church is encountered as an equal. That the radical power of encounter of the gifts of grace does not come wholly to bear is, however, evident from the fact that the often painful ecclesiastical and theological differences are seldom considered explicitly. Difficult conflicts are avoided in a sub-culture of 'love one another'. And in the Pentecostal movement, while women may make an equal contribution to the meeting, this contribution is in theory seen apart from their otherness as women (the gift is 'something' that they give, not their unique self) so that in practice their subordination is maintained.

(b) A creative process

It is perhaps not superflous to emphasize once again that there is a legitimate place in our world for 'what belongs to who' relations, practical transactions, in short the giving and receiving of something. Without this, society would not function. The only problem is that our humanity threatens to languish under the uncontrolled growth of these it-relations orientated on utility. To repeat an earlier quotation from Buber: 'Anyone who lives only by "it" is not human.'

I now want to sum up my findings on the charisms with the help of a model provided by the practical theologian Jaap Firet.[28] In it he compares the workings of the gifts of grace with the phases in a creative process.

1. The preparatory phase. In the creative process here one comes up against the problem that requires a solution. From the charismatic perspective this is the confrontation with the otherness of the neighbour – quite often in the form of a specific need. This provokes the dread of death (the 'other' *par excellence*), so that the false self fixes this otherness into a picture; the other is 'such and such'. The neighbour remains an 'it' and I concentrate on something of him or her that is useful for me, something that I can use in the struggle to justify my own existence. I see the other as someone who can make a contribution to my programme, or as the object of the help I give. I cannot separate myself from my false self which fossilizes my identity (Word) and smothers my interaction with the other (Spirit).

2. The phase of incubation. In this stage (which is not always present), there is detachment from the problem, although people unconsciously continue to brood until a solution is found. This process is furthered by the charismatic celebration, which stimulates

the play of Word and Spirit of the true self. Morover, the answer to the 'you' is often given in the context of a celebration. But here we are already in the next phase.

3. The phase of illumination. This is the moment of inspiration: the penny drops, the solution is found. From being a threat, the otherness of the neighbour becomes a 'you' and is transparent to God, the eternal 'You'. In the self of the other I receive Christ's self that overcomes death in Word and Spirit, so that in one and the same movement I experience 'that Christ dwells in me', take courage to go through the 'school of anxiety' and depart from the false self in a playful interaction with the other. For me, this is an end in itself. I allow myself to be touched by the other, and as one who has been touched give myself to the other. My self-giving can take many forms, like a prophecy, a form of ministry or support, or an empathetic prayer. But the nucleus is always my true self, which pours itself out in the play of Word and Spirit to the other, who on the other hand wholly gives himself or herself to me. This results in the reception of a 'presence as power', a transformation that will be worked out in the world.

4. The phase of verification. In the creative process here the solution of the problem is tested. In his extensive study of the grace and liberation of God in Jesus, Schillebeeckx concludes that this amounts to losing oneself in others, and within this 'conversion' also having a structural effect on peace and justice for humankind.[29] So the question is: have I given myself to the other in a liberating and healing encounter? If not, then my gift was not a gift of grace, since true freedom is an expression of grace. Then I remain imprisoned (as probably does the other) in my anxiety and drive towards self-preservation, and basically untouched. In that case the gift was not really for the 'upbuilding' of the church as the body of Christ. Nor was any power received for mission to the world, to renew the static order through the crazy sabbath play of God's kingdom.

An important cause of the churches' orientation on order lies in the increasing isolation of the ministers. As a result of this, the possibility of a charismatic encounter between them and the 'laity' is often limited, as a result of which the ministers become rigid (and are isolated). The rise of Pentecostalism has shed new light on the nature of the church as a charismatic community.

3

The Church as the Body of Christ

Men and women are beings concerned for community. As Aristotle put it in the classic view, we call the attempt to form community politics. The practice of politics may have its origin in the struggle for existence, but in addition to that it aims above all to further the good life. This is a life which is as far as possible free from pressing need and limiting anxiety. Now the New Testament depicts the community of Christ as the politically ideal community. For scripture, everything that blocks our relationship with God and our fellow human beings is sin, since it damages God's covenant with all men and women. The experience of Christ's Word and Spirit represents a real liberation from this.

(i) Unity in difference

The church is a consistently charismatic community: 'Through one Spirit we are all baptized into one body, whether Jew, Greek, slave or free' (I Cor.12.13). The baptism with Word and Spirit makes human beings with all their ethical, social and sexual differences gifts of grace, and so reconciles them with one another. They need not deny their own identity and situation in life, as the social order with its bias towards uniformity and predictability often requires, but are confirmed and purified in this in the charismatic encounter with one another. In this way countless people belonging to the nameless poor masses of the Third World or to the anonymous mass of our Western, reified consumer society find a new sense of their own worth in Pentecostalism. They are 'built up'; 'becoming I, I say you'. In the sphere of encounter of the charism they know that they are 'seen' in the other by God who unconditionally accepts them (by grace) in their unique identity. Human differences which are usually threatening and therefore are denied or suppressed by a Babylonian order thus lead to a community which consists of a dynamic unity in difference. Only the common experience of grace in and through the gifts makes what Mary Grey calls this 'redemptive mutuality' possible. Because the gifts realize God's covenant in union with all men and women, in a daring metaphor Paul can call the charismatic community the body of Christ (Rom.12.5: I Cor.12.12-17). Just as a body consists of a dynamic whole made up of many different members, all of which are necessary, so the community is an interplay of many different but equal gifts of grace. Indeed the weakest members – the people who have least to give – are even treated 'with greater honour' (I Cor.12.22-25). For the poor, the handicapped, the unemployed and others who have been cast aside by society have a power in their weakness to evoke gifts. Through their need they stimulate the functioning of giving and thus the encounter with God in Christ, so that the community is enriched. 'What you have done for one of the least of these you have done for me' (Matt.25.40). Moreover it is no wonder that precisely this category of people is markedly present in Pentecostalism – the wisdom of God but foolishness as far as the world is concerned.

By the expression 'body of Christ' Paul also means very concretely that the believers partake in the life of the crucified and risen Lord.[30] In the charismatic encounter they receive Christ's Word and Spirit, through which they 'die' to their false self and 'rise' to the new life from the true self. Only in this way is a community of unity in difference possible and can the church be the continuation of the mission of Christ in the world, in which the Word and the Spirit already perfectly embody the eternal sabbath play. So in the letter to the Ephesians Christ is seen as the head of his body, the church (1.22-23).[31] The background to this is the Median thought of this time in which the head is regarded as the source of a dynamic which fills the body with its power and sets in motion. So the 'fullness' of Christ's Word and Spirit fills the community, and this is the way in which God 'perfects all in all' – in other words is on the way towards indwelling the whole creation. The community is simply that part of the world which already feels liberated through God's rule in Christ. For the letter to the Ephesians, too, this liberation is manifested in the play of the gifts of grace (4.1-16), through which the differences between people, like Jew and Greek, does not bring any division but an enrichment (2.11-3.1). So through its sabbath play the community constantly criticizes and renews the fossilized it-world and makes known the 'manifold wisdom of God' (3.10) to it. Without charisms the church cannot be a body of Christ. Charisms are more fundamental to the church than the ministries or sacraments.[32] I have already observed that in a society like ours which is poor in relationships God is by definition experienced as absent (Buber's 'darkening of God'). Today, therefore, the awareness and experience of the church as charismatic community seems to be the most relevant form of evangelization. The community experience of the Pentecostals in any case to a large extent explains their effectiveness.

From a survey of church history it emerges that the church has constantly denied its charismatic call and adapted itself to the order of the it-world. Think, for example, how much the unique contribution of blacks, women and homosexuals is systematically rejected, a situation which can change only if the charismatic identity and structure of the church is taken seriously again. In the preface to his Schmalkald Articles of 1537 Luther wrote that the church is provided by God's grace with the pure Word and the right use of the sacraments and with 'the granting of all kinds of callings and states and just works'. The last clauses still echo the importance of the gifts of grace through which believers can manifest the new life in church and world. However, for fear of the Spirit movements of his time Luther drastically limited this 'priesthood of all believers'. In an extreme bias towards order the ministry took all important tasks in the church to itself, reducing the believers to onlookers. So Calvin was content with describing the church in terms of the objective word and the sacraments. The community itself is completely absent from this definition, which is still always orientated on the priesthood. Up to the Second Vatican Council in the 1960s it was not really important for the Roman Catholic mass whether believers were present or not. The eucharist was not a communal meal but a bloodless offering of the cross performed on the altar by a priest who stood with his back to the believers and spoke a language (Latin) which most people did not understand. Only in the Second Vatican Council's text *Lumen Gentium* are the believers recognized as 'people of God', although (in contrast to the New Testament) they are still qualitatively distinguished from the priest. Furthermore the Decree on the Lay Apostolate emphasizes the right of all believers to use their charisms 'for the good of humankind and for the building up of the church'. However, the results of this return to the sources of scripture are not laid down in church order, so that in practice the charismatic interplay did not emerge much in the Roman Catholic Church. Here a change came about only when some years later the charismatic renewal and other base movements came into being.

(ii) Celebration and the world

The German theologian Ernst Käsemann has shown that Paul's doctrine of the gifts of grace is the church counterpart to his doctrine of justification by faith.[33] Moreover the development of an order of ministry in which all kinds of conditions are imposed on those who perform certain tasks in the community (from being male to possessing the right diploma) went hand in hand with the disappearance of the apostolic doctrine of justification. Nothing is so revolutionary and radical as God's grace, which attacks the roots of our selfishness, the oppression of the other and passive acceptance of this, by overcoming our fear of death in Christ's Word and Spirit. With the dimming of the sense of justification through faith/grace alone (the baptism with Word and Spirit) the charisms also disappear as expressions of grace and thus the nature of the church as a guarantee of the eternal play of the sabbath. As I described it earlier, this play becomes visible above all in the charismatic celebration on a useless Sunday.

The present-day charismatic celebration is very similar to the early Christian meeting described in I Corinthians 14.[34] There Paul gives some rules of the game, so that everyone present can in principle make a contribution. Loud talk in glossolalic sounds which are not interpreted can be disruptive for others. They cannot understand it, so do not say 'amen', and thus they are left out. Those who want to speak a prophetic word must do so in a well-mannered way, one after another, otherwise they cannot be followed. The same goes for those who want to read out or sing a psalm or to shed light on a biblical text. The rules of the game make it possible to improvise and for all present to contribute. If an outsider enters, 'all can prophesy' (presumably one after the other). As a result he is 'seen' (met) by different members of the community. They become a prophetic gift for the outsider through which he comes to know both himself and God: 'then he is convicted by all, he is called to account by all, the secrets of his heart are disclosed; and so, falling on his face, he will worship God and declare that God is really among you' (vv.24-25). His false self is unmasked and overcome and his true self blossoms in the encounter with the 'you' – and thus with the 'You'. In line with his argument (the importance of rules of the game in the celebration), Paul here calls only the members of the community gifts, but probably they themselves will also be drawn into this 'mutually inward' encounter by the outsider. Just before this Paul has already said that it is a matter of mutual knowledge (13.12). Very much in this style, Paul ends his argument about the rules of the game (14.34-36 is probably a later addition) by saying that the nature of the celebration must correspond to the character of God himself: 'God is not a God of disorder but of peace' (v.33). He does not write that God is a God of order, as most churches, given the character of their ministries, seem to think. For the apostle it is not order, but the order of the game that is the alternative to disorder. God's being finds expression in the creative play of Word and Spirit that is first revealed to the world in Christ and then in the charismatic community. This is the 'game of peace' in which men and women come into their own in their uniqueness. Only the order of the game resonates with God's own being.

Because those who participate in the charismatic celebration deliberately want to live by faith and to encounter God and one another, the gifts of grace are most clearly expressed here. However, they are certainly not limited to the celebration, though there is a greater orientation on the charism and an expectation of it there. The liberation theologian José Bonino rightly warns against making the critical function of the liturgy an ideology so that it remains abstract, at the expense of the concrete expression of God's liberation in the world.[35] The gifts are aimed at filling the whole creation with God's presence in Christ's Word and Spirit (Eph.1.23). Buber already emphasized that the religious dimension is not limited to the sabbath or to the synagogue or church. The sabbath is experienced every day, at different times on one day, whenever the divine realizes itself in the 'mutually inward'movement between people. This corresponds to Paul's view of the charisms. In the gifts of grace the gift of God's grace and the task of love combine in surrender to the other/Other, and this is not limited to church life. In Romans 12.1-8 Paul calls this our 'spiritual service'.[36] Through Christ's Word and Spirit the body becomes a temple of God. The body makes possible the play of the encounter with the other and with the world. Moreover with an 'appeal to the grace of God' he urges the Romans to give their bodies as a 'living sacrifice, holy and well-pleasing to God' (v.1). In 'temple language' he thus encourages them to make their physical life a daily liturgy through the charisms (vv.4-11). For the revolutionary power of God's grace has also abolished the division between the holy and the worldly, between the sabbath (or Sunday) and the working week. Since the death and resurrection of Christ, the presence of God can be experienced in any charismatic encounter with the neighbour. No longer is this limited to specific times and places, like temple worship in Jerusalem. This means a sanctification of the world which is focussed on the eternal play of the sabbath. It is no coincidence that this passage is preceded by a doxology which celebrates a variation of 'God all in all' (11.36). Life in faith (from grace) implies the expectation that people can at any moment, at any place, become a gift of grace. This expectation makes people different from the rigid order of this world with its anxious, rational grasp on life and therefore represents a 'renewal of thought' (v.2).

(a) Charismatic ethics

This renewed thought, Paul concludes, can discern and recognize (*dokimazein*) God's will. The word he uses denotes the spontaneous capacity to make a correct (ethical) decision in any concrete situation. The believer does not follow one moral law or another slavishly, but 'walks in the Spirit'. At every step he or she knows what the will of God is.[37] Reality is too great and too multicoloured to be capable of being summed up in absolute moral laws. Any attempt at this results in a caricature, a lie which is then served as an idol. So one can ask how far the absolute prohibition by some churches of the use of contraceptives at a time of Aids still indicates a sense of reality. Such a legalistic ethic reduces not only reality but also its members to objects who become slaves of an alienating law outside. In contrast to love, a law can never motivate even its most ardent adherents wholly from within. Therefore the Torah is fulfilled only in love (Rom.12.8-10), and the commandments and even Paul's instructions (12.9-14.23) serve as what Käsemann calls 'navigation lights'. Sometimes the commandment must be broken out of love in a broken world. Then the choice of the least evil is the only right solution (though it still remains evil). Thus in Nazi Germany Dietrich Bonhoeffer, initially a pacifist preacher, took part in the plot to murder Hitler, which meant that he was ready to transgress ths commandment not to kill. Scripture also knows similar situations. Rahab denies to their pursuers that she has a group of Jewish spies in her house, a lie for which she is praised in the New Testament as a heroine of faith (Josh.2.1-6; Heb.11.31). Thus one could give many examples of situations in which the commandment has to be transgressed for the sake of love and righteousness. This makes the taking of decisions a risky business which calls for courage to face the possibility of making mistakes, a reason why those who want to justify themselves go along with the 'safe' law.

However, Paul rejects this as conformity to the order of this world and points the way to a playful atittude to life in which, in interaction with the ethical demand and the concrete situation which is always new, choices must constantly be made. This is possible only through the charisms, experiences which open people up and in which those involved are really encountered and known in their situation. Thus in the book of Acts new times of 'being filled' with Christ's Word and Spirit at critical moments put the disciples in a position to have charismatic encounters in which they see through the intentions of the Sanhedrin (4.8-12) and unmask those who threaten them (13.52). This accords with Jesus's promise that in such situations his disciples need not be anxious about what to say, because at the decisive moment the Spirit will support them (Mark 13.11). Liberated from our false self in the charism, we can receive the 'other' of the neighbour without this being distorted by our anxious prejudices and our legalistic thought. Indeed we intuitively begin to understand others better than they understand themselves (a process that Schleier-macher called 'divination'). So the Word and Spirit, as the Paraclete of the Gospel of John, lead us 'into all truth', and in the concrete situation we can discern 'what is the good, well pleasing and perfect will of God'.[38] For the early desert fathers this capacity to discern was the basis of all the virtues. However, Paul admonishes his readers (with a reference to God's grace) to be modest here (Rom.12.3). A charism is always *my* gift of grace 'to the degree of faith' that I have, so that I can never be absolute in what I say. My finitude means that I need to listen to the results of the charismatic encounters of other members of the 'body' so that together, in a dialectical process, we can come to a right decision. The same process takes place in the celebration, in which a prophetic expression has to be tested by 'others' (I Cor.14.29). This corresponds with the custom in the synagogue of discussing the exposition of scripture together. The notion that the final decision has to be taken by one person (e.g. the bishop according to Roman Catholic doctrine) is thus wrong. From a biblical perspective the Protestants had a good intuition in emphasizing the role of the community in decision-making. Thus in the sixteenth century the London refugee community of the Pole John à Lasco knew a form of prophecy which came close to a public testing of preaching. And the first article of the acts of the Synod of Emden (1571) already says: 'No church shall have rule over another church, no minister of the Word, no elder, no deacon shall have rule over another.' However, this leads to many meetings which are often unnecessarily long and tedious because they get stuck at the level of the false self with its defence mechanisms. This makes authentic conversation unclear. A sense of the importance of the charisms and deliberate prayer for them might perhaps make the average gathering rather more meaningful, more pleasant (and shorter)!

The importance of charismatic community for making correct ethical decisions also applies to the interpretation of the church tradition and Scripture. Thus for example in the sexual sphere the biblical rule seems to be a lasting, monogamous, heterosexual relationship which leads to children (Gen.1.26-28). But already within scripture itself there are exceptions which are not seen as a threat to this rule, like polygamy, levirate marriage, concubinage and celibacy. Open interaction with the possibilities and impossibilities of the concrete situation leads to deviations from the rule. Thus Jesus and (probably) Paul opted for celibacy, although the rabbinic interpretation of scripture was: 'Anyone who does not have a wife is not a man.' Jesus' absolute prohibition of divorce in the earliest Gospel (Mark 10.2-12) was moderated both in Corinth, by Paul (I Cor.7.10-16), and by the community in which Matthew wrote his Gospel (19.9). So scripture itself shows us what the church's task is in this respect. In a playful interaction with ever-new, concrete situations, a biblical rule needs constantly to be interpreted anew and adapted by the community, which is called to life and nurtured by the same Bible.[39] Scripture and tradition do not need to be revered as reliquaries and handed down unchanged to the next generation. If that happens, they degenerate into a rigid law which enslaves people instead of helping to liberate them to a life in love. However, this process of interpretation is possible only through charismatic encounters in which the 'otherness' of the other is received and known, and scripture and tradition can be illuminated anew. The neglect of the charismatic dimension therefore explains why the church remains so stuck in antiquated, rigid views and has fallen behind society in the play of Word and Spirit. Unlike previous generations of Christians, we have realized, for example, in the last century that slavery is unworthy of humanity, and since then that Jews do not deserve punishment for crucifying Jesus, women need not be inferior to men and homosexuality is not a voluntarily chosen perversion. All are equal players in the sabbath game, in which their otherness is purified and confirmed as a gift.

The New Testament really calls only I-you encounters with other people charisms, because these are mainly treated in the framework of instruction about the community. If language is to make a real dialogue possible, moreover, here the 'mutually inward' movement with the other/Other comes most into its own. However, we saw that I-you relations with nature, expressions of science and art are also possible in which these are no longer experienced as useful objects but as ends in themselves. The play of Word and Spirit is not limited to human beings, but involves the whole of creation in a cosmic, mutual bond between all things. These encounters, too, are therefore expressions of grace in which we are liberated from my drive to make the other subservient to our effort at self-justification. A flower, a painting or a mathematical formula can then touch us and move us. In our turn we then become gifts for the other whom we encounter; we want to begin to dedicate ourselves to the preservation of the environment, to the advancement of the arts or to pure, 'purposeless' scientific investigation. In this way we break through and renew the it-world in which nature, the arts and sciences are reduced to useful instruments. So we can call these I-you encounters gifts of grace (partial, since they are not completely reciprocal). This connects with the view of the early church that human beings can really fulfil their task to rule over creation only through Christ. As priests of creation they let this come into its own in the light of the eternal sabbath. The whole world has a part in the liberating rule of Christ (Eph.1.10).

In Romans 8 we find the only possible model for a charismatic encounter with the world (including the non-human world). Here Paul seems exceptionally to allude to what concerns us so much today: the suffering of the masses from poverty, sickness and violence; unjust political and economic structures; the dying woods and seas and the break-up of the ozone layer. In short the whole creation 'groans' and suffers 'birth-pangs' (v.22). The background to this is the Jewish notion of the messianic woes which precede the coming of the new world. The community of Christ groans with creation, since it forms part of it (v.23). First of all because it itself lives in the charismatic tension betwen the Spirit and the 'flesh', the true and the false self (this is the theme of Paul's preceding argument). But also, it recognizes this same tension in the world, so that a solidarity comes about in the struggle in which believers express the groans of the world as priests of creation, in lamentation and intercession. Here the community knows what the world does not know, namely that the human indignation over and opposition to evil are inspired by Christ's Word and Spirit, which fight against the rule of death with its many forms – a struggle which in principle has been resolved with the resurrection of Jesus. Therefore in the lamentation and intercession of the community, in a flash the groaning of the world turns into hope. Very often, however, the suffering of the world is too great to be put into words. Moreover, anyone who lives by the false self must end up with a Stoic attitude, for fear of being overwhelmed by the 'nothingness' of the world's need. Then there is no longer any interaction with the world and the person's identity becomes fossilized. The charism of glossolalia gives strength in the face of this to remain open to the suffering of the world; to allow ourselves to be touched by this suffering and to pray for it with 'sighs which cannot be uttered', but which need no explanation before God (vv.26-27).[40]

(b) Gifts of grace outside the church

Do the charisms also occur outside the church? Calvin thought that they did because Christ's rule extends over the whole creation, and theologians within the charismatic renewal like Hollenweger and the Lutheran Arnold Bittlinger follow him in this.[41] We saw that as God's Wisdom, the Word and the Spirit are creatively present throughout the world, most clearly in human beings who create culture, and perfectly in Jesus. Through his death and resurrection they have also become Christ's Word and Spirit, his 'word of power' that 'supports all things' (Heb.1.3).

Thus the baptism with Word and Spirit is not limited to those who know Christ. The Pentecost play of Word and Spirit also makes possible outside Christianity charismatic encounters which have an upbuilding and transforming power, expressions of grace in which people live by their true self and become an unsuspected gift. Buber was a Jew and not a Christian. Bittlinger names among other things the prophetic gifts of some Indian gurus, and there are many other non-Christian charismatic leaders. Pentecostalism itself is an explicit version of the holistic spirituality of the Third World. I expect that this is also the explanation of the positive influence exercised by some 'paranormal' healers on people, an influence which can hardly be attributed to their often obscure ways of healing. It is well known that unlike most regular doctors, they make time for their clients. They are concerned not just with the specific complaint ('something') but with the whole person. They encounter the client as a 'you', and this is experienced as healing. *Mutatis mutandis*, the same is true of all kinds of therapy groups, as in Gestalt psychology. On another level, sociology has discovered that taking employees seriously as subjects and stimulating their creative contributions are essential for a healthy organization. Hence a recent book on building up community which starts from the charismatic structure of the community can with virtually no difficulty link up with modern organizational sociology.[42] Thus there are further examples of an increased awareness in which there is action against an absolutized it-world that makes people objects. I am thinking of the intentions of the ideologies of the Enlightenment and other movements of emancipation and also of the transformation of a paternalistic treatment of the Third World into an attitude of cooperation between equal partners. The universal, painful contrast-experiences of an order which reduces people to passive objects and victims is in itself already a sign of the inspiration through Christ's Word and Spirit which stimulates the sense of concern for a reality in which people are given their due.

Both these things mean that other religions, too, are not without gifts of grace. The modern awareness of the existence of other world religions nevertheless seems to be as much a great shock to Christian self-sufficiency as the breakthrough of science in the previous century. John Hick remarks that the roots of all the great religions lie in roughly the last millennium before Christ.[43] In the time before this the religious sense generally emphasized the manipulation of the dominant world order. By contrast, the present world religions teach the possibility of change and liberation and of an infinitely better world. All came into being as a reaction to the alienation and chaos of their time, like the Jewish exile, the violent kingdoms rising on the Ganges at the time of Buddha and the downfall of the Chinese Chou

dynasty in the period of the Tao writers. All were looking for a new
human order and believed in one transcendent Reality which by
religions like Christianity and Islam is called 'God' (the personal
God), but, for example, by Buddhism Nirvana. According to
Hick, they also have similar concepts of liberation, namely the
transformation of an existence bent back on itself into a life orientated
on the infinite Reality. This is a life of love (or compassion). God's
Word and Spirit are therefore not absent from the other religions,
whose adherents, according to Paul in his address at Athens, live,
move and have their being in God (Acts 17.28). Already in pre-
literate cultures the remarkable I-you encounter with a mountain, a
tree or a spring led to the rise of holy places.[44] Mystics from the great
religions have always been able to agree on the experience that there
is one infinite Reality. Precisely because God by definition always
transcends human beings, many different interpretations of the divine
religions have come into being, conditioned by experience and
culture. The differences between the religions can to some degree be
regarded as the world-wide counterparts of the differences within
each particular religion. We saw how already within Pentecostalism
there is an enormous variation in views which is sometimes mutually
contradictory. But Pentecostals recognize one another in the charismatic experience of the baptism with Word and Spirit. As with almost
any other subject discussed here, in this case too there is far more to
be said than is possible in a book (moreover I am no specialist in the
field of world religions). But the charismatic attitude at all events
seeks to encounter believers of other religions, too, as an 'I'. Mission
is the call and task to encounter 'the other'. (The explanation of the
attraction of Pentecostalism is not the often aggressive drive for
mission among the Pentecostals, which makes non-Christians objects
that must be 'converted', but the playful character of their charismatic
celebration.)

The charism makes possible an authentic inter-religious dialogue
in which anxiety and prejudices are overcome. So in any faith God's
truths can be reciprocally received as an enrichment, while the
untruths come to life and are corrected. For Buber, from his youth
Jesus was 'my great brother' and the Hindu Gandhi was strongly
influenced by the Sermon on the Mount. On the other hand, many
Christians have experienced a deepening of their faith through Zen
Buddhism. So in such a dialogue a person's own religious views are
not suppressed. Experience teaches that precisely those who have

most appropriated the truth of their own tradition are most open to the truth in other religions, which they welcome as familiar strangers. Misunderstandings are avoided if a person's own specific views are not presented in a rigid, exclusive way (where this happens, the false, defensive self is speaking). So the missiologist John Taylor rightly observes that to say 'Jesus Christ is divine' leaves far less room for dialogue than to say 'Whatever else God is, I believe that he is Christlike'.[45] The other is now free to discover what being Christlike is. In the end, the important issue is the one Reality which the great religions all serve and worship. Just as Jesus is the end (fulfilment) of the Jewish Torah (Rom.10.4), so he can become the fulfilment of the writings of other religions which teach love and learn a playful attitude. The exodus experience is not limited to Israel: 'As I brought Israel out of Egypt, so I brought the Philistines from Caphtor and Aram from Kish,' says God according to the prophet Amos (9.7). Christ's Word and Spirit give everyone power within their own cultures and religions to be liberated from the false self and take the way to God's kingdom.[46]

If my view is right, since the death and resurrection of Christ the capacity for authentic encounter among humankind (including those who are not Christians) has increased to an important degree through the charisms. Before this it was limited to exceptional individuals like Buddha and Socrates and some heroes and prophets from the First Testament who were bold enough to confront their fellow human beings (and thus death). However, this has to be examined closely – the melancholy fate of any strict theological position. Certainly the Pentecost event of the outpouring of Christ's Word and Spirit on 'every living creature' is regarded as a decisive new change in the relationship between God and the world and thus also in the relationship between human beings (Acts 2.16-20; Rom. 5.1-11). We saw that for Luke and Paul the baptism with Word and Spirit explains the Christian community's radical power of encounter, beyond rigid barriers, a power of encounter which is also characteristic of all kinds of charismatic currents in history. I have already mentioned the increasing, world-wide, awareness of human beings as unique and inviolable subjects. Nevertheless the orientation of (NB!) the church itself on order and, in our age, the rise of the technocratic and ideological it-world shows how stubborn is the dread of death which leads the 'flesh' to escape into an enslaving order. Hence large parts of Pentecostalism, which above all consists of people who have to suffer most under this order, cannot believe in a fluid transition from the present world into the kingdom of God. Before that they expect a cosmic crisis, the return of Christ. Apocalyptic expectations have always been the dreams of the oppressed, who long for their future satisfaction in the kingdom of God. Moreover, since the Word and Spirit are a guarantee of the eternal play of the sabbath, it is no wonder that charismatic trends have almost always had a marked eschatological expectation. Rejected by the church and society, charismatics were often led to flee from the world. However, at least as often, the vision of the coming kingdom of God led to opposition to the oppressive *status quo*. This is the right response to the baptism with Word and Spirit, since God seeks to become 'all in all' (with no exceptions). Thus Paul describes the end of a development which has begun through God with the resurrection of Jesus (I Cor.15.12-28). As far as I know, it has not been noted previously that this development, through Christ's liberating rule, is a charismatic process. In and through the gifts of grace God, according to Paul, is now active for 'all in all' (I Cor.12.6) and Paul's discussion of the charisms in Romans follows praise of God from whom, through whom and to whom are all things (11.36). We find the same pattern in the letter to the Ephesians, where God is named 'above all and through all and in all' (4.6), after which there is a discussion of the charismatic character of the community. Finally, in a passage about the new life in Colossians (3.15-17), the charismatic unity is stressed once again: there is no difference 'between Greek and Jew, circumcised and uncircumcised, barbarian and Scythian, slave and free, but Christ *is all and in all*' (v.11). The charisms, as encounters in which the other/ Other already becomes 'all' for me, are all over the world the divine way to the eternal play of the sabbath.

If Christ's Word and Spirit are at work in the whole creation, what then is the specific identity and task of the Christian church? The church names what the Word and the Spirit are doing in the world. It knows that God in Christ, the Wisdom and 'firstborn from the dead', has reconciled all things with himself and established this world-wide through the charism in those who 'were alienated and hostile'. So Christ exercises his liberating rule, especially as head of the community, 'the body', but also as the 'first' of all creation (the Greek notion of the cosmos as a body lies behind the image of the community as a body, Col.1.18-21). The church thanks God for the moments in which the dead order is broken through and renewed by the gifts of grace, and it complains about and prays to God for liberation from the rigid political and economic structures which reduce human beings and the environment to an 'it'.[47] It stimulates a policy which embodies its own experience of unity-in-difference in the world, both in furthering a dialogue between peoples and religions, supporting an institution like the United Nations, and in attempts to achieve a just distribution of prosperity. The church also does what it can to help the victims of the prevailing order by, for example, working for their emancipation. But above all it proclaims and celebrates as an explicitly charismatic community that God in Christ has overcome death. Thus the church is the exodus community which knows that it is justified through faith/grace alone. In the gifts of grace it keeps departing from the false self in order to play the crazy sabbath game – first in the celebration, but as a result also in society. Precisely in those places where people suffer most under an oppressive order the charismatic celebrations are the most exuberant and the concern for diaconal service is the greatest. In the conscious interplay of the gifts of grace the church is a living guarantee of God's kingdom, salting the world with fiery love. In its prophetic preaching and celebration of the uselessness of God and the world, it puts the axe to the roots of all objectivizing power-thinking and all passive slave mentalities.

The minister equips the commuity for this sabbath play and can be compared with a trainer or producer. The sacraments are the normative, objective expression of charismatic life and represent as it were the rules of the game.

(iii) The minister as religious producer

Many people think that charism and ministry are opposed. This is understandable, since out of anxiety over the play of Word and Spirit in the community, at a very early stage ministers ensconced themselves in an authoritarian order and more or less took over the monopoly of the gifts. Even in recent statements on the ministry by the Roman Catholic Church (*Lumen gentium*) and the World Council of Churches (*Baptism, Eucharist and Ministry*) less than ten per cent of the text is devoted to the priesthood of all believers. This is a sign that this is still not taken very seriously in the established churches.

A well known fact, but one which is still disconcerting for some, is that the New Testament does not use the existing Jewish terms for the ministry and even seems to avoid them. The justifying power of God's grace in Christ excludes a separate 'caste' of priests or levites, for whom particular tasks in the community are exclusively reserved. What is described in I Thessalonians 5.12-13 as the task of a particular group within the community is expected of the whole community in the following two verses: the 'seeing' of the other and thus the bringing in of the idlers, the encouraging of the fearful and the defence of the weak. This community must also test the prophecies (vv.19-21), something which is not limited to particular persons. Apostles, prophets and teachers, functions which in our thought directly conjure up the image of people set apart who stand 'over against' the community in the name of Christ, are usually part of the lists of gifts (I Cor.12.28; Eph.4,11). This radical view is not limited to Paul. The whole letter to the Hebrews itself turns on the argument that the priestly system is 'antiquated and outdated' as a result of the coming of Christ. On the other hand the 'lay' Jesus is named priest. In the renewed covenant the Torah is written on every heart, and all may boldly enter the Holy of Holies, i.e. encounter God (4.16; 7-8). The relationship with God is no longer exclusively mediated through the ministry. And I Peter calls the whole community a 'holy priesthood' which makes 'spiritual sacrifices'; that means that the members with their unique identity and situation can become a charism for one another and can speak 'words as of God' (2.5; 4.10-11). Because in a gift of grace the game is played of the love which rejoices in the truth, every charismatic encounter has a critical, judging force in which those involved are freed from their false self. So in every charism one also encounters God in Christ as a prophetic 'counterpart'. This is a fiery baptism with Word and Spirit.

All this does not mean that there is no certain basis in the New Testament for the traditional view of a group of separate ministers. There are charisms which are specifically at the service of the charismatic interplay of the community. Therefore Paul mentions apostles, prophets and teachers first in his summing up of individual gifts of grace. These charisms make the functioning of the other gifts possible where they equip members to play the sabbath game and lead and co-ordinate it.[48] This emerges more clearly in the later letters (I Tim.4.24; II Tim.1.6). The apostle Paul himself gives an example in his own pastoral work, of which we have an account in his epistles. In his instruction, admonitions and encouragement he respects the fact that the community members themselves have received the guarantee of the Spirit and the life of faith. He does not want to rule over them, but to collaborate with them for their delight (II Cor.1.21-24). He does not appear as an authoritarian super-apostle, but encounters them vulnerably in the charism (with 'Spirit and power', I Cor.2.1-5). Only when the gospel itself is threatened does he pull his rank (II Cor.10-13). The minister is a religious producer who makes the sabbath play possible. This emerges very clearly in the letter to the Ephesians. After a summons to 'walk' in love and unity, the author goes into the different charisms in the community (4.1-16). With an interpretation of Psalm 68, which is read at Pentecost in the synagogue, he explains that the risen Christ gave gifts to men and women (v.8). According to the British exegete G.B.Caird, he then continues by stating that these gifts (Christ's 'descent' to earth in the outpouring of the Spirit at Pentecost) manifest the rule of the risen Christ to 'bring all things to fullness' (vv.9-10).[49] In the same way, for Peter too on the first day of Pentecost the gifts which 'you see and hear' are an expression of Christ's rule at the right hand of God (Acts 2.33). The letter to the Ephesians then goes further in summing up of some of these gifts: apostles, prophets, evangelists, pastors and teachers (v.11). These serve to equip the members of the community for charismatic service 'for the building up of the body of Christ' (v.12). So the believers achieve union in their unique otherness and become mature and responsible adults. The fact that each member can become a gift of grace ('the power which each member exercises in his or her way') determines the essence and dynamic of the community. Thus the liberating rule of Christ manifests itself in a community which encounters one another as 'you' and becomes rich in love (v.16).

However, the charism of the minister, too, is no obvious trait that one might possess through study or ordination. Of course knowledge of scripture and liturgy, of some of the human sciences and of the complexities of society, are necessary. But this is only the raw material, and does not of itself yet make a person a minister, as anyone is aware when painfully confronted with a pastor (or other helper) who is completely in his or her world. Gifts of grace are dynamic and must be waited for from moment to moment. They make possible an authentic encounter in which people are 'seen' and healed. In this encounter the gift of the minister takes the specific form of encouragment and equipment for the sabbath play. Weber therefore quite rightly derived from Paul his concept of the 'charismatic' leader who liberates people to give themselves. Here we see the nature of the charism of the minister as it were greatly magnified. So ministers should not take all tasks upon themselves, but first of all inspire and enable community members to do the work. Only in this way can they become mature Christians, open to the gifts of grace, and thus live in faith, from the true self. The way of self-giving is the only way to human perfection. Someone's identity (Word) embraces a specific disposition and talents which only come into their own in interaction (Spirit) with appropriate surroundings like pastoral work, diaconal work or administration. The minister identifies these talents and helps to deploy them on appropriate tasks (like the casting of actors in certain roles in a film or play). This calls for a way of thinking which the community consistently sees as an interplay of gifts. If the minister takes the monopoly on to his or her ground, then the game is spoilt.

On the other hand, many members of the community are afraid of responsibilities because they are asked to perform tasks which do not suit their talents and feel that they are being used as a means to an end ('If you don't do it, it won't get done'). A minister with a charismatic awareness will begin from the people in the community, not from the tasks, and not be afraid, if necessary, to leave a gap in the team. Quite often in this way a tired way of being a community ('We've always done it this way') is renewed by surprising insights which had no chance before. Furthermore the existence of the charismatic renewal which has flared up in all the church traditions, from low church to high church, indicates that the gifts of grace are not tied to a particular theology of the ministry, There are Roman Catholic bishops who powerfully awaken the gifts in believers, and Pentecostal ministers who are so dominant that celebration has become a solo. A certain church order and structure is a sociological necessity. However, this must constantly be renewed by the charismatic sabbath play if it is not to degenerate into the it-world which often makes church history such an oppressive story. To use the words of the Reformed theologian O.Noordmans, the closed forms must constantly be broken through by the Spirit.[50] A minister who blindly opts for the preservation of the existing order denies the very nature of the ministry.

What applies to views of ministry also applies to the different forms of organization in the church. In principle these are determined by culture and can all give space to the charismatic interplay of believers. This, too, is shown by the practice of charismatic renewal. The contours of the most important features of present-day church order are already evident (along with the many house communities) in the New Testament. So we find an almost episcopal structure in the community in Jerusalem, with James standing at the head of a college of elders (Acts 5.13-21). A more presbyterian form existed in the community at Antioch, where important decisions were taken by a council of prophets and teachers (Acts 13.1-3). Finally, the community in Corinth had congregationalist features: every member had an equal say and all were involved in the making of decisions. This emerges among other things from the fact that in his admonitions about division, immorality, the celebration of the Lord's supper and order in the celebration, Paul addresses all members of the community and not a council of elders or a bishop (in contrast to I Tim.4.6, 11, where Timothy is addressed about the state of the community, good or bad).

The different views of ministry are the greatest stumbling block in the ecumenical world today. In a visionary address, W.A.Visser't Hooft, the first Secretary General of the World Council of Churches, in 1951 described the charismatic model as the only possible ecumenical model.[51] Just as in the local community the members are distinguished by various talents but one through the gifts of grace, so the world-wide Christian church is divided by different traditions which can form a dynamic unity only through the charisms. Only in this way can the self-sufficient attitude be overcome which says to the other within the one body of Christ, 'I have no need of you' (I Cor.12.21). The World Council of Churches, Visser't Hooft concludes, is therefore essentially an attempt to manifest the principle of the gifts of grace. From this reading it emerges that it was certainly not the fault of the Secretary General that it was not until 1968 (Uppsala) that the doctrine of the Spirit appeared on the agenda of the World Council of Churches. His theory is now in a sense confirmed by the practice of charismatic renewal.

The ministry, as a commission to stimulate the dynamic of the charismatic encounter, by definition has an ecumenical orientation. Far from being a cause of division, as in the present church order, the ministry needs to be a ministry of reconciliation (see II Cor.5.18).

The same thing applies, in my view, to the dialogue with the religions. Ministry stimulates encounter not only in one's own local community and with believers of other church traditions, but also with believers of other religions. An open dialogue in which 'the other' is really received and known is a charism. The call by Hans Küng for a dialogue with the religions because this is the only way of arriving at world peace[52] thus presupposes a new awareness of the gifts of grace. The Christian church, to which the news of the death and resurrection of Christ is entrusted and which is explicitly aware of the charisms, should be taking the lead in this dialogue. Had Pentecostalism not so quickly been infiltrated by fundamentalist views, there might perhaps already have been a charismatic renewal of the religions. Thus the Christian charismatic renewal is clearly related to the Hasidim in Judaism, Sufism in Islam, and definite mystical currents in other religions.

(a) The sacraments as objective rules of the game

There is also far more to be said about the sacraments than is possible here. I must limit myself to baptism with water and the Lord's table (supper or eucharist), and moreover to two aspects which are particularly illuminating from a charismatic perspective: their relationship to the exodus and the fact that they are the normative, dramatized expression of the call of the community to the charismatic life. As 'visible Word' (Augustine), a sacrament symbolizes the objective rules of the sabbath play. In water baptism the centre is the individual as a unique person; in the Lord's supper the community is the centre.

I wrote earlier that the expression 'baptize with Spirit' was probably coined by John from the practice to which he owed his name 'the Baptist'. The baptism with Word and Spirit is bound up with water baptism, but does not coincide with it, as is often thought. Baptism with Word and Spirit realizes the truth expressed in water baptism and can be chronologically dependent on this sacrament; therefore some Pentecostal communities and many churches of the charismatic renewal can practise infant baptism. In the immersion (*baptizein*, customary in the Pentecostal movement and the indigenous non-white churches) and rising again from the water, baptism is a dramatized prayer for the exodus experience in Christ's Word and Spirit. Baptism aptly expresses the 'dying' to the false, Egyptian self in the terrifying waters and the 'rising' to a life from the true self that alludes to the coming, promised land. This is not an experience which applies once for all but a constantly repeated event in and through the gifts of grace. Standing at the beginning of Christian existence, water baptism thus depicts the dynamic, charismatic structure of the new life.

This emerges clearly from Romans 6, where Paul goes into water baptism at length.[53] It is a participation in the death and resurrection of Christ 'through the majesty of the Father' (this is the Spirit of understanding [Word] and sanctification, see Test. Levi 18.7-11), so that 'we should walk in a new way of life' (v.4). Moreover traditionally water baptism is administered on Easter Eve, at the boundary of the change from death to life. In the Eastern church baptism does not stand first of all for the remission of sin, as it has done since Augsutine in the West, but for liberation from our mortality. Because of the anxiety which it evokes, this is the main cause of sin and guilt, as I have tried to show. Paul very soberly begins from the fact that everyone has to die. The only question is, how? As James Dunn emphatically concludes after his extensive exegetical study of the gifts of grace: '*If man chooses to live his own life* [this is the false self], *then he will die his own death* – and that will be that. *But if by the power of the Spirit he dies Christ's death now, then he will lead Christ's life* [this is the true self] *both here and hereafter.*'[54] This new life is a charismatic way in which we 'die' at every step to the old man, which falls under the rule of death, and 'rise' to the life of Christ. Here too the apostle thinks in very concrete terms. 'For just as you once yielded your members to impurity and to greater and greater iniquity, so now yield your members to righteousness for sanctification' (v.19b). For Paul, righteousness and sanctification are closely connected. For the charism as an expression of our being justified by God in Christ involves a painful dying of the false self (sanctification) which, driven by the fear of death, seeks to justify itself. To experience that God accepts us unconditionally, by grace, is at the same time the most attractive and most difficult thing that can happen to us. It is like a fire which in every encounter with the other burns away all one's activistic attempts to give oneself a foundation. Moreover, the most visible fruit produced by the charismatic process of transformation to a life from the true self is humility, as we heard Simeon the New Theologian say. Life from faith is characterized by an enduring and increasing sense of our dependence on grace (the gifts of grace). Moreover Paul ends his discussion on water baptism and the new life expressed in it with a reference to the source of all gifts: 'the charism of God is eternal life in Christ Jesus our Lord (of the exodus)' (6.23).

> Often justification is regarded as the beginning of the new life and sanctification as its realization in the life of the believer (Roman Catholic doctrine sees this precisely the other way round: there sanctification – *gratia infusa* – is the cause of justification). But justification is not only the start but also the condition of the new life. To be 'in Christ' is to become 'God's righteousness' (II Cor.5.21) or, in other words, 'a new creation' (II Cor.5.17). So justification implies a transformation (sanctification) and thus a healing for fragmenting anxiety. On the other hand sanctification does not first of all have an ethical significance, but indicates the fact of our salvation. Like the believers in the New Testament, the holy men and women in the First Testament are those who are set apart, in other words who belong to God. Both justification and sanctification are dynamic concepts. The suggestion of a growth towards moral perfection would immediately be used by the false self to justify itself. The only authentic growth is an increasing knowledge of God and of oneself in which 'Christ becomes more and more necessary'.[55]

The celebration of the Lord's table is rooted in the Jewish *pesach* meal, in which the participants are involved in the Exodus from Egypt and look forward to complete liberation through God's Messiah.[56] As Jesus parted from his disciples, he renewed the significance of this meal by making the bread and the wine symbols of his liberating death and resurrection, the 'new covenant' (Mark 14.22-25; I Cor.11.23-26). The Lord's table is *par excellence* a community sacrament and therefore occupies a central place in most churches. It is celebrated more often in the Pentecostal movement than in Calvinist churches: usually every month or even every Sunday. The celebration of the Lord's table also occupies an important place in the charismatic renewal. The sacrament expresses the new charismatic community, as is evident from Paul's instructions to the Corinthians. In their community there were different rival groups which had enslaved themselves to a leader – 'I am of Apollos! And I of Cephas!' – to which the apostle replies with a rhetorical question: 'Is Christ divided?' (I Cor.1.12-13). Later in the letter, having reminded them of their baptism with Word and Spirit and water baptism (their baptism 'in the cloud and in the sea', 10.2), he warns them against idolatry, using Israel as an example (vv.6-14). This is his introduction to a discussion of the Lord's table.

The exact opposite of idolatry which leads to division is the life that is liberated in the exodus of Christ's death and resurrection and expressed in the drinking of the wine and the eating of the bread: 'Because there is one bread, we who are many (and different) are one body' (v.17). The charismatic community symbolized by the celebration of the Lord's table is the exact opposite of idolatry (v.21). Paul then emphasizes the charismatic difference in which even the weaker members and the women who prophesy are to be heard as equals (10.23-11.16), and criticizes the abuses in the Corinthian community. For the community is divided and needs are denied (11.17-22). This is no less than contempt for Christ himself, not only because he identified himself to the death with the poor and oppressed but also above all because the liberating power of his death and resurrection which manifests itself in the charisms is also denied. Therefore the apostle emphasizes in the so-called words of institution that the significance of the wine and bread of the Lord's table lies in the experience (remembrance) of Christ's death and resurrection (11.23-26), and then goes at length into the gifts of grace (12-14). Through one Spirit, the Corinthians are baptized into one body in which their differences do not lead to division but through the charisms become a dynamic interplay in which the members build one another up in love.

The Catholic theologian Kilian McDonnell, who has already been involved with the charismatic renewal for a long time, describes the rite of initiation to be found in the writings of the church father Tertullian who lived round about 200. Tertullian set this down (in his *De Baptismo*) not long before he went over to charismatic Montanism. McDonnell nevertheless also finds largely the same rite in later, official teachers of the church like Cyril and Hilary. Here the sense that the celebration of the Lord's table is an expression of charismatic community is still clearly present.[57] The ritual consisted of water baptism with immersion, followed by anointing and laying on of hands as a welcoming of the Holy Spirit; the raising of his or her hands by the candidate in a prayer for the charisms, the assurance by the priest that this prayer for the gifts of grace has been answered,

and finally the celebration of the eucharist. In my view this whole
rite has a charismatic orientation. Water baptism is the sacrament
which expresses the participation of believers in the death and
resurrection of Christ. Anointing, laying on of hands and prayer are
focussed on the realization of this truth in baptism with Word and
Spirit which manifests itself in the gifts of grace. Only through the
charisms does the believer function as a member of the one body of
Christ, to use the terminology of the Lord's table, as a piece of the
one bread (and no one piece is like another). This is aptly expressed
in a practice to be found in some more intimate celebrations of the
eucharist: the plate with the bread is handed round, and each person
gives a piece to the next as an expression of the sesne that one can be
a gift to others. In Tertullian's description the charism still clearly
combines water baptism and the Lord's table and actualizes the truth
of these sacraments. This truth is the covenant of renewal, or the
experience of a bond with God and one another in the charismatic
encounter.[58] So the sacraments are the objective expression of the
authentic life embodied and made possible by Jesus. Anyone who
wants to save his or her life (false self) will lose it (since it remains
imprisoned in a superficial life orientated on self-preservation). But
everyone who wants to lose his or her life for Christ's sake (and thus
live from the true self, following Jesus) will save it (see Mark 8.35).
All who lose themselves in encounter with the neighbour will
find themselves. The charismatic 'way of life' in which people are
constantly a self-gift in the playful interaction with the other/Other
is a life in faith: a life in love, wonderment and great joy. It is no
coincidence that in Greek the words grace and gift of grace (*charis,
charisma*) are related to the word for joy (*chara*). This is the joy
which flashes out in the Easter hymns, from of old sung by the church
as the liberated community of Christ.

(b) The pastorate

Liturgically, the charismatic pastorate has led to a revaluation of the
early church's ministry of healing and the ministry of liberation (a
form of exorcism). In addition, the pastorate is also focussed on
'inner healing', also called the 'healing of memories'. The method
here is a therapy which gives insight with the imaginative help of
faith. Traumatic situations (which are sometimes hidden) are re-
experienced, but now with the figure of Jesus as it were projected

back on them. In this notion the pain of the trauma is shared with him, and this often has a positive effect. The healing power of the charismatic encounter is one of these various forms of the pastorate. It is not reserved for the pastorate in the charismatic renewal. Any form of pastorate consists in achieving respect for others in a relationship between subjects which is experienced as liberating and healing (and is thus a charismatic encounter, though this is not interpreted as such). I have worked this out elsewhere with the help of the model of the transitional sphere described by the Dutch-American psychologist of religion Paul Pruyser, who has associations with the Menninger Foundation.[59]

The transitional sphere mediates between the instinctive drives which strive for satisfaction in each person and the outside world, the reality which calls for adaptation and a certain reification of a person's own wishes and needs. The instinctive drives are expressions of the mortal 'flesh' which is concerned for self-preservation and which, when it gets the upper hand, reduces the outside world to a useful it-world. There is then no dynamic interaction with the other. This is what I have called the false self, which consists of a fossilized identity (Word) and a heightened interaction with the outside world (Spirit). It objectifies the outside world so that it becomes a fixed image, and this can lead to a polarization of good and evil, a rationalistic no-nonsense attitude or a bias towards authoritarian leadership. On the other hand the false self is thus thrown back on its own inner world. As we have already seen, this is a subjective world full of illusions (since it has no relation to reality), in which a person's own feelings can be absolutized so that they become divine or demonic experiences. The transitional sphere is now as it were an intermediate zone in which the inner drive to self-preservation and the real outside world coincide in a tension which leads to creative solutions. This is what I have called the true self, which constantly grows in identity (Word) in a playful interaction with reality (Spirit). In Kierkegaard we already found the view that the mentally healthy person exists in this interplay of subjective and objective world. Moreover according to Pruyser, the transitional sphere is the sphere of religion, myths, rites and symbols; of an intuitive 'feeling something', dreams and art. This 'intermediate zone' in people is the sphere of play which makes human growth and culture possible: '... the discovery of an attitude to reality (in both its interpersonal and external aspects) calls for the discovery of an attitude to play'.[60] An inactive transitional sphere (and thus a situation in which the true self is overgrown by the false self) therefore results in an inability to deal with refractory reality in a creative way, so that people 'get stuck'. They are caught in a fossilized situation in which no movement is possible and with which nothing can be done. Pruyser mentions as causes of an underactive transitional sphere a general lack of trust (in my terms, anxiety about death and life) and the modern shortage of myths, symbols and other forms of play. So he expects a great deal from the renewal of liturgy. In my view the most important contributions of the pastorate as practised in the charismatic renewal lie here.

The basic form of all pastoral work is encounter in the assembly. It is from this that the pastorate has arisen, and in the charismatic renewal this is still quite clearly visible. For the charismatic pastorate usually takes place in the context of a celebration. First of all the celebration itself has a pastoral force, because in the charismatic encounter with the other one receives Christ in the Word and the Spirit (the eternal 'You'), which overcomes the dread of death and gives trust. I know that I am 'seen' and known. In this encounter, on the one hand the other can give me an insight which helps me in my situation. On the other, I myself can become an unexpected gift in my being touched by the other with his or her need for trust, consolation or encouragement (as long as the dread of death dominates I cannot authentically know the other nor give myself for fear of losing myself). This gift need not be verbal. I have often noticed how in a charismatic celebration people are deeply touched and a process of healing is set in motion in them because someone spontaneously danced for them or sang a song with glossolalic sounds. This last has much of the Hasidic *nigun*:

> The rabbi of Ladi once noticed among his hearers an old man who clearly was not understanding the meaning of what he heard. He called to him and said, 'I see that my conversation is not clear to you. Listen to the melody and then you will know how to approach God.' The rabbi began to sing a *nigun*, a song without words. It was a song of trust in God, a song of the Torah, of longing for the Lord and a song of love for God.
>
> 'Now I know that you wanted to teach me,' exclaimed the old man: 'I feel a very deep longing in me to be united with God.' And

the rabbi's melody became part of his daily devotion to God, although it had no words.[61]

Thus in the charismatic encounter one not only receives confidence but through one's self-giving also takes part in the play of the celebration. People live from their true selves (in Pruyser's terms, the transitional sphere is activated), as a result of which it is possible to deal more creatively with life's challenges. Here, through the interaction in celebration, the sense of community grows and with it the courage to ask for pastoral help, if that is still necessary. It is amazing how many people who otherwise never get so far, feel free in a church or inter-church charismatic celebration to approach a pastoral worker. Pastoral help is usually given directly after (sometimes during) the celebration by one or two workers who are suited to it by virtue of personality, talent, training or experience. These can be 'professional' pastors, but also non-theologians. The pastoral conversation is above all a charismatic encounter which is more concentrated than is possible in the celebration or in everyday life. At its best it is like the patient interplay between the potter and his or her clay, in which each is shaped by the other. The pastorate can take the form of listening to the person asking for help, giving moral support, resolving conflicts and the like. But the charismatic pastorate is more than a conversation and often has a playful element: silence, penitence, prayer, humour, laying on of hands, anointing, rites, symbols, icons and dance can all be involved here. In all this the pastor tries as receptively as possible to be there for the other (to have his or her own transitional sphere activated), and here the purposeless glossolalic prayer is often experienced as a help. In the charismatic encounter the person asking for help is then liberated from anxiety and thus from the false self (his or her transitional sphere is activated, which means that there is a possibility of entering into a playful interaction with the reality of his or her own stuck situation. The function of the charismatic pastorate, embedded in the celebration, is thus above all the activation of the transitional sphere (the true self) of the person asking for help. Then this person becomes free in his or her turn to become a gift for others. This also explains why the pastoral activity of those taking part in the charismatic renewal often began with their own experience of healing in a pastoral encounter.

In his response to my description of the charismatic pastorate
A.van Hoogen rightly points out that this pastorate is characterized
by an experience which leads to unity and therefore cannot be put
into one of the usual categories.[62] However, he asks whether
the charismatic pastorate is not one-sidedly about an aesthetic
(integrating) experience through which concrete social reality is
lost sight of. This last is certainly a danger in Pentecostalist practice.
There is little investigation of structural and social factors which
lead to sickness. But this has other causes (above all fundamentalist
theology), as I indicated earlier. However, the charismatic pastorate
calls for the integration of the inner world of drives with the
concrete outside world, so that the person involved can refer to
the challenges of his or her situation. The experience of union
in the charismatic encounter puts the person asking for help in a
position to counter the chilly order of the it-world in the practice
of his or her own life and renew it. So he or she lives as a covenant
partner with God, who is concerned to change and consummate
this world in the eternal sabbath play.

(iv) God 'all in all'

The fact that God reveals himself in history in the Word and Spirit,
and so, in and through the charisms, is on the way to becoming 'all
in all', led at an early stage to the notion that God from eternity exists
as a Trinity. In addition to the wish to safeguard the divinity of Christ
(and later of the Spirit), this development was caused above all by
the dominant static image of God. For the Greeks, change was a sign
of imperfection, so that the divine existence must have been the same
from eternity.

This compelled the church to defend Christ's's existence with God
before his birth on earth (his pre-existence). Here use is made of the
passages in scripture which describe the life and work of Christ in
terms derived from the poetical wisdom literature. As we have seen,
here the Word and the Spirit are celebrated as the Wisdom through
whom God from the beginning calls creation into being and who
descends from heaven in order to dwell among human beings. But
that God's Word and Spirit expressed themselves perfectly in the
human being Jesus of Nazareth, so that he came to be called
the Wisdom of God, does not mean that we must conclude retrospec-
tively that he exists with God from eternity, indeed *is* God. Even the

Gospel of John, which, strongly influenced by the Wisdom tradition, points most strongly to the pre-existence of Christ with God, frequently emphasizes the initiative of God who has sent Jesus. The Son 'can do nothing of himself, but only what he sees the Father doing' (5.19). God the Father has set his seal on him (6.27), so that Jesus can say that the Father is in him and he is in the Father (10.38). The relationship between God and Jesus already consists in a perfect, uninterrupted encounter in the play of Word and Spirit, anticipating the kingdom in which God will be 'all in all'. So on earth Jesus was transparent to God, the light of the world. Anyone who encountered Jesus always encountered God in him. Thus precisely in his perfect humanity, as the image of God he can be called truly divine (*vere Deus*). The static idea that God exists irrecovably from creation as Father, Son and Spirit irrevocably prompts the misunderstanding that this is polytheism. This has seriously hampered the dialogue with Judaism and Islam and has caused much confusion among Christians themselves. Anyone familiar with present-day pastoral practice knows that most people regard this doctrine as abstract theological speculation which has little or no value for their own life of faith. This is ironic, because the doctrine of the Trinity emerged in the first instance from the experience of faith of the early Christians.[63] In their fellowship with one another they experienced *God's* Word and Spirit as *Christ's* Word and Spirit. In the framework of the dominant Logos philosophy, however, Christ was then rapidly identified with the Word (with whom Wisdom was also identified), after which the Spirit, which was left over, also gained a separate 'divine status' (first explicitly through Gregory of Nazianzus in the fourth century). The essential play of Word and Spirit symbolized in biblical wisdom thus came to be forgotten.

This somewhat simple summary of complex material at any rate shows that the doctrine of the Trinity can be understood better dynamically. This corresponds with the course of evolution, which leads from elementary particles through animal populations and human society to ever higher forms of community. God is what I. Carter Heyward calls the 'power in relationship' which makes this union possible. From eternity there is one God who 'from before the foundation of the world' longs to share himself in the Word and the Spirit – in the creation and afterwards completely in Christ, in order after his death and resurrection to flow through them in a new way to all of humankind. For God created without reason and without aim, 'for nothing' and 'out of nothing'. Death is an expression of this 'nothing', of the fact that no creature is grounded in itself. As long as the creation is not perfected, people cannot live in real union with God and with one another because of the threat of this 'nothingness'. They are dominated by the fear of death and have to justify their existence through 'works' in which they reduce the other and thus the Other to an object. So in the Word and Spirit God becomes 'all' in the man Jesus and in him has overcome the principle of death. Easter has made possible an outpouring ('baptism') of Christ's Word and Spirit, and in the charismatic encounter people are liberated from their fear of death and thus slavery to idols which are 'all' for them, whether represented by a loving partner, an ideology or a career. In the gifts of grace, along with others they can play the play of the totally other God and grow as human beings. This is a pledge of the eternal sabbath, of the creation as this is meant to be. For in the playful interaction of the charismatic encounter which is an 'mutually inward' relationship we receive in the self of the other the self of God in Christ (we are 'filled' with Christ's Word and Spirit and thus become a 'temple of God'). Touched by this, we give our own selves (Word and Spirit) to the other and thus to God in Christ. Thus in the charisma a reciprocal permeation has a place so that we already experience something of our eschatological identity. The way by which God becomes 'all in all' is charismatic. One day we shall be perfectly ourselves, our true selves, in the play of Word and Spirit.

Like Hendrikus Berkhof, moreover, I regard the Trinity as the perfected covenant.[64] This is the perfect bond (in mystical terms the union) of the creation of God and thus among its members. The view that God is triune is therefore an expression of faith which looks forward to the new creation. Since God's Word and Spirit have become Christ's Word and Spirit in the resurrection, Christ continues to mediate the encounter with God. In the vision of the book of Revelation, in the perfect and renewed creation God himself will be its temple (as we will be filled with God, so God will be filled with us) 'and the lamb' (2.22). Moreover Paul says in militant language that when after the conquest of death all is subjected to the Son, last of all the Son will subject himself to God 'so that God is all in all' (I Cor.15.28). The encounter with God remains social; in the other we encounter Christ, and in him God. Elsewhere God encounters us in Christ and thus in the other. The consummated covenant is a dynamic triune community in which God through the Word and the Spirit dwells completely in Christ and thus in his 'body' (the world) and so makes all things 'to fullness'. On the other hand human beings will dwell in this 'mutually inward' movement with one another completely in Christ and thus in God. Then the prayer of Jesus, 'I in them and you in me, that they may be perfectly one' (John 17.23) will be heard fully. The difference betwen the false self as a limited and crippled ego and the true self, which as a person is concerned for others, means that in the process of fulfilment we become constantly less ego and constantly more person. In God's kingdom, ego-limits will disappear and every person will merely be a living consciousness, transparent to the other human consciousness in a community of love which now we can hardly imagine. In the words of François Varillon, then 'all will simply be themselves by standing outside themselves (namely in the other)'.[65] Then there will be only 'you'/ 'You'. This mutual indwelling can be called *perichoresis*, using a classical theological term (from the Greek *chorein*, step or dance). We saw that Huizinga regards the dance as one of the most perfect forms of play. Now the perfect covenant is like a mutual dance of Father, Son and holy community of creation. In it the play of Word and Spirit, now already visible in and proclaimed through the church as the charismatic body of Christ, will come to perfect expression in a divine unity in difference in which the whole creation will come into its own. In this way the apostolic prayer of blessing will be fulfilled which has been spoken down the centuries over believers as representatives of humankind; 'The grace of our Lord Jesus Christ, and the love of God, and the fellowship of the Holy Spirit (and Word) be with you all.'

Brief summary

Present-day Pentecostalism comprises the Pentecostal movement, the church charismatic renewal and the non-white indigenous churches of the Third World. It goes back to the great revival which took place between 1906 and 1909 in Los Angeles and was led by the black Bill Seymour. From his African roots he underwent a holistic experience of faith which exercised an attraction unprecedented in church history. This spirituality, which above all also attracts the poor, draws no distinction between the spiritual and the earthly-physical reality and therefore can leed to social and political involvement. However, in Pentecostalism it is often damped down by the white fundamentalism which has crept in. The essential contribution of Pentecostal spirituality lies in its playful character. This is evident above all from the charismatic celebration which is not characterized by either order or chaos but by the dynamics of play. Through the gifts of grace (charisms), everyone has a contribution to make – regardless of race, gender or status.

This play of celebration is the play of Word and Spirit, which is summed up in scripture in the term Wisdom. In and through this Wisdom God creates the world to be an eternal sabbath, the kingdom of God. In it the Word represents order (the rules of the game) and the Spirit the dynamism and interchange (the 'enthusiasm') which bring the church to life. Thus creation has no necessity and no reason, consisting as it does in this purposeless play of Word and Spirit. In it human beings find their direction, since they are freed from the obsession with usefulness and necessity. This playful, creative dynamic is clearly visible in the life and work of Jesus, in which no one was left out of the game.

However, the established church has usually emphasized order (the Word) at the expense of the Spirit. It opted for the *status quo* without taking much account of the victims of the prevalent system.

This applies to the Roman Catholic, the Protestant and the Eastern Orthodox traditions. At the same time, on the other hand, there have always been charismatic counter-movements in which the play of Word and Spirit continued and, for example, women, blacks and the uneducated were welcomed as equals. On closer inspection, this play of Word and Spirit finds its highest expression in the human self, which consists of a defined personal identity (Word) and a dynamic interaction with the world (Spirit); and because Word and Spirit are an expression of God's being, the unique human self shares in God's self. So human beings are the image of God and can deal creatively with the absurdities of existence. However, this true human self is sometimes taken over by the false self, which is not bound to God but is bent back on itself and escapes into a rigid order. Directly opposed to this is the crazy play of the charismatic movement which gives it a prophetic and re-creative power.

The expectation and experience of baptism with Word and Spirit explain why Pentecostals can play. This is not possible as long as one is dominated by the dread of death, as this is typical of the false self. Death symbolizes *par excellence* that our existence is not necessary. This sense makes possible a grateful life of grace, in the freedom of the play of Word and Spirit. The false self, however, understands death as the denial of the right to live. This forces it to justify its existence. The false self disguises the truth of our mortality by grounding itself in idols, like a career, status or ideology which is served slavishly. Personal identity (Word) becomes rigid because it is not in real interaction (Spirit) with the world, which is reduced to an object serving the struggle for self-justification. This anxious reaction to death explains the one-sided emphasis on order in history and is possibly the most important cause of human evil, including the misuse of nature. In the resurrection of Jesus, God's Word and Spirit have now also become Christ's Word and Spirit. God's self is mediated through Christ and has taken on as it were the 'colour' of his cross and resurrection. The experience of this resurrection power brings freedom from the false, crippled self and helps the true self to live in communion with God and the creation. Through this baptism with Word and Spirit the renewed covenant is written in the heart of reality, namely a life of love which fulfils the Torah. In the New Testament, this is the central Christian experience, which for all kinds of reasons is not fully expressed in Pentecostalism.

Baptism with Word and Spirit is the experiential dimension of the life of faith and manifests itself in countless charisms. In every gift of grace we experience that our existence is justified 'for nothing', since it is grounded in God, who in Christ has overcome death. For a gift of grace is a concrete relationship with the neighbour, in whom we encounter God in Christ. This liberates the true self to live in the playful interaction of Word and Spirit with the other/Other. This is a reciprocal giving and receiving which has a healing and upbuilding power. Only through the power of the gifts of grace to bring about openness can the otherness of the neighbour be welcomed as an enrichment. This makes possible the unity in difference that characterizes the community as the body of Christ. The call of the church is in the first place to play this game of Word and Spirit in charismatic celebration. In this way people are equipped to renew the oppressive political and economic order as a guarantee of the eternal sabbath in which death will be dethroned and God become all in all.

Notes

Part One: The Origin and Characteristics of Present-Day Pentecostalism

1. C.M.Robeck, 'The Social Concern of Early American Pentecostalism', 104, 106.

2. Quoted in C.van der Laan, 'Portret van William Joseph Seymour (1870-1922)', 9.

3. I.MacRobert, *The Black Roots and White Racism of Early Pentecostalism in the USA*, 9-23, 33-36.

4. M.E.Suurmond-Vonkeman and J.-J.Suurmond, 'Een tandem relatie van Woord en Geest', 56-8.

5. D.W.Dayton, *Theological Roots of Pentecostalism*, 35-8; D.Brandt-Bessire, *Aux sources de la spiritualité Pentecôtiste*, 41-156.

6. D.J.Nelson, *For Such a Time as This: The Story of Bishop William J.Seymour and the Azusa Street Revival*.

7. L.J.Oudeman, 'Het Dilemma van het Gevangen Denken. Een Persoonlijke Frustratie-analyse en Kritisch Theologische Reflectie op Twintig Jaar Functioneren binnen de Pinksterbeweging,' 141-61.

8. I. MacRobert, *The Black Roots of Pentecostalism*, 81.

9. W.J.Hollenweger, *The Pentecostals*, 157.

10. Quoted in C.van der Laan, *De Spade Regen*, 174-5.

11. Ibid., 127-8, 158-62.

12. G.A.Wumkes, *De Pinksterbeweging*, 3.

13. Quoted in C.van der Laan, *De Spade Regen*, 160.

14. C.M.Robeck, 'The Social Concern of Early American Pentecostalism', 98-100.

15. W.J.Hollenweger, *The Pentecostals*, 105, 100-4.

16. J.Comblin, *The Holy Spirit and Liberation*, xii-xiv, 8-9, 25-6, 158.

17. G.te Haar, *Spirit of Africa. The Healing Ministry of Archbishop Milingo of Zambia*.

18. J.M.Horn, 'The Experience of the Spirit in Apartheid: The Possibilities of the Rediscovery of the Black Roots of Pentecostalism for South African Theology', 117-39.

19. W.J.Hollenweger, 'Het Pentecostalisme: Onstaan, Bijdragen en Wenken voor Onderzoek', 23-33; J.-J.Suurmond, 'Een Introductie tot de Charismatische Vernieuwing', 41-50.

20. M.Oomen and J.Palm, 'Excursie: Allochtoon Christendom', 60.

21. D.B.Barrett, 'The Twentieth-Century Pentecostal/Charismatic Renewal in the Holy Spirit. With its Goal of World Evangelization', 1-10; id., 'Signs, Wonders and Statistics in the World of Today', 189-96.

22. W.J.Hollenweger, 'Introduction', 2-3.

23. W.J.Hollenweger, 'Het Pentecostalisme: Onstaan, Bijdragen en Wenken voor Onderzoek', 36-8.

24. A.J.Heschel, *The Insecurity of Freedom*.

25. Cf. W.J.Hollenweger, 'Het Pentecostalisme: Onstaan, Bijdragen en Wenken voor Onderzoek', 27.

26. W.J.Hollenweger, 'The Social and Ecumenical Significance of Pentecostal Liturgy', 209-11.

27. Cf. G.von Rad, *Old Testament Theology* II, 357-87.

28. J.-J.Suurmond, 'Engeln en Demonen: Exegetisch-theologische en Pastorale Notities', 221-35.

29. K.H.Miskotte, *When the Gods are Silent*, 173-302.

30. J.V.Taylor, *The Go-Between God*, 198.

Part Two: Sabbath Play: Biblical Passages

1. Cf. C.Delhez, *Ce Dieu inutile*; J.Moltmann, *Theology and Joy*, 80-2.

2. John of the Cross, *Complete Works*, I, 63ff.

3. A.A.van Ruler, *Gestaltwerdung Christi in der Welt*, 50-2.

4. J.Moltmann, *God in Creation*, 276, 296.

5. Cf. R.A.Gueling, *Mark 1-8.26*, 129.

6. P.C.Craigie, *Psalms 1-50*, 1-5, 107-10.

7. J.Huizinga, *Homo Ludens*, Foreword (unnumbered), passim.

8. Cf. K.Waaijman, *De mystiek van Ik en Jij*, 35-49.

9. J.Huizinga, *Homo ludens*, 45.

10. Plato, *The Collected Dialogues*, 803 cde.

11. Cf. G.von Rad, *Wisdom in Israel*, 151f., passim.

12. Cf. J.D.G.Dunn, *Christology in the Making*, 164-5, 217-20.

13. G.Theissen, *Biblical Faith*, 135-62.

14. P.T.O'Brien, *Colossians, Philemon*, 32-63.

15. R.E.Brown, *The Gospel according to John I-XII*, cxxii-cxxv.

16. P.J.A.M.Schoonenberg, 'Opmerkingen over Geest-christologie: Tussen Van de Kamp en Suurmond', 34-5; cf. id., *De Geest, Het Woord en de Zoon*, chs.2-3.

17. R.E.Brown, *The Gospel according to John I-XII*, 519-24.

18. Cf. J.D.G.Dunn, *Jesus and the Spirit*, 68-92.

19. J.A.Fitzmyer, *The Gospel according to Luke I-IX*, 678-9.

20. Cf. E.Schillebeeckx, *Jesus*, 154-72.

21. J.D.Crossan, *The Dark Interval*, 119-22.

22. G.Theissen, *The Miracle Stories in Earliest Christianity*, 302.

23. M.Grey, *Redeeming the Dream*, 95-108.

24. Cf. W.F.Orr and J.A.Walter, *I Corinthians*, 152-67.

Part Three: Sabbath Play: A Closer Look at Church History

1. L.Kolakowski, *Chrétiens sans Eglise*; cf. C.Duquoc, 'Charism as the Social Expression of the Unpredictable Nature of Grace'.

2. Plato, *The Collected Dialogues*, 667e.

3. Cf. D.W.Hardy and D.F.Ford, *Jubilate*, 96-107, 140-5; P.Tillich, *Systematic Theology* III, 114-20.

4. W.J.Hollenweger, *The Pentecostals*, 459.

5. J.Comblin, *The Holy Spirit and Liberation*, 26-7.

6. M.F.G.Parmentier, *Spiritus donorum, Spiritus ministeriorum*, 5, 30.

7. J.Comblin, *The Holy Spirit and Liberation*, 13-15.

8. P.Tillich, *Systematic Theology* III, 126, 162-282.

9. O.Steggink, 'Het Kerkelijk Verbod op Ervaring en het Verzet van Mystieke', 23-32.

10. H.Berkhof, 'Het Hedendaagse Zoeken naar de Heilige Geest en het Antwoord van de Bijbel', 15.

11. J.Rodman Williams, 'Charismatische Theologie: Een Calvinistisch-reformatorisch Benadering', 119-32; K.Froelich, 'Charismatic Manifestations and the Lutheran Incarnational Stance', 136-57.

12. J.-J.Suurmond, 'De Pneumatologie van Karl Barth', 42-53.

13. A.F.S.Emmert, 'Charismatische Theologie: Een Oosters-orthodoxe Benadering', 85-99.

14. F.O.van Gennep, *De Terugkeer van de Verloren Vater*, 72-202.

15. R.M.Anderson, *Vision of the Disinherited*.

16. J.Wesley, *Works* II, 204.

17. G.Strachan, *The Pentecostal Theology of Edward Irving*.

18. C.van der Laan, *De Spade Regen*, 177, 182-3.

19. See K.McDonnell (ed.), *Presence, Power, Praise*.

20. G. van der Leeuw, *Der Mensch und die Religion*, 25-35.

21. P.Tillich, *Systematic Theology* I, 180-2.

22. D.Donnelly, 'Divine Folly: Being Religious and the Exercise of Humor', 385-98.

23. Leontios von Neapolis, *Leven van Symeon de Dwaas*.

24. R.A.Baer, Jr, 'Overeenkomsten tussen de Glossolalie, de Stilte van de Quakers en de Katholieke Liturgie', 173-87.

25. R.Niebuhr, 'Humour and Faith', 135-49; see also A.R.Eckardt, 'Divine Incongruity: Comedy and Tragedy in a Post-Holocaust World', 399-412.
26. T.H.Zock, *A Psychology of Ultimate Concern*, 83-9.
27. S.Weil, *Waiting on God*, 66-75.
28. Cf. G.Wainwright, *Doxology*, 149-283.
29. Huizinga, *Homo Ludens*, 28.
30. J.Moltmann, *Theology and Joy*, 57ff.
31. D.Bonhoeffer, *Ethics*, ch.V.
32. H.Andriessen, 'Psychologie, Spiritualiteit en de Stadia van Geestelijke Gezondheid', 151-2.
33. R.Guardini, *Vom Geist der Liturgie*, 48-60.
34. Huizinga, *Homo Ludens*, 15-19, 53-6.
35. Cf. Moltmann, *Theology and Joy*, 65-8.
36. D.Bonhoeffer, *Ethics*, 131-3.
37. V.Havel as reported in *Trouw*, 28 November 1992.
38. Cf. V.E.Frankl, *Psychotherapy and Existentialism*, 136-54.
39. D.W.Hardy and D.F.Ford, 'Lofprijzing en profetie', 191-8.
40. Cf. R.Burggraeve, *Het gelaat van de bevrijding*, 51-69.
41. Huizinga, *Homo Ludens*, 164-5.
42. H.Cox, *The Feast of Fools*, 63-71.
43. J.Moltmann, *God in Creation*, 244-57.
44. E.Wiesel, *Four Hasidic Masters and Their Struggle Against Melancholy*, 167.
45. J.F.White, *Protestant Worship. Traditions in Transition*.

Part Four: Baptism with Word and Spirit

1. Cf. L.Newbigin, *The Household of God*, 93-8.
2. H.I.Lederle, *Treasures Old and New. Interpretations of 'Spirit Baptism' in the Charismatic Renewal Movement*.
3. Thomas Aquinas, *Summa Theologiae*, q.43.
4. Cf. J.D.G.Dunn, *Baptism in the Holy Spirit*.
5. W.Foerster, *Der Heilige Geist im Spätjudentums*, 130-1.
6. W.Eichrodt, *Theology of the Old Testament*, I, 228-32.
7. Cf. M.Noth, *Exodus*, 160f.
8. K.Nielsen, 'Das Bild des Gerichts (Rib Pattern) in Jes.I-XII', 309-24.
9. Cf. R.A.Guelich, *Mark 1-8:26*, 18-20.
10. E.Schillebeeckx, *Jesus*, 274-319.
11. G.Strachan, *The Pentecostal Theology of Edward Irving*, 134.
12. R.E.Brown, *The Gospel according to John I-XII*, 14-18.
13. L.Kohlberg, 'The Claim to Moral Adequacy of a Highest Stage of Moral Judgment', 630-46; J.W.Fowler, *Stages of Faith*, 199-213; cf. P.Tillich, *Systematic Theology* II, 118-120.

14. P.J.A.M.Schoonenberg, *Hij is een God van Mensen*, 9-48.

15. Cf. C.Brown, *Miracles and the Critical Mind*, 290-2.

16. J.A.Fitzmyer, *The Gospel According to Luke I-IX*, 799-800.

17. J.Moltmann, *The Spirit of Life*, 33-8.

18. Cf. R.E.Clements, *Isaiah 1-39*, 121-4.

19. Cf. J.Moltmann, *The Spirit of Life*, 138-44; H.Mühlen, *Het Hart van God; Nieuwe Aspecten van de Triniteitsleer*, 207-16.

20. A.J.Hultgren, *Christ and His Benefits*, passim.

21. H.D.Goverts, *Het Lied van de Doortocht*, passim.

22. H.Jonas, 'The Concept of God after Auschwitz: A Jewish Voice', 8-11.

23. P.B.Suurmond, *God is Machtig – Maar Hoe?*, passim.

24. R.Burggraeve, *Het Gelaat van de Bevrijding*, 130 (and 125-33).

25. Cf. J.V.Taylor, *The Christlike God*, 170-4.

26. Cf. J.D. Crossan, *The Dark Interval*, 15-18.

27. E.Becker, *The Denial of Death*.

28. Cf. P.Tillich, *Systematic Theology* II, 25, 34-36, 66-78; III, 11-110.

29. E.Becker, *The Denial of Death*, 115-9.

30. S.Kierkeegard, *The Concept of Dread*, 113-16; id., *The Sickness unto Death*, 60c; E.Becker, *The Denial of Death*, 67-92, 176-207.

31. D.Bonhoeffer, *Ethics*, 60.

32. F.O.van Gennep, *De Terugkeer van de Verloren Vader*, 72-83.

33. A.Vergote, *Religieuze Moed en Deemoed*, 93-5.

34. Cf. H.Cox, *The Feast of Fools*, 30f., quoting Rubinstein, *After Auschwitz*.

35. S.Kierkeegard, *The Concept of Dread*, 124.

36. V.S.Goldstein, *The Human Situation. A Feminist View*, 165.

37. E.Becker, *The Denial of Death*, 175.

38. V.P.Furnish, *II Corinthians*, 197-201.

39. J.D.G.Dunn, *Jesus and the Spirit*, 325.

40. G.D.Fee, *The First Epistle to the Corinthians*, 786-95.

41. A.J.Hultgren, *Christ and his Benefits*, 11-39.

42. S.Kierkeegard, *The Concept of Dread*, 139-45; id., *Sickness unto Death*, 78; E.Becker, *The Denial of Death*, 85-92, 257f.

43. Cf. V.P.Furnish, *II Corinthians*, 234-42.

44. Cf. R.E.Brown, *The Gospel According to John XIII-XXI*, 637-53, 698-701, 703-117, 1135-44.

45. E.Franck, *Revelation Taught*, passim.

46. Cf. R.E.Brown, *The Epistles of John*, 342-7, 374-77.

47. J.Calvin, *Institutes*, III.2, 39; cf. III.2, 33-36; III.1, 1; III.1, 4; III.2, 15-16; also J.J.Suurmond, 'Ethical Aspects of the Inner Witness of the Holy Spirit', 3-16.

48. G.A.Maloney, *The Doctrine of St Symeon the New Theologian on the Baptism of the Holy Spirit*, 289-304.

49. W.J.Hollenweger, *The Pentecostals*, 334.

50. J.D.G.Dunn, *Baptism in the Holy Spirit*, 226 and passim.

51. J.Moltmann, *The Spirit of Life*, 188-90.

52. Cf. J.D.G.Dunn, *Baptism in the Holy Spirit*, 124-7.

53. Cf. E.Becker, *The Denial of Death*, 48-50.

54. O.Steggink and K.Waaijman, *Spiritualiteit en Mystiek*, I, 79-108.

55. J.V.Taylor, *The Christlike God*, 47.

56. Cf. S.Baynes, *Poetry and the Gift of Tongues*, 8-17.

57. Quoted in O.Steggink and K.Waaijman, *Spiritualiteit en Mystiek*, I. 1-3.

58. Ibid, 1-3, 7; cf. E.Underhill, *Mysticism*, 169-70, 176-443.

59. Cf. J.W.Maris, *Geloof en ervaring*, passim.

60. P.J.A.M.Schoonenberg, *De Doop met Heilige Geest*, 148-52.

61. K.Rahner, *The Spirit in the Church*, 9–31.

Part Five: The Gifts of Grace

1. J.Veenhof, 'Charismata – Bovennatuurlijk of Natuurlijk?', 156-72.

2. Quoted by J.W.Naris, *Geloof en Ervaring*, 174.

3. Cf. J.D.G.Dunn, *Jesus and the Spirit*, 201-9; E.Schillebeeckx, *Christ*, 82-178.

4. Cf. J.Moltmann, *Spirit of Life*, 9, 17, 31f.

5. A.McGrath, *IUSTITIA DEI* I, 4-16; cf. E.Käsemann, *Commentary on Romans*, 21-32.

6. J.Moltmann, *Spirit of Life*, 188.

7. E.Käsemann, 'Ministry and Community in the New Testament', 76, cf. 63-6.

8. Ibid., 69-74.

9. Cf. ibid., 66, 71-4; J.D.G.Dunn, *Jesus and the Spirit*, 318-26.

10. J.Beuner, *Intimitet en Solidariteit*, passim.

11. J.D.G.Dunn, *Jesus and the Spirit*, 312-16.

12. Cf. P.Tillich, *Systematic Theology* III, 107-10, 134-8.

13. Cf. K.Waaijman, *De Mystiek van Ik en Jij*, 127-243.

14. M.Buber, *I and Thou*, 44.

15. S.M.Panko, *Martin Buber*, 151-6.

16. K.Waaijman, *De Mystiek van Ik en Jij*, 266-7, 283-6.

17. Ibid., 276.

18. M.Buber, *I and Thou*, 135.

19. Ibid., 52.

20. K.Waaijman, *De Mystiek van Ik en Jij*, 487-93.

21. E.Levinas, *Le temps et l'autre*; cf. R.Burggrave, *Het Gelaat van de Bevrijding*, 135-52, 155-68.

22. Cf. E.Becker, *The Denial of Death*, 171-5, 186-9, 221f.

23. Cf. H.G.Gadamer, *Truth and Method*, 104-6; cf. P.Tillich, *Systematic Theology*, III, 112.

24. John of the Cross, *Complete Works*, III, 16ff.

25. D.W.Dayton, 'Theological Roots of Pentecostalism', 87-113; N.Hardesty, L.S.Dayton and D.W.Dayton, *Women in the Holiness Movement: Feminism in the Evangelical Tradition*, 225-54; M.Grey, *Redeeming the Dream*, passim.

26. M.Buber, *I and Thou*, 91.

27. M.Buber, *I and Thou*, 46.

28. J.Firet, 'Psychologische Notities met Betrekking tot de "Geestesdoop" ', 80-1.

29. E.Schillebeeckx, *Christ*, 838.

30. M.Barth, 'A Chapter on the Church – The Body of Christ', 131-56.

31. M.Barth, *Ephesians* 1-3, 183-210.

32. J.D.G.Dunn, *Jesus and the Spirit*, 298.

33. E.Käsemann, 'Ministry and Community in the NT', 76, 85.

34. Cf. G.D.Fee, *The First Epistle to the Corinthians*, 653-98.

35. J.M.Bonino, *Doing Theology in a Revolutionary Situation*; M.Grey, *Redeeming the Dream*.

36. E.Käsemann, *Commentary on Romans*, 323-31.

37. O.Cullmann, *Christ and Time*, 220; cf. D.Bonhoeffer, *Ethics*, 38-41; V.Furnish, *Theology and Ethics in Paul*, 188-203.

38. Cf.T.J.Gorringe, *Discerning Spirit*, passim.

39. Cf. L.Cahill, *Between the Sexes*, 139-54; E.Schillebeeckx, *Church*, 59-62.

40. Cf. E.Käsemann, *Commentary on Romans*, 241f.

41. W.Krusche, *Das Wirken des Heiligen Geistes nach Calvin*, 122-4; W.J.Hollenweger, 'All Creatures Great and Small: Towards a Pneumatology of Life', 41-53; A.Bittlinger, 'A "Charismatic" Approach to the Theme', 107-13.

42. J.Hendricks, *Een Vitale en Aantrekkelijke Gemeente*, passim.

43. J.Hick, *An Interpretation of Religion*, 1-69 and passim.

44. J.V.Taylor, *The Christlike God*, 56-62.

45. Ibid., 256-7.

46. Cf. C.H.Kraft, *Christianity in Culture*, 113-15; J.Macquarrie, *Jesus Christ in Modern Thought*, 415-22.

47. Cf. E.Schillbeeckx, *Church*, 17-25.

48. Cf. *Baptism, Eucharist and Ministry*, no. 40.

49. G.B.Caird, 'The Descent of Christ in Ephesians 4.7-11', 535-45.

50. Cf. O.Noordmans, *Gestalte en Geest*, passim; P.Tillich, *Systematic Theology* III, 114-20.

51. W.A.Visser't Hooft, 'The Economy of the Charismata and the Ecumenical Movement', 321-3.

52. H.Küng, *Global Responsibility*, 71-138.

53. Cf. E.Käsemann, *Commentary on Romans*, 159-65; V.P.Furnish, *Theology and Ethics in Paul*, 155-7, cf.171-6, 225-7.

54. J.D.G.Dunn, *Jesus and the Spirit*, 338.

55. R.Prenter, *The Word and the Spirit*, 105.

56. I.H.Marshall, *Last Supper and Lord's Supper*, 21-3, 143-4.

57. K.McDonnell, 'Charismatic Renewal: On the Periphery or at the Center?', xiv-xxvii.

58. Cf. D.L.Gelpi, 'Charismatische Theologie: Een Rooms-katholieke Benadering', 107-13; J.Veenhof, 'Charismata – Bovennatuurlijk of Natuurlijk?', 167-8.

59. J.-J.Suurmond, 'Charismatisch Pastoraat', 3-21; P.W.Pruyser, *Tussen Geloof en Ongeloof*, 118-25, 203-9, 240-51.

60. P.W.Pruyser, *Tussen Geloof en Ongeloof*, 247.

61. L.Newman, *Uit de Wereld der Joodse Mystiek*, 37.

62. A.van den Hoogen, 'Pastorale Arbeid in het Charismatisch Pastoraat, Een Theologische Analyse', 22-30.

63. Cf. J.D.G.Dunn, *Jesus and the Spirit*, 326.

64. H.Berkhof, *Christian Faith*, 330-37.

65. F.Varillon, *L'Humilité de Dieu*, 107; cf. J.H.Hick, *Death and Eternal Life*, 459-60.

Bibliography

R.M.Anderson, *Vision of the Disinherited. The Making of American Pentecostalism*, Oxford University Press, New York 1979.

H.Andriessen, 'Psychologie, spiritualiteit en de stadia van geestelijke gezondheid', in J.van der Lans (ed.), *Spiritualiteit*, 147-60

Thomas Aquinas, *Summa Theologiae*, Blackfriars, London 1964-76 (60 volumes)

R.A.Baer, Jr, 'Overeenkomsten tussen de glossolalia, de stilte van de quakers en de katholieke liturgie', in J.J.Suurmond (ed.), *'Och, ware het geheel volk profeten!'*, 173-87

Baptism, Eucharist and Ministry, Faith and Order Paper 111 (The Lima Report), World Council of Churches, Geneva 1982

D.B.Barrett, 'Signs, Wonders and Statistics in the World of Today', in J.A.B.Jongeneel et al. (ed.), *Pentecost, Mission and Ecumenism*, 189-96

– , 'The Twentieth-Century Pentecostal/Charismatic Renewal in the Holy Spirit, With its Goal of World Evangelization', *The International Bulletin of Missionary Research* 12, July 1988, 1-10

M.Barth, 'A Chapter on the Church – The Body of Christ', *Interpretation* 12, 1958, 131-56

– , *Ephesians 1-3*, Anchor Bible 35, Doubleday, New York 1982

S.Baynes, 'Poetry and the Gift of Tongues', *Theological Renewal* 12, June 1979, 8-17

E.Becker, *The Denial of Death*, Collier Macmillan, New York 1973

H.Berkhof, *Christian Faith. An Introduction to the Study of the Faith*, Eerdmans, Grand Rapids and T. & T.Clark, Edinburgh 1980

– , 'Het hedendaagse zoeken naar de Heilige Geest en het antwoord van de bijbel', *Bulletin voor Charismatische Theologie* 9, Pentecost 1982, 15-25

J.Beumer, *Intimiteit en Solidariteit. Over het Evenwicht tussen Dogmatiek, Mystiek en Ethiek*, Ten Have, Baarn 1993

A.Bittlinger, 'A "Charismatic" Approach to the Theme', *The Ecumenical Review* 42, 1990, 107-13

D.Bonhoeffer, *Ethics*, ed E.Bethge, SCM Press, London and Macmillan, New York 1955

J.M.Bonino, *Doing Theology in a Revolutionary Situation*, Fortress Press, Philadelphia 1980

D.Brandt-Bessire, *Aux sources de la spiritualité Pentecôtiste*, Labor et Fides, Geneva 1986

C.Brown, *Miracles and the Critical Mind*, Eerdmans, Grand Rapids 1984

R.E.Brown, *The Epistles of John*, Anchor Bible 30, Doubleday, New York 1982

– , *The Gospel According to John I-XII*, Anchor Bible 29, Doubleday, New York ²1980

– , *The Gospel According to John XIII-XXI*, Anchor Bible 29A, Doubleday, New York ²1980

M.Buber, *I and Thou*, T. & T.Clark, Edinburgh 1984

R.Burggraeve, *Het gelaat van de bevrijding. Een Heilsdenken in het Spoor van Emmanuel Levinas*, Woord en Beleving 8, Lannoo, Tielt 1986

L.Cahill, *Between the Sexes. Foundations for a Christian Ethics of Sexuality*, Fortress Press and Paulist Press, Philadelphia and New York 1985

G.B.Caird, 'The Descent of Christ in Ephesians 4.7-11', in F.L.Cross (ed.), *Studia Evangelica*, Akademie Verlag, Berlin 1964, II, 535-45

J.Calvin, *Institutes of the Christian Faith* (2 vols), Library of Christian Classics, SCM Press, London and Westminster Press, Philadelphia 1960

R.E.Clements, *Isaiah 1-39*, The New Century Bible Commentary, Marshall, Morgan and Scott, London 1980

J.Comblin, *The Holy Spirit and Liberation*, Liberation and Theology 4, Orbis Books, Maryknoll, New York and Burns and Oates, Tunbridge Wells 1989

H.Cox, *The Feast of Fools*, Harvard University Press 1969

P.C.Craigie, *Psalms 1-50*, Word Biblical Commentary 19, Word, Dallas 1983

J.D.Crossan, *The Dark Interval. Towards a Theology of Story*, Argus, Allen 1975

O.Cullmann, *Christ and Time. The Primitive Christian Conception of Time and History*, SCM Press, London and Westminster Press, Philadelphia 1951

D.W.Dayton, *Discovering an Evangelical Heritage* (1976), Hendrickson, Peabody 1988

– , *The Theological Roots of Pentecostalism*, Studies in Evangelicalism 5, Scarecrow Press, Metuchen, NJ 1987

C.Delhez, *Ce Dieu inutile...Éloge de la gratuité*, Lumen Vitae, Brussels 1988

D.Donnelly, 'Divine Folly: Being Religious and the Exercise of Humor', *Theology Today* 48, January 1992, 385-98

J.D.G.Dunn, *Baptism in the Holy Spirit. A Re-Examination of the New Testament Teaching on the Gift of the Spirit in Relation to Pentecostalism Today*, SCM Press, London 1970

– , *Christology in the Making. An Inquiry into the Origins of the Doctrine of the Incarnation*, SCM Press, London and Trinity Press International, Philadelphia 1980

– , *Jesus and the Spirit. A Study of the Religious and Charismatic Experience of Jesus and the First Christians as Reflected in the New Testament*, SCM Press, London and Westminster Press, Philadelphia 1975

C.Duquoc, 'Charism as the Social Expression of the Unpredictable Nature of Grace', *Concilium* 109, 1978, 87-98

A.R.Eckardt, 'Divine Incongruity: Comedy and Tragedy in a Post-Holocaust World', *Theology Today* 48, January 1992, 399-402

W.Eichrodt, *Theology of the Old Testament* (2 vols), SCM Press, London and Westminster Press, Philadelphia 1961, 1967

A.F.S.Emmert, 'Charismatische Theologie: Een Oosters-orthodoxe Benadering', in J.J.Suurmond (ed.), *'Och, ware het gehel volk profeten!'*, 85-99.

G.D.Fee, *The First Epistle to the Corinthians*, The New International Commentary on the New Testament, Eerdmans, Grand Rapids 1989

J.Firet, 'Pyschologische notities met betrekking tot de "Geestesdoop"', in G.P.Hartvelt (ed.), *Op het spoor van de Geest, Theologische Opstellen. Vragen aan en Kanttekeningen bij de Charismatische Beweging*, Kok, Kampen 1980, 77-91

J.A.Fitzmyer, *The Gospel according to Luke I-IX*, Anchor Bible 28, Doubleday, New York 1981

W.Foerster, 'Der Heilige Geist im Spätjudentum', *New Testament Studies* 8, 1961-62, 117-34

J.W.Fowler, *Stages of Faith. The Psychology of Human Development and the Quest for Meaning*, Harper and Row, San Francisco 1981

E.Franck, *Revelation Taught. The Paraclete in the Gospel of John*, Coniectanea Biblica, New Testament Series 14, CWK Gleerup 1985

V.E.Frankl, *Psychotherapy and Existentialism. Selected Papers on Logotherapy*, Penguin Books, Harmondsworth 1973

K.Froelich, 'Charismatic Manifestations and the Lutheran Incarnational Stance', in P.D.Opsahl (ed.), *The Holy Spirit in the Life of the Church. From Biblical Times to the Present*, Augsburg Publishing House, Minneapolis 1978, 136-57

V.P.Furnish, *II Corinthians*, Anchor Bible 32A, Doubleday, New York 1984

– , *Theology and Ethics in Paul*, Abingdon Press, Nashville 1978

H.-G.Gadamer, *Truth and Method*, Sheed and Ward, London 1976

D.L.Gelpi, 'Charismatische Theologie. Een Rooms-katholieke Benadering', in J.J.Suurmond (ed.), *'Och, ware het geheel volk profeten!'*, 100-18

F.O.van Gennep, *De Terugkeer van de Verloren Vader. Een Theologisch Essay over Vaderschap en Macht in Cultuur en Christendom*, Ten Have, Baarn 1989

V.S.Goldstein, 'The Human Situation: A Feminist View', in S.Doniger (ed.),

The Nature of Man in Theological and Psychological Perspective, Harper and Row, New York 1962, 159-70

T.J.Gorringe, *Discerning Spirit. A Theology of Revelation*, SCM Press, London 1990

K.D.Goverts, *Het Lied van de Doortocht. Bijbels-theologische en Liturgische Studie naar Aanleiding van Exodus 15, 1-17*, Unpublished dissertation, University of Amsterdam 1992

M.Grey, *Redeeming the Dream. Feminism, Redemption and Christian Tradition*, SPCK, London 1989

R.Guardini, *Vom Geist der Liturgie*, Ecclesia Orans, Herder, Freiburg [18]1953

R.A.Guelich, *Mark 1- 8.26*, Word Biblical Commentary 34A, Word, Dallas 1989

G.ter Haar, *Spirit of Africa. The Healing Ministry of Archbishop Milingo of Zambia*, Hurst, London 1992

N.Hardesty, L.S.Dayton and D.W.Dayton, 'Women in the Holiness Movement: Feminism in the Evangelical Tradition', in R.Ruether and E.McLaughlin (eds.), *Women of Spirit. Female Leadership in the Jewish and Christian Traditions*, Simon and Schuster, New York 1979, 225-54

D.W.Hardy and D.F.Ford, *Jubilate, Theology in Praise*, Darton, Longman and Todd, London 1984

– 'Lofprijzing en profetie', in J.J.Suurmond (ed.), *'Och, ware het geheel volk profeten!'*, 188-206

V.Havel, 'Ik was gezwicht voor het so vernietigende ongeduld', *Trouw*, 28 November 1992

J.Hendriks, *Een Vitale en Aantrekkelijke Gemeente. Model en Methode van Gemeenteopbouw*, Kok, Kampen 1990

A.J.Heschel, *The Insecurity of Freedom*, Jewish Publication Society of America, Philadelphia 1966

J.H.Hick, *Death and Eternal Life*, Macmillan, London and Harper and Row, San Francisco 1980

– , *An Interpretation of Religion, Human Responses to the Transcendent*, Macmillan, London and Harper and Row, San Francisco 1989

W.J.Hollenweger, 'All Creatures Great and Small: Towards a Pneumatology of Life', in D.Martin and P.Mullen (eds.), *Strange Gifts? A Guide to Charismatic Renewal*, Blackwell, Oxford 1984, 41-53

– 'Introduction', in A.Bittlinger (ed.), *The Church is Charismatic. The World Council of Churches and the Charismatic Renewal*, World Council of Churches, Geneva 1981, 1-4

– 'Het Pentecostalisme: Ontstaan, Bijdragen en Wenken voor Onderzoek', in J.J.Suurmond (ed.), *'Och, ware het geheel volk profeten!'*, 23-44

– , *The Pentecostals*, SCM Press, London and Augsburg Publishing House, Minneapolis, 1972

– , 'The Social and Ecumenical Significance of Pentecostal Liturgy', *Studia Liturgica* 8, 1971-72, 207-15

A.van den Hoogen, *Pastorale Arbeid in het Charismatisch Pastoraat. Een Theologische Analyse*, Praktische Theologie 19, 1992, 22-30

J.M.Horn, 'The Experience of the Spirit in Apartheid. The Possibilities of the Rediscovery of the Black Roots of Pentecostalism for South African Theology', in J.A.B.Jongeneel (ed.), *Experiences of the Spirit. Conference on Pentecostal and Charismatic Research in Europe at Utrecht University 1989*, Studies in the Intercultural History of Christianity 68, Peter Lang, Frankfurt am Main, etc. 1991, 117-39

J.Huzinga, *Homo Ludens. A Study of the Play Element in Culture*, Routledge, London 1949

A.J.Hultgren, *Christ and his Benefits. Christology and Redemption in the New Testament*, Fortress Press, Philadelphia 1987

John of the Cross, *Complete Works*, Burns and Oates, London 1963

H.Jonas, 'The Concept of God after Auschwitz: A Jewish Voice', *Journal of Religion* 67, 1987, 1-13

J.A.B.Jongseel et al. (eds.), *Pentecost, Mission and Ecumenism. Essays in Intercultural Theology. Festschrift in Honour of Professor Walter J.Hollenweger*, Studies in the Intercultural History of Christianity, 75, Peter Lang, Frankfurt am Main 1992

E.Käsemann, 'Ministry and Community in the New Testament', in *Essays on New Testament Themes*, SCM Press, London 1964, 63-94

– , *Commentary on Romans*, Eerdmans, Grand Rapids and SCM Press, London ²1982

S.Kierkegaard, *The Concept of Dread*, Princeton University Press 1944

– , *The Sickness unto Death*, Oxford University Press, London 1941

– , *Fear and Trembling*, Oxford University Press, London 1939

L.Kohlerg, 'The Claim to Moral Adequacy of a Highest Stage of Moral Judgment', *The Journal of Philosophy* 70, October 1973, 630-46

L.Kolakowski, *Chrétiens sans Église. La Conscience Religieuse et le Lien Confessionel au XVIIe Siècle*, Bibliothéque de Philosophie, Gallimard, Paris 1969

C.H.Kraft, *Christianity in Culture. A Study in Dynamic Biblical Theologizing in Cross-Cultural Perspective*, Orbis Books, Maryknoll, New York 1979

W.Krusche, *Das Wirken des Heiligen Geistes nach Calvin*, Vandenhoeck & Ruprecht, Göttingen 1957

H.Küng, *Global Responsibility*, SCM Press, London and Crossroad Publishing Company, New York 1991

C.van der Laan, 'Portret van William Joseph Seymour (1870-1922)', *Parakleet* 11.38, 1991, 7-33

– , *De Spade Regen. Geboorte en Groei van de Pinksterbeweging in Nederland 1907-1930*, Kok, Kampen 1989

J.van der Lans (ed.), *Spiritualiteit. Sociaalwetenschappelijke en Theologische Beschouwingen. Voor Willem Berger*, Ambo, Baarn 1984

R.Laurentin, 'Charisms. Terminological Precision', *Concilium* 109, 1978, 3-12

H.I.Lederle, *Treasures Old and New. Interpretations of 'Spirit Baptism' in the Charismatic Renewal Movement*, Hendrickson, Peabody 1988

G. van der Leeuw, *Der Mensch und die Religion, Anthropologischer Versuch*, Philosophia Universalis 2, Haus zum Falken, Basel 1941

Leontios van Neapolis, *Leven van Symeon de Dwaas*, Monastieke Cahiers 5, Kerckebosch, Zeist 1990

E.Levinas, *Le temps et l'autre*, Presses Universitaires de France, Paris 1983

J.Macquarrie, *Jesus Christ in Modern Thought*, SCM Press, London and Trinity Press International, Philadelphia 1990

I.MacRobert, 'The Black Roots of Pentecostalism', in J.A.B.Jongeneel et al. (eds.), *Pentecost, Mission and Ecumenism*, 73-84

– , *The Black Roots and White Racism of Early Pentecostalism in the USA*, Macmillan, Basingstoke 1988

G.A.Maloney, 'The Doctrine of St Symeon the New Theologian on the Baptism of the Holy Spirit', *Journal of Spiritual Formation* 13, November 1992, 289-304

J.W.Maris, *Geloof en Ervaring. Van Wesley tot de Pinksterbeweging*, Groen, Leiden 1992

I.H.Marshall, *Last Supper and Lord's Supper*, Paternoster Press, Exeter and Eerdmans, Grand Rapids 1983

K.McDonnell, 'Charismatic Renewal: On the Periphery or at the Center?', in K.McDonnell (ed.), *Open the Windows. The Popes and Charismatic Renewal*, Greenlawn, South Bend, 1989, ix-xxvii

– (ed), *Presence, Power and Praise. Documents on the Charismatic Renewal*, Liturgical Press, Collegeville 1980 (3 vols)

A.McGrath, *IUSTITIA DEI. A History of the Christian Doctrine of Justification* (2 vols), Cambridge University Press 1986

K.H.Miskotte, *When the Gods are Silent*, Collins, London and Harper and Row, New York 1967

J.Moltmann, *The Spirit of Life*, SCM Press, London and Fortress Press, Minneapolis 1992

– , *God in Creation*, SCM Press, London and Fortress Press, Minneapolis 1985

– , *Theology and Joy*, SCM Press, London and Harper and Row, New York 1973

H.Mühlen, 'Het Hart van God: Nieuwe Aspecten van de Triniteitsleer', in J.J.Suurmond (ed.), *'Och, ware het geheel volk profeten!'*, 207-25

D.J.Nelson, *For Such a Time as This; The Story of Bishop William J.Seymour and the Azusa Street Revival*,Unpublished PhD Dissertation, University of Birmingham 1981

L.Newbigin, *The Household of God. Lectures on the Nature of the Church*, SCM Press, London and Friendship Press, New York 1953

L.Newman, *Uit de Wereld der Joodse Mystiek*, Servire, Katwijk aan Zee 1976

R.Niebuhr, 'Humour and Faith' (1946), in C.Hyers (ed.), *Holy Laughter. Essays on Religion in the Comic Perspective*, Seabury Press, New York 1969

K.Nielsen, 'Das Bild des Gerichts (Rib Pattern) in Jes.I-XII', *Vetus Testamentum* 29, 1979, 309-24

O.Noordmans, 'Gestalte en Geest' (1954), in J.M.Hasselaar et al. (eds.), *Verzamelde Werken. Meditaties*, Kok, Kampen 1980, VIII, 347-451

M.Noth, *Exodus* (1959), Old Testament Library, SCM Press, London and Westminster Press, Philadelphia 1962

P.T.O'Brien, *Colossians, Philemon*, Word Biblical Commentary 44, Word, Dallas 1982

M.Oomen and J.Palm, 'Excursie: Allochtoon Christendom', in H.Schaeffer (ed.), *Handboek Godsdienst in Nederland*, De Hostrink, Amersfoort 1992, 56-62

W.F.Orr and J.A.Walther, *I Corinthians* Anchor Bible 32, Doubleday, New York 1981

L.J.Oudeman, 'Het Dilemma van het Gevangen Denken. Een Persoonlijke Frustratie-analyse en Kritisch Theologische Reflectie op Twintig Jaar Functioneren binnen de Pinksterbeweging', in *Religieuze Bewegingen in Nederland, De Tegenbeweging*, VU, Amsterdam 24, 1992, 141-62

S.M.Panko, *Martin Buber*, Makers of the Modern Theological Mind, Word, Waco 1978

M.P.G.Parmentier, *Spiritus Donorum, Spiritus Ministeriorum. Over de Werkingen en de Werken van de Heilige Geest en over de Mensen die daarin Werkzaam Zijn*, VU, Amsterdam 1993

Plato, *The Collected Dialogues*, ed. E.Hamilton and H.Carins, Bollingen Series LXXI, Princeton University Press, Princeton 1980

R.Prenter, *The Word and the Spirit*, Augsburg Publishing House, Minneapolis 1965

P.W.Pruyser, *Tussen Geloof en Ongeloof. Een Psychologische Studie van de Twijfel*, Ambo, Baarn 1976

G.von Rad, *Old Testmeant Theology II, The Theology of the Prophetic Traditions of Israel*, Oliver and Boyd, Edinburgh 1965 reissued SCM Press London 1975

– , *Wisdom in Israel*, SCM Press, London and Abingdon Press, Nashville 1970

K.Rahner, *The Spirit in the Church*, Seabury Press, New York 1979

C.M.Robeck, 'The Social Concern of Early American Pentecostalism', in J.A.B.Jongeneel et al (eds.), *Pentecost, Mission and Ecumenism*, 97-106

A.A.van Ruler, *Gestaltwerdung Christi in der Welt. Über das Verhältnis von Kirche und Kultur*, Bekennen und Bekenntnis 3, Moers, Neukirchen 1956

E.Schillebeeckx, *Jesus*, Collins, London and Crossroad Publishing Company, New York 1979

– , *Christ*, SCM Press, London and Crossroad Publishing Company, New York 1980

– , *Church. The Human Story of God*, SCM Press, London and Crossroad Publishing Company, New York 1990

P.J.A.M.Schoonenberg, 'De doop met Heilig Geest', in J.J.Suurmond (ed.), *'Och, ware het geheel volk profeten!'*, 137-55

– , *De Geest, het Woord en de Zoon. Theologische Overdenkingen over Geest-Christologie, Logos-Christologie en Drieëenheidsleer*, Altiora/Kok, Averbode, Kampen 1991

– , *Hij is een God van Mensen*, Malmberg, 's-Hertogenbosch 1969

– , 'Opmerkingen over Geest-christologie: Tussen Van de Kamp en Suurmond', *Bulletin voor Charismatische Theologie* 14, St Maarten 1984, 33-6

T.Smail, A Walker, N.Wright, *Charismatic Renewal. The Search for a Theology*, SPCK, London 1993

O.Steggink, 'Het Kerkelijk Verbod op Ervaring en het Verzet van Mystieken', *Speling* 30, 1978, 23-32

– , and K.Waaijman, *Spiritualiteit en Mystiek, I. Inleiding*, Gottmer, Nijmegen 1985

G.Strachan, *The Pentecostal Theology of Edward Irving* (1973), Hendrickson, Peabody 1988

J.J.Suurmond, 'Charismatisch pastoraat', *Praktische Theologie* 19, 1992, 3-21

– , 'Engelen en demonen: exegetisch-theologische en pastoral notities', *Gereformeerd Theologisch Tijdschrift* 90, 1990, 221-35

– , 'Ethical Aspects of the Inner Witness of the Holy Spirit', in *Studia Biblica et Theologica* 13.1, 1983, 3-16

– , 'Een Introductie tot de Charismatische Vernieuwing', *Kerk en Theologie* 40, 1989, 33-50

– (ed.), *'Och, ware het geheel volk profeten!' Charismatisch-theologische Tektsten*, Sleutelteksten in godsdienst en theologie 16, Meinema, Zoetermeer 1992

– , 'De pneumatologie van Karl Barth', *Bulletin voor Charismatische Theologie* 18 (Christus Koning 1986), 42-53

P.B.Suurmond, *God is Machtig – Maar Hoe? Relaas van een Godservaring*, Ten Have, Baarn 1984

M.E.Suurmond-Vonkeman and J.-J.Suurmond, 'Een Tandemrelatie van Woord en Geest', *Mara* 2, 1989, 56-62

J.V.Taylor, *The Christlike God*, SCM Press, London 1992

– , *The Go-Between God*, SCM Press, London 1979

G.Theissen, *Biblical Faith*, SCM Press, London and Fortress Press, Philadelphia 1984

– , *Miracle Stories of the Early Christian Tradition*, T.& T.Clark, Edinburgh 1983

P.Tillich, *Systematic Theology*, London, SCM Press and University of Chicago Press 1967

E.Underhill, *Mysticism. A Study in the Nature and Development of Man's Spiritual Consciousness* (1911), Methuen, London [12]1960

F.Varillon, *L'Humilité de Dieu*, Centurion, Paris 1974

J.Veenhof, 'Charismata – Bovennatuurlijk of natuurlijk?', in J.J.Suurmond (ed.), *'Och, ware het geheel volk profeten!'*, 156-72

A.Vergote, 'Religieuze Moed en Deemoed', in J.van der Lans (ed.), *Spiritualiteit*, 84-98

W.A.Visser't Hooft, 'The Economy of the Charisma and the Ecumenical Movement', *The Ecumenical Review* 41, 1989, 321-23, a revised reprint of his article in *Paulus-Hellas-Oikumene*, Student Christian Association of Greece, Athens 1951

K.Waigman, *De Mystiek van Ik en Jij, Een Nieuwe Vertaling van 'Ich und Du' van Martin Buber mit Inleiding en Uitleg en een Doordenking van het System dat eran ten Grondslag Ligt*, Kok, Kampen 1990

G.Wainwright, *Doxology. The Praise of God in Worship. Doctrine and Life: A Systematic Theology*, Epworth Press, London and Oxford University Press, New York 1980

S.Weil, 'Reflections on the Right Use of School Studies with a View to the Love of God', in *Waiting on God*, Collins, Fontana Books, London 1959, 66-75

J.Wesley, *Works*, Complete and Unabridged (1878), Eerdmans, Grand Rapids 1978 (14 volumes)

J.F.White, *Protestant Worship, Traditions in Transition*, Westminster/John Knox Press, Philadelphia 1989

E.Wiesel, *Four Hasidic Masters and Their Struggle Against Melancholy*, University of Notre Dame Press 1986

J.Rodman Williams, 'Charismatische Theologie: Een Calvinistisch-Reformatorische Benadering', in J.J.Suurmond (ed.), *'Och, ware het geheel volk profeten!'*, 119-32

G.A.Wumkes, *De Pinksterbeweging, Voornamelijk in Nederland*, Polman, Amsterdam 1917

T.H.Zock, *A Psychology of Ultimate Concern. Erik H.Erikson's Contribution to the Psychology of Religion*, Rodopi, Amsterdam, etc., 1990

Index of Biblical References